GIRLTALK

ALL THE STUFF YOUR SISTER NEVER TOLD YOU

GIRLTALK

ALL THE STUFF YOUR SISTER NEVER TOLD YOU

CAROL WESTON

BARNES & NOBLE BOOKS

A DIVISION OF HARPER & ROW, PUBLISHERS
New York, Cambridge, Philadelphia, San Francisco
London, Mexico City, São Paulo, Singapore, Sydney

Grateful acknowledgment is made for permission to reprint adaptations of:

"How Well Do You Know Your Best Friend?" "Icebreakers," "Are You and He a Good Match?" and "Are You Too Nice?" reprinted with permission from *Young Miss* Magazine. Copyright © 1983, a division of Gruner + Jahr, USA Publishing.

"10 Sticky Dating Situations and How to Handle Them" and "35 Dating Ideas Guaranteed to Steal His Heart" reprinted with permission from *Young Miss* Magazine. Copyright © 1984, a division of Gruner + Jahr, USA Publishing.

Library of Congress Cataloging in Publication Data

Weston, Carol.
   Girltalk: all the stuff your sister never told you.

   1. Adolescent girls.   2. Adolescent girls—Conduct
of life.   I. Title.
HQ798.W43   1985   646.7'0024055   84-48631
ISBN 0-06-463711-5 (pbk.)

85 86 87 88 89 10 9 8 7 6 5 4 3 2 1

Dedicated to the memory of my father,
William Weston

CONTENTS

ACKNOWLEDGMENTS

I want to be brief, but I'm feeling awfully grateful. So here's a bouquet of thanks to:

Sally Ackerman, for being my friend, surrogate younger sister, and inspiration for this book. Sally was thirteen when I met her and is eighteen now. She read the entire rough draft and scribbled wonderfully insightful *goods* and *yuks* all over it.

Rob Ackerman, my husband, for being a first-rate (if ruthless) editor, for his excellent suggestions, and for being so supportive and loving.

Irv Levey, director of Barnes & Noble, for his warm encouragement, for coming up with the original idea with me, and for taking a gamble on an article writer.

Marybeth Weston, my mother and role model, for reading my first draft, red pencil in hand.

Dawn Raffel and Jeanne Flagg, my terrific editors.

Jane Wilson, my terrific agent.

Ragdale Foundation, a writers' and artists' colony, for my five productive and peaceful stays there. What an idyllic place to work!

Dr. Irving Distelheim, who looked over my sections on acne and sexually transmitted diseases with dermatological expertise.

Dr. Stephanie Bird, who filled me in on the nitty-gritty of abortions with gynecological savvy.

Dr. John FitzGibbon, Jr., who reviewed the *Drinks, Drugs, Etc.* chapter and never tired of answering questions.

Dr. Seth Berkley, at the Centers for Disease Control, who explained recent findings on toxic shock syndrome.

Christopher Athas, vice president of the National Association of Anorexia Nervosa and Associated Disorders, who made sure my section on eating disorders was accurate and up-to-date.

My two writing groups: Monday-night friends Rochelle Distelheim, Anne Brashler, Barbara Nodine, Barbara Polikoff, Diane Williams, Roslyn Lund, Mary James. And Wednesday-morning friends Dolores Weinberg, Janice Rosenberg, and the rest of the Deerfield, Ill., crowd.

John Carlo Mariani, Andy and Lisa Jeffrey, Mark, Eric and Cynthia Weston, Laurel Davis, and everyone else who helped out.

The libraries I holed up in.

Young Miss for permitting us to reprint and adapt six articles.

Last but not least, my teenage cat Chanda. She sat on my lap as I wrote, purring as my word processor hummed. Because Chanda hates to be disturbed, and because purring and humming are happy sounds, I kept on plugging.

GIRLTALK

ALL THE STUFF YOUR SISTER NEVER TOLD YOU

HELLO

I'm impressed with you already. I don't always read introductions.

I hope you'll also read the *Body* chapter, which tells how to have clearer skin and a better figure, explains menstruation, body talk, and what guys worry about, and gives the latest information about bulimia, anorexia, and toxic shock syndrome. The chapter on *Friendship* will interest you if you adore your best friend but sometimes feel smothered, or if you ever wish you could ease into a different group. The *Love* chapter can help if you wonder how to flirt without sounding like a jerk, how to break up without breaking down, or what to do if you've told a guy you're busy all this Saturday and next, but he doggedly invites you out for the following three.

Turn to *Sex* to learn the myths and facts about everything from cooties to herpes, what you should know before saying yes, and how to get and use contraceptives. Flip to *Family* if it's hard to believe your parents were both teenagers seven years apiece, if it's difficult to get used to a stepsibling, or if you fear your family might be a ripe candidate for counseling. *Education* offers ways to deal with touchy teachers, improve your grades, and get into college—if that's where you're heading.

Are you wondering about summer jobs and careers? The *Money* chapter is full of lucrative ideas and can help you plot your future, write your résumé, and ace an interview. Want to know more about tobacco, pot, cocaine, or alcohol? Read *Drinks, Drugs, Etc.* Take the *Quintet of Quizzes* to find out how observant or jealous you are, how well you know your best friend, how compatible you and your boyfriend are, and whether you are *too* nice.

GIRLTALK: All the Stuff Your Sister Never Told You lends a hand in your leap from confusion to confidence. Read it from cover to cover, or skip around, pausing whenever you're curious. It's your personal encyclopedia.

Even if you do have an older sister, I bet you have a few questions you'd feel funny asking. This book is loaded with answers. It's full of the stuff I wanted to know when I was growing up and the stuff it took me years to figure out.

Although shaping your life isn't easy, growing up shouldn't have to hurt too much. There's no such thing as a true grown-up anyway, just as there's no such thing as a typical teen.

What's great about being your age is that you have it in you to become whomever you want—and you're becoming yourself.

1
BODY

LOOKING AND FEELING YOUR BEST

Too fat, too flat, too tall, too small—hardly any of us is 100 percent happy with our appearance. It's especially hard for you now. Your body may be growing in all directions, blemishes may freckle your face, hair may be sprouting here and there, your period may be a mystery. What is going on inside you anyway? Are you stuck with your features and figure?

Beauty does make a difference in first impressions. But so do friendliness, sense of humor, intelligence, thoughtfulness. And who said you had to be "flawless" to be pretty? With a little effort, anybody can look attractive.

Since you and your body are together for the long haul, you need to learn to take care of it. This chapter will show you how to make the most of your attributes and how to be your most healthy and radiant.

DO GUYS WORRY ABOUT THEIR BODIES?

Before we launch into a discourse about breasts, periods, diets, cosmetics, and other female concerns, you might be wondering if guys ever worry about their bodies. Answer: They certainly do.

Sure, a few wink in the mirror each morning and think they're God's Gift to Manhood—and Womankind. But most wrestle with some puberty-related anxiety.

Guys wonder whether they're tall enough, whether their biceps bulge enough, whether their chest and facial hair will ever grow in. They wish their voices would get deeper and stop croaking. They wish they weren't hungry all the time. They're tired of having braces and pimples and being clumsy and lanky. They wish they were more handsome and that their hands wouldn't sweat when they ask you to slow dance. A few may even fret about someday turning bald and beer-bellied.

Guys worry extra in gym showers, club saunas, and public or school bathrooms, because they figure someone might be checking out their private parts. Someone probably is. Guys want to be "well hung," though penis size isn't that important in a sexual relationship. Some boys even worry that their organ is crooked!

Here's another male concern. Most guys in their mid-teens begin to have wet dreams. They wake up to find they've ejaculated during the night, and they wonder if that's normal. Yes. It's also normal for guys to get erections at odd times—when they wake up, or in math class, or when they're minding their own business on the school bus.

Many guys feel uneasy about their sexuality. Are they oversexed if they masturbate a lot, or undersexed if they don't? If they have an orgasm quickly when they masturbate, does that mean they'll be premature ejaculators in years to come? If they haven't started dating, or if they've played sex games with other guys or admire their male coach, does that mean they're gay? If they have an X-rated fantasy involving an "old lady" teacher, does that mean they're perverted? No, no, no, and no. Guys grow at different sexual speeds and need not be alarmed by early tame or wild imaginings or experiences.

In one important way, girls have an advantage over guys in the Worry Department. Most guys don't discuss their growing pains, whereas, luckily for us, most girls do. It's not uncommon for a girl to complain, "Mom, I wish my breasts were bigger." But rare is the guy who would say, "Dad, I wish my penis were bigger." It's a shame guys aren't more open and honest together, and it's their loss. They have as many questions, troubles, and fears of inadequacy as girls, but fewer outlets. Guys tease and taunt each other, yet usually worry alone. They don't even have many magazines or books to consult. But you do. So keep reading!

EVERYTHING YOU EVER WANTED TO KNOW ABOUT BREASTS

Back to us girls.

If you're like me, you sometimes get fed up with your figure. Why can't it just settle into a shapely 36-24-36? Why can't your breasts be medium instead of mountains or molehills?

It's frustrating that your body's timetable answers to hormones and heredity rather than to your own wishful thinking. If you haven't started developing yet, you may be feeling shortchanged. If you've been developing for years, you may worry you'll wind up with watermelons. Either way, you might envy the average girls who strut around the locker room parading their bra-and-panty sets.

I envied them. I was in a mad rush to grow up. I couldn't wait to get my breasts on and my braces off, to start getting periods and stop getting pimples. At fourteen, I was a restless late-blooming flatso. I dressed behind curtains and cringed at breast jokes.

Why are you a sailor's delight? Because you have a sunken chest! What do members of the Itty Bitty Titty Committee wear instead of bras? Band-Aids! Pretend you're a boy for a minute. Ahh . . . doesn't that take a load off your chest? Quips circulated about ironing boards, mosquito bites, pancakes, and string beans, as well as jumbo jugs, bouncing bazooms, and knockout knockers. Poor Denise, girls said, was so flat she could wear her bra inside out. And people teased Erica that she'd knock down passersby if she turned without warning.

At first hardly anybody was happy. My friend Alice was as distressed about being buxom as I was about being flat. She sported baggy shirts to hide her dramatic décolletage.

It was Alice who told me of the Best Breast Test. "To find out if you need a bra, place a pencil underneath one of your boobs and see if it stays up," she explained. I ducked into the bathroom . . . and my pencil clattered to the floor. Alice handed me two of her outgrown training bras anyway—"booby" prizes since she'd graduated to larger sizes.

Status was at stake when classmates discussed bra size. The ideal seemed to be As in school and Bs in bust. I earned no grade: just an incomplete. Later when the subject switched to boys, books, baby-sitting, I'd sometimes still be thinking bosoms, boobs, breasts. Would mine ever grow?

I wish I could have realized that I'd make it safely to womanhood. I wish I could have foreseen that although I'd never rival Dolly Parton, I'd end up perfectly content with my own measurements, just as Alice now feels good about her curves.

Yes, *Playboy*'s pages do tend toward the well endowed, and not long ago, some breast-oriented fellow paid $1040 at a London auction for a 36-D bra worn by Marilyn Monroe. But small-breasted women have admirers too. What's more, sagging is not a problem for us, and while it's hard to look voluptuous, it's sometimes easy to look slim.

Most girls' breasts start swelling when they're between ages ten and fifteen, usually twelve or thirteen. Some girls grow just the "right" amount just when their friends are developing. But many are ahead of or behind the pack and feel self-conscious or impatient. It's nice to know you're not the only one who has anxiously compared your chest with the next girl's. It's even nicer to know that ultimately almost everybody ends up with the bust that goes best with her figure and learns to accept and enjoy her own shape.

The catch is that if you feel like a freak in the meantime, that's the image you project. Who wants to hang out with a girl who is totally preoccupied with her bust? It's not true that guys favor girls who are "built." Guys like girls who feel good about themselves.

Although many girls are concerned about being concave or convex, I hope you can appreciate your own curves. Bodies look their most attractive when they are firm and in shape, whether they resemble hourglasses, pears, or beanpoles. The days of girdles, bustles, corsets, falsies, and bandoes are behind us. Now big is beautiful and flat is fine and medium is marvelous. So throw back your shoulders when you walk. Take off your T-shirt when you swim. Get out of the slumber party sleeping bag when you undress. Don't be like me who agonized too long over nothing—if you'll pardon the pun.

Have you ever wondered about women who have surgery to change their breast size? Breast surgery is not a neat option; it's a last resort. Still, you may be curious about mammoplasty, so let me tell you about Tammy.

In high school, Tammy's body was petite, but her bosom was enormous. She got shoulder cuts from her tight bra straps and backaches from supporting her heavy, drooping bosom. She felt out of proportion and never got used to her vital statistics, or to the constant comments she used to draw. "I felt like walking breasts," she said.

When Tammy was eighteen and fully developed, she and her mother visited a few doctors. They agreed she might be better off with a little off and that she was old enough to undergo the major surgery of breast reduction. She went to the hospital, was given general anesthesia, stayed several days, paid over $2500 (some of it covered by insurance), put up with a lot of pain—and emerged less buxom.

Most people thought she'd lost weight but they didn't guess where. Tammy already had a boyfriend, so her love life didn't change, but she did begin to feel better about herself. Scars? Yes. She doesn't skinny-dip anymore because the scars are noticeable under her breasts and around her nipples. She also lost some sensitivity in her breasts, and never will be able to nurse. Nonetheless, she has no regrets. Yet her case is highly exceptional.

How about the other extreme? Can you make your bosom more bountiful? Ads in the back of magazines are mostly rip-offs. Some feature exercises that make your back wider, not your front. Your measurement increases, not your cup size. Others feature creams that temporarily irritate the bust, making it bigger because it is swollen.

Surgery to increase breast size is not as involved as the operation to make the bust smaller. Some 72,000 American women are fitted for breast implants each year. Not teens, but middle-aged women who have had a mastectomy due to cancer, are usually first in line for reconstruction surgery.

Breast cancer among girls and young women is exceedingly rare, and ten out of eleven women will never get breast cancer. Even lumps or some discharge from the nipple may be normal. But consult your doctor, particularly if your breasts start changing after you are seventeen, or if your mother has had breast cancer. And check your breasts regularly. Do it after your period each month; it only takes a few minutes. It's a matter of life and breasts! Here's how.

1   In the bath or shower (since wet skin is slippery), keep your fingers flat and move them all over your breasts, checking for lumps, knots, or thickening.

2   Lie down in bed or on the floor. Put your right hand behind your head, and with your left hand, check your right breast. Move your fingers in circles around your nipple, including the area around your armpit. Repeat with opposite hand and breast.

3   Sit up, and with arms overhead, inspect your breasts in front of a mirror to check for changes. Squeeze each nipple gently to check for discharge.

Since you are probably still developing, your breasts should be changing. But it's wise to get in the habit now of doing this monthly three-step routine. If your breasts change when you're older, alert your doctor immediately.

Does anyone have her bust enlarged who hasn't had cancer? Yes. Mariel Hemingway, for instance, had it done for the movie *Star 80*.

It's rarely recommended, but this is how breast augmentation surgery works. The woman sits up, and the plastic surgeon marks the creases where her breasts fall. She is given a local anesthetic; then the surgeon cuts along the creases, making two-inch incisions about a half-inch deep, to free a pocket in each breast. Inside each, the surgeon tucks a silicone-gel-filled plastic bag, both of equal size. (If the woman's breasts are very uneven, an implant is put in just one breast to match the other in size.) The surgeon puts in a few sutures and binds the patient with a supportive dressing. That's it. Often it takes just thirty minutes, although the woman wears the dressing and a special supportive bra for several weeks. One woman I know said that the first week after surgery, she had trouble sleeping and felt as though someone were stepping on her chest. She's fine now, and her scar is minimal.

The cost is not minimal and is not usually covered by insurance. It can run to $2000, especially if there is a hospital stay or if implants are put into both breasts. How do the new breasts feel? Like natural breasts but firmer. Unlike natural breasts, which may soften with age, silicone pouches stay firm forever. Some women complain that they are downright hard and never jiggle. And many doctors aren't convinced that breast implants are absolutely safe.

If you are healthy, you aren't physically uncomfortable, and your breasts aren't extremely uneven, is it worth the money and complication to change your silhouette? I don't think so. I'd rather have my own soft mini-breasts than expensive bigger, stiffer ones. It's sensible to make peace with your body.

The best breast advice of all is to grin and bear them—whether they're big, small, or slightly asymmetrical.

IS YOUR PERIOD A QUESTION MARK?

Can you imagine how scary it would be to start menstruating if you didn't know anything about it? Suddenly you'd be bleeding! Down there! I'd have been petrified if I hadn't known that the menarche (first period) is as much a part of puberty as developing breasts. Even if you've had your period for years, you may not understand it completely or know what to do about cramps or tampons.

My first encounter with the paraphernalia of periods came when I was about six. My brother and I found white cylindrical cardboard tubes in my mother's bathroom wastebasket. We slipped them on our fingers and played puppets. Little did we know they were Tampax applicators!

Years later, in fifth grade, my friend Alice (the one who was practically born with a bra on) was sleeping over and we compared what we knew about menstruation, which wasn't much. We made a pact to tell each other when it happened, and sure enough Alice started her period that year.

Most American girls start when they are twelve or thirteen, but starting anywhere from nine to sixteen is not uncommon, and when you start depends not just on age but also on weight, percentage of body fat, and dietary habits. A girl's first period usually occurs after her breasts have begun to develop and her pubic hair has begun to appear.

My body was in no hurry. I still remember when my lab partner Colleen came by after school in seventh grade. At the doorstep she announced, "I have my friend."

"She can come in too," I said, then noticed she was alone.

Colleen rolled her eyes. "I mean my period," she said.

By ninth grade, almost all the girls I knew whispered about their "time of the month." Colleen told the same joke to everybody: "How do you know when an elephant is menstruating? There's a dime on the bed and the mattress is missing!"

When I finally got my period, I was fifteen and a half and had been going out with a guy for six months. The first time is rarely a dramatic flood for anybody; usually it's just a little red on the toilet paper you're using, or a few drops of blood on your underpants, with little warning beforehand. (Wash stains out with cold, not hot, water.) When I started, I felt relieved, and my friends seemed to think it was cause to celebrate. My mother said, "Congratulations, welcome to the sorority."

This is the gist of what menstruation is all about. Once you start menstruating, you are capable of having a baby, and every month your body gets revved for possible motherhood. A tiny egg (you're born with thousands) matures in one of your ovaries, is released and sent down a fallopian tube, and eventually reaches the uterus. Meanwhile, your uterus, or womb, has been preparing for the egg's arrival, and its lining is now thick and velvety. If the arriving egg is fertilized by a sperm, your uterus is ready to protect and nourish it. The fertilized egg, or ovum, will grow in your uterus, and in about nine months, you'll have a baby. If your egg hasn't been fertilized (you haven't had sex or you've been careful about contraception), then you're not pregnant. Your uterus has no use for the thick, spongy lining it has been building up. Much of the lining is therefore cast off, and that, along with some blood, body fluids, and the disintegrated egg, comprises the six or so tablespoons of reddish brown menstrual flow that flushes out through your vagina for three to six days each month. Once you start menstruating and your cycle becomes regular, you'll have periods (except during pregnancy) until they stop at menopause, which usually occurs when you're between forty-five and fifty-five.

Are your periods already regular? Mine didn't become regular for over a year. Even if yours are, you may sometimes miss a month or several months. As long as you know you're not pregnant, some irregularity shouldn't worry you. Nerves, plane rides, poor nutrition, weight gain or loss, even a cold can throw off your cycle. Mysteriously, sisters' or roommates' menstrual cycles sometimes become synchronized when they live together, so their periods may be off schedule as this first happens. And one-third to one-half of very athletic women often skip periods, although they are still fertile. (I know a marathon runner who hadn't menstruated in years, but when she and her husband decided to have a family, she had no problem getting pregnant.) If you are extremely thin and are skipping periods, try to gain weight and they may begin again. If you're worried about your cycle—it's very irregular or painful—keep track of when you get your periods and talk to a doctor.

Do you know when you're about to get your period? I usually mark a small *x* on my calendar on the first day of each period so I'll know approximately when to expect it the next month. Most girls' cycles are about twenty-eight days, but they range from twenty-two to thirty-four days. Some girls may worry that their period is late, when if they'd kept track, they'd realize that they simply have a long cycle.

Sometimes I'll be supersensitive or weepy or strung out, and the next day, bingo—I'll get my period. I don't usually suffer from headaches, backaches, cramps, cold sores, or nosebleeds as a few of my friends do, but I'm prone to a blemish or two, I feel heavy, and once in a while my breasts get so tender, it hurts just to walk down the stairs! That's nature's way of warning me that my period is on its way. Other times I'll have no symptoms at all, or my symptoms will come a full week or ten days before my period.

It's smart to be aware of your own premenstrual symptoms so you'll carry a tampon or pad in your purse (a good idea anyway), wear panties at night if you think you'll start (not your new white ones), and try not to scream at some innocent person just because you are short-tempered. (Studies show there are more family arguments, traffic accidents, crimes, and even suicides among women who are in their premenstrual week than among other women.)

Symptoms vary from woman to woman and from month to month. They depend on your body and your attitude. If you think, "This is the week I get depressed and bitchy," you'll probably get depressed and bitchy. But if you think it's kind of neat that your body has rhythms, and you stay busy and don't make a fuss over it, your period may come and go before you know it. Don't skip gym or postpone tests just because your body is functioning normally.

If you are among the minority who hate that time of the month because you feel sluggish, edgy, bloated, and sore, you should know that your periods will probably become easier in a few years, and that in the meantime, several nonprescription and prescription drugs can help relieve premenstrual syndrome (PMS) and painful periods (dysmenorrhea). But don't reach for medication every time you have a slight ache. Perhaps a brisk walk, a cup of tea, or a hot bath can make you feel better. Or try a heating pad or hot water bottle. Or gentle exercises: lie on your back with your knees up and move them in a small circle, or lean facedown on your forearms and shins and let your abdomen (and uterus) relax. Because your uterus is swollen and taking up more room than usual at the start of your period, you may want to avoid heavy meals.

Women who are on the Pill rarely suffer premenstrual discomfort and are as regular as clocks, but the Pill has some disadvantages—more on that in the *Sex* chapter.

What should you do when you have your period? Everything you'd do otherwise! Swim, play tennis, dance, go out. Shower each day, eat healthfully, get lots of sleep and exercise. If you have intercourse, use contraception, because menstruation is no guarantee that you won't get pregnant.

Using too much salt is never good for you, and it's particularly smart to avoid it now, since it makes you retain fluids and look puffy. You're losing iron, so eat meat, eggs, raisins, whole grain bread. Liver is also wonderful for you if you can stand it—I can't! The calcium level in your blood is down, so drink plenty of milk. Your blood sugar is down, so eat small healthful snacks (not sweets) to keep it up. Now is an especially good time to take daily vitamins. Alcohol, by the way, affects you more than usual at this time, so beware.

Constipation can be a problem around your period. If it is for you, exercise and eat bran, vegetables, salads, apples, prunes, and other fruits; drink plenty of water, juice, or even coffee. (Have you tried reading on the john?) Regular bowel movements are crucial to overall health and extra important now to avoid cramping.

Which should you wear, tampons, or pads? Do you realize how great it is to have a choice? Before 1921, women wore a cloth diaper they washed and reused. Next came bulky napkins attached with belts. Nowadays it's so easy!

Most pads have an adhesive side that sticks to the inside of your panties. You can choose thin or thick pads—also called napkins, shields, liners—depending on your flow. If you're not having your period but are scared you might spot or start in the middle of a class or movie, wear a pad as a safety precaution. (Some spotting may be normal, particularly if you use the IUD or the Pill or if you've gained or lost weight. Otherwise, see your doctor. Some white or yellow discharge is also normal, but if yours is clumpy or unusual for you, call your physician.)

What about tampons? I find them more convenient than pads for the first day or two because they're smaller, less messy, more comfortable, and there's no odor. They're a must when you go swimming. Some tampons come with tube applicators (such as Tampax), others with stick applicators (such as Kotex), others with plastic applicators (such as Playtex), and others you push in with your finger (such as o.b.).

Manufacturers also make deodorant tampons, but some women are allergic to them. There is no odor anyway until your menstrual flow meets the air, and by then you're throwing the used tampon away—in the trash wrapped in lots of paper, or in the toilet, if you are positive the plumbing is excellent.

Most tampons come with directions for first-time users. If you haven't tried them, buy small tampons (the stick applicator kind or a slender or junior tampon) and give it a go when you next have your period. Relax, read the guidelines, aim the tampon toward the small of your back, and push it in just far enough so it's comfortable. You may go through several before you pop one in right, but inserting tampons is like whistling— once you get the hang of it, you'll never forget how.

The only possible reason you might not be able to use a tampon is that most girls have a thin layer of skin, called the hymen, that partially covers the opening of the vagina. But rarely does the hymen seal the opening completely, so just as there's room for your flow to come out, there's room for your tampon to go in. (In case you've heard otherwise, you're a virgin if you haven't had intercourse, whether your hymen is or isn't intact.)

When your flow is light or medium, use a regular tampon. When your flow is heavy, usually on day two and three, use a super tampon. (Heavier girls sometimes have heavier flows.) Still worried? You can always wear a tampon with a pad as a backup. Change your tampons at least every four to six hours. Changing too often can cause irritation. It's best to wear a pad at night and during the last day or two of your period to minimize chances of toxic shock syndrome.

In high school, my friends and I used to be afraid we'd stain our white pants or skirts. If you're careful, you need not worry. Maybe I've been lucky, but I've never yet sprung a serious leak.

We also worried that tampons would get lost in our bodies. That can't happen because your cervix, which is the gateway to your uterus, is too small for a tampon to slip through. If it did somehow slip up your vaginal canal, you'd just wash your fingers and tug it out. But that possibility is highly unlikely. And it can't slip down because your vaginal muscles hold it up.

The more serious worry is toxic shock syndrome, or TSS. You've probably noticed the warning printed on every box of tampons. A lot of research has been done since May of 1980 to learn about this rare and sometimes fatal disease associated with tampon use. Anybody can get it, but young women who are menstruating are the most susceptible; only 20 percent of the cases occur in nonmenstruating women. Symptoms include a sudden fever (102° or over) accompanied by vomiting or diarrhea, rash, dizziness, faintness, and a drop in blood pressure. If you have these signs, contact your doctor immediately, and if you are wearing a tampon, yank it out!

Now that I've got you in a total panic, let me stress how rare this illness is. According to the Federal Centers for Disease Control, in 1980 886 cases of TSS were reported among 52 million menstruating women.

In 1981, 586 cases. In 1982, 400. In 1983, 324. (So far, there have been 114 deaths.) Fewer cases of TSS have been reported since then, probably because Rely high-absorbency tampons, which seemed less safe than other brands, have been taken off the market. And since more women are now aware of this illness, more are alternating tampons with pads and steering clear of the super-plus absorbency kind and the kind that opens into a balloon or umbrella shape. So be informed, but don't lose sleep, okay?

Some women like to douche after their periods. That's unnecessary because your vagina is like a cat—it cleans itself! If you do douche, don't do it more than once a week and don't mistake it for contraception. Some douches actually kill helpful bacteria and can cause rashes or infections.

By the way, do you ever feel embarrassed when you buy tampons or pads? You shouldn't. Half the population buys or has bought or will buy them. Besides, you don't quake when the guy at the counter sees your toothpaste, soap, deodorant, or cologne, do you? Tampons or pads are just one more way of keeping clean and confident. So no blushing in the drugstore!

On the other hand, while you should never feel ashamed of menstruation, you don't need to get out the megaphone every time your period comes. Menstruation has been a taboo subject in the past, and I'm not encouraging you to be hush-hush about it, but don't go to the other extreme, either.

(For what it's worth, I feel the same way about getting up to go to the bathroom. You can say, "Excuse me, I'll be right back," or "I've gotta take a leak." I prefer discretion. But then I'm the type who runs the tap water when I'm in the powder room and others are within earshot.)

Once you've begun your period, you may want to start seeing a gynecologist (male or female) instead of your pediatrician. Before your pelvic exam, the doctor will ask about your medical history, your cycle, and when you had your last period. Keep a menstrual record chart and a list of questions you may have and bring them in.

What to expect next? You'll probably slip into a paper smock and lie back, your feet in stirrups. The doctor will check your breasts, put on a rubber glove and check your vagina and rectum (ugh!), and take a Pap smear with a cotton swab to send on a slide to the laboratory. (If you start to feel embarrassed, try silently spelling your best friends' last names backward.) Annual checkups are less expensive at Planned Parenthood or a city clinic than at a private office. Examinations aren't fun, but once you're a woman, they're important. And knowing you're in perfect health gives you a great sense of well-being.

THE RIGHT HEIGHT

Just as you can't control how big your breasts will be or when your period will come, you can't control your height. It's a given, so the sooner you accept it, the better.

My short story is that I was the runt of the litter. My brothers are both over a foot taller than I. Even my mother is an imposing 5 feet 7 inches, but, as she explained, "You take after Grandmother." And Grandmom was a shrimp.

In school, I was always at the end when the teacher lined us by height. Instead of seeing eye-to-eye with people, I saw eye-to-neck.

I finally put my size in perspective and stopped fretting. I also stretched a few inches skyward and am now a towering five foot two, eyes of blue. (Over half the women in America are 5'3" and under.) For me, the bright side of being petite was that I went out with lots of guys, tall and small. I still receive terrific hand-me-downs (actually hand-me-ups) from my teenage sister-in-law. And I'm the last one to get wet when it rains!

Are you tall? "Giraffe" girls may be frustrated now but are lucky in the long run. (Aren't you tired of waiting for the long run?) Tall women look elegant in clothes that make shorties look frumpy. On the job, they look authoritative. Another plus? Tall women can eat more than their short sisters. Be grateful, too, that you can reach the top closet shelf and can see the movie no matter who plunks down in front.

If you are afraid you'll soon be ducking under doorways, take heart. You may have reached the end of your growth spurt. A girl's growth spurt starts about the same time as her period and usually lasts one or two years. That's when you're shooting up up up, and past the guys. It takes them a couple of years, but most catch up.

If you ever feel you're all arms and legs, fear not. That's normal, and your body will sort itself out sooner than you think.

Whatever your height and proportions, stand straight and learn to wear clothes and shoes that suit you. If you're short, don't wear high heels constantly though, because they aren't good for your feet or back. Shopkeepers, friends, magazines, and moms can help you figure out which styles work best for you.

WINNING THE WEIGHT WAR

Do you eat to live or live to eat? Most people do both, and even if you would briefly consider trading in your brother for a pepperoni pizza, that doesn't necessarily mean there's cause for concern.

However, weight control *is* a problem for too many of us. No one wants to be roly-poly fat or starvation skinny. Yet it can be difficult to eat healthful, balanced meals and maintain a comfortable in-between weight. Are you so calorie-conscious that weight is controlling you rather than the other way around? Are you dieting desperately or feeling guilty every time you eat even though friends swear you're a toothpick? Or are you chubby but unwilling to recognize it, or chunky just to spite your gymnast mother or health-nut father?

The media may be partly to blame. Food commercials say eat! eat! eat! but the actress munching the brownie is skinny! skinny! skinny! Fashion magazines also brim with mixed messages. On one page: the latest fad diet of grapefruit and alfalfa sprouts. On the next: new recipes for mocha cheesecake and gooey chocolate pie.

What do you do? Your boyfriend gawks over svelte models in intimate apparel ads, but if you're together at a fancy restaurant, he doesn't want you to order just a salad. Your mother says you could stand to lose a few pounds, then prepares lasagna, your favorite, because she loves you.

In my house, it was my father who stuffed turkeys, fried bacon, stirred gravies, rolled dumplings, flipped crêpes, whipped cream, grated chocolate. I cleaned my plate with gusto.

Somehow I managed to get away with it and be a bit of a stick— until senior year of high school. That's when I went to France to live with a French family. France! Home of tempting breads, pastries, cheeses, and haute cuisine! Suffice it to say I overindulged. And my metabolism caught up with me.

I scarcely realized I was gaining weight because I thought of myself as the skinny-bones I'd always been. Yet when I returned to Armonk, New York, everyone seemed more interested in the dozen pounds I'd put on than in my newly acquired fluency in French or my impressions of the Louvre. Most frustrating was that I'd gone from underweight to overweight without ever having appreciated the time when I might have been "just right."

I cut back on my munching, bought a calorie counter, and stayed seated at dinner while my brothers hopped up for seconds and thirds. Most of the weight fell off pretty fast. Since then, however, I've had to watch myself, exercise, and not gobble chocolate chip cookies with abandon.

Just last week, a friend seemed surprised when I declined her offer of a milkshake. "C'mon," she said, "you don't have to worry about your weight." Wrong! The only reason I occasionally look as though I don't have to worry about my weight is that I *do* worry about it.

The trick is to be sensible. You don't want to be a blimposaurus, a Renoir model, a Miss Piggy lookalike—but you also don't want to be neurotic about every half-inch of flesh on your body. I prefer to be two pounds over my ideal weight than to be obsessive and frantic about calories.

Even if you do lose a pound per thigh and trim two off your behind, you still won't be tall and blond (like Cheryl Tiegs) if you're short and brunette (like me). And your life won't change just because you get rid of your spare tire. It might change because after losing weight, you may start to feel more cheerful, self-assured, outgoing. People respond to a gain in confidence as much as they do to a loss in weight.

Work to become fit instead of fat now, because you are setting your eating patterns (good habits now mean good health later), and because, as the saying goes, if you don't watch your figure, no one else will.

The following section on weighty worries offers fifty-five dieting tips. I hope you don't spend your life jumping on and off the diet merry-go-round. Nor should you be on a perpetual diet, because your body will simply make do on less food by slowing your metabolism.

Confidence is cumulative. So accept yourself or change. How much you weigh is up to you, but think nutrition if you diet. It's especially vital now while you're still growing.

DON'T WINDOW-SHOP AT THE BAKERY
AND 54 OTHER DIETING DO'S AND DON'TS

Dieting is not hard if you alone have decided you are ready to lose weight. The secret is to eat less. The average teenage girl burns up about 2200 calories each day. You'll lose weight if you consume fewer. A pound of body weight equals 3500 calories. Adults generally need about 15 calories per pound per day. For instance, since I weigh about 110 pounds, I need about 1650 calories.

You should exercise to improve muscle tone, but playing an hour of volleyball burns about 200 calories and does not entitle you to scarf down a thick slice of pecan pie à la mode. An hour's jog burns about 600 calories—a lot, but still less than the calories in that dessert. Why not pass on the pie? Or just have a taste of a friend's.

The idea is to eat like a bird instead of a horse. Dieting isn't fun, but when your tight pants feel loose and your flabby belly is firm, you'll be glad you slimmed down. So if you are overweight (and only if you are overweight), summon your willpower and win by losing.

    1   **Don't** eat if you're not hungry.
    2   **Do** eat slowly, putting your fork down between bites and talking during the meal. A table is not a trough.

3 **Don't** take big portions. Take small portions. Think slivers, not slabs.

4 **Do** stop before you're full, because it takes about twenty minutes for your belly to figure out what your mouth has been up to.

5 **Don't** take big bites. Take small bites.

6 **Do** brace yourself when you're going to eat at someone's home. Don't arrive famished. Decline politely on seconds.

7 **Don't** eat absentmindedly. Enjoy what you're consuming, or don't bother. (The first two cookies are scrumptious. Can you really taste the sixth?)

8 **Do** exercise at least two hours a week, and remember that muscle weighs more than flab—and looks better. Swimming, jogging, gymnastics, dancing, skiing, bicycling, and even jumping rope are great for all-over trimming. Think appearance and inches, not just pounds.

9 **Don't** waste calories on soda. Drink calorie-free herbal teas or nutritious juices, such as tomato or grapefruit.

10 **Do** keep peeled carrots, celery sticks, cherry tomatoes, green grapes, radishes, and other vegetables and fruits ready for snacking or for taking on a trip.

11 **Don't** buy fattening foods, and ask the family shopper to skip the candy aisle. It's easier to resist the stuff when it's not around. Never market on an empty stomach.

12 **Do** stock up on sugarless gum. (Chain-chewing is sometimes my way of coping with stress.)

13 **Don't** take diet pills without a doctor's go-ahead. Some are dangerous; others make you irritable; others make you lose water, not fat.

14 **Do** eat well-balanced meals daily that include foods from the four major food groups: grains and cereals; fruits and vegetables; meat, poultry, and fish; and dairy products. Avoid "empty," non-nutritious calories, and realize once and for all that crash diets are unhealthy.

15 **Don't** weigh yourself every day, because your scale won't immediately register last night's bag of Fritos. Weigh yourself at the same time every few days. Don't expect to lose more than one or two pounds a week.

16 **Do** be patient if you're dieting wisely but losing slowly, or if you've reached a plateau. Some people have faster metabolisms than others, and the very plump usually lose faster than the slightly pudgy. Keep dieting and you'll keep losing.

17 **Don't** get discouraged if people don't notice your weight loss right away. You don't notice every two pounds others gain and lose.

18 **Do** take a walk or call a friend or write a letter when you get a food craving.

19 **Don't** skip breakfast. Your body will thank you more for breakfast than it will for an extra seven minutes' sleep. Instead of skipping any meals, eat small meals. (According to some studies, if you consume 1500 calories divided into six small meals, you'll lose weight faster than if you consume the same calories in just three meals.)

20   **Do** learn that spumoni is more fattening than spinach—and potatoes, more caloric than tomatoes, etc. Without memorizing charts, learn which foods can turn you into a Goodyear Blimp. (Surprise! It's usually not the noodles but what goes on top that makes pasta fattening.)

21   **Don't** talk about your diet all the time. You'll bore everybody silly.

22   **Do** keep busy, and food will become less important.

23   **Don't** blow the rest of your diet day just because you snuck a Snickers at lunch.

24   **Do** order fish, chicken salad, or something light when eating out.

25   **Don't** have one potato chip. It's easier to have none.

26   **Do** remember that calories count even when it's your birthday, even when you're on a date, even when you have a test that day, and even when the cookie dough is raw.

27   **Don't** mistake the new womanly roundness of your breasts, bottom, and thighs for unsightly flab.

28   **Do** use a small plate if your dietetic dinner looks pitiful on a big one.

29   **Don't** start a diet right before finals or your period or when other concerns are making you tense.

30   **Do** cut down on salt and avoid crackers, pretzels, and chips, because salt makes you retain excess water. Season your food with pepper and spices. (Canned veggies come salted; eat fresh ones.)

31   **Don't** pig out on Sunday in preparation for the diet you might start on Monday.

32   **Do** drink lots of water between meals. Drinking will make you less hungry. Keep ice water in the refrigerator and a teapot on the stove. Sip juice or broth before dinner.

33   **Don't** fill your plate at a salad bar or smorgasbord until you've checked out all the offerings.

34   **Do** consider taping a picture of you-at-your-tubbiest *or* sleekest on your fridge. (I know a man who wired his fridge with a gadget that asks, when the door is opened, "Are you really hungry, Fatso?")

35   **Don't** leave a knife on the cake plate. It makes it too easy to slice off a taste when you really were just passing by.

36   **Do** brush your teeth when you want to put something in your mouth. The just-brushed feeling will cut down on your desire to munch.

37   **Don't** fry when you can boil, broil, steam, grill, or bake.

38 **Do** buy tuna packed in water instead of oil; canned fruit in its juice, not in syrup; skim milk, not whole milk; thin-sliced bread, not regular bread; white meat (e.g., chicken, fish), not red meat (e.g., burgers, steak).

39 **Don't** guide yourself by weight charts, because your bone structure may not be average. Ask your doctor or school nurse what he or she thinks you should weigh.

40 **Do** consider writing down everything you eat during one week. That can help you figure out when extra calories slip into your diet. It also curbs eating when you report cheating.

41 **Don't** snack without asking, "Is this worth the calories?"

42 **Do** pick up a five-pound bag of flour after you lose your first five: That's how much weight you no longer lug around. Mirrors and scales don't lie, but it takes time to adjust your self-image.

43 **Don't** become a vegetarian unless you research exactly what you'd need to eat each day to get enough protein.

44 **Do** learn how to use chopsticks. They'll slow you down when you eat Chinese food, and at other meals, too.

45 **Don't** let your menu get boring. Experiment with herbs, and try vegetables such as leeks and pea pods, and seafood such as mussels and squid. Learn to adore salad, but go easy on dressings.

46 **Do** resist. Mere minutes of fudge joy equal flab that could take days of dieting to lose.

47 **Don't** sit through TV food commercials—change the channel.

48 **Do** consider making rigid rules for yourself. It may be easier to know you won't allow yourself to snack after 9 P.M. than to have to test your willpower every evening.

49 **Don't** window-shop at the bakery.

50 **Do** use a serrated (grapefruit) spoon if you must taste the ice cream. You'll be aware of each bite.

51 **Don't** underestimate the pleasure of holding back. When you pass up the blintzes, you'll feel strong and virtuous.

52 **Do** think of getting through one day at a time rather than bumming out over the prospect of surviving three weeks without Häagen Dazs.

53 **Don't** drink diet sodas or use sugar substitutes that specifically warn they contain "saccharin which has been determined to cause cancer in laboratory animals." (Granted we're talking rats, not people, and doses, not packets, but I'll take my tea plain, thanks.)

54 **Do** consider meeting instead of eating. You could try Weight Watchers, Overeaters Anonymous, TOPS, the Diet Center, or another organized group if you can't lose on your own.

55 **Don't** keep dieting when you've reached your ideal weight. (If

you look like Nastassja Kinski in the Richard Avedon photo, don't worry that you have a big belly and an outie.) You may want to lose a few extra pounds since you may gain a few back. But quit when it's quitting time, and then work on maintaining. Don't congratulate yourself with Fig Newtons. Treat yourself to a pair of pants—in your new smaller size.

LOSING TOO MUCH: EATING DISORDERS

If preoccupation with food interferes with your life, if you see yourself as plump even though others swear you're underweight, or if you truly believe that if you were thin, you'd be happy, you may be prone to an eating disorder. Eating disorders are diets gone wrong, diets that are self-destructive instead of self-improving. Anorexia and bulimia have become increasingly common—there may be more than a million sufferers in America—and young women are the prime victims. One teen friend of mine said that eating disorders have become practically a fad.

Anorexics and bulimics starve or stuff themselves compulsively, and some abuse laxatives or make themselves throw up. Many are so pleased to be looking slim that they overlook the permanent damage they may be doing to their bodies. If you are anorexic or bulimic, or exhibit symptoms of both disorders, you are not alone. But you also probably can't cure yourself alone. Start taking vitamins, and try to go three days without feasting or fasting. If you can't, immediately call a doctor or one of the centers listed on pages 21–22. Proper treatment is available. And the sooner you get help, the sooner you'll get better.

Anorexia Nervosa

Pam is in her late teens. She is a perfectionist. She is as emaciated and bony as a prisoner of war or a famine victim, but she insists that her belly sticks out and she wants to lose a little more weight.

Her friendships have changed. Her family is concerned. They think she looks skeletal and urge her to eat more. But that just makes her defiant, so she hardly touches the food on her plate. Pam thinks about food a lot, and she cooks for others. But while food fascinates her, eating repels her. So she feeds her dinner to the dog, or hides it, or throws it out when no one is looking. When someone *is* watching, she may eat, but may later take a laxative or an enema. Occasionally her willpower falters and she binges, but afterward she vomits or fasts with added determination.

Losing weight makes Pam feel in control. Her parents have always demanded a lot of her, and she expects a lot of herself. She found it was easier to diet than to get straight As or master the piano. After Pam shed the five pounds she wanted to lose, she kept dieting and exercising rigidly. She is plugged into the idea of putting as little as possible into her body. It gives her a sense of power, even of superiority, to know she can live almost without food, that she can resist what others find irresistible.

From 120 pounds, she's down to below 90. She's lost some hair as well as weight. Some of her skin is scaly. She feels cold and bundles up. She has problems sleeping and suffers from constipation and sudden muscle cramps. When her periods stopped (amenorrhea), Pam wondered if her whole system was shutting down. But she hadn't felt too comfortable about menstruation anyway or the prospect of dating and future pregnancy. What finally scared Pam was that she went from feeling super-energetic to feeling debilitated. And when her sister came home from college, she took one look at Pam and started to cry.

Pam has a classic, all-too-common case of anorexia nervosa. If she doesn't get help soon, she could die or suffer lifelong problems. There *is* such a thing as being too thin.

Anorexia nervosa has been described as a psychosomatic and psycho-social illness in which irrational fear of being overweight leads to compulsive dieting. It can affect anybody, but statistics show that 90 to 95 percent of sufferers are women, especially young women. Some women diet success-fully or lose weight in an illness, then continue dieting until they've lost as much as 25 percent of their original body weight. As many as 1 in 100 women may be anorexic, and 6 percent of those with serious cases die. They starve to death or die of infections or heart failure. Others wait too long before they seek help; although they recover, they've done irreparable damage to their bodies due to drastic chemical imbalances and malnutrition.

Anorexia contributed to the untimely death in 1983 of singer Karen Carpenter, a former anorexic who died of heart failure when she was thirty-two. Princess Di's sister Lady Sarah also suffered from anorexia for two years.

What should you do if you recognize that you or a friend may be anorexic? Seek help. Talk to your family. Or the school nurse. Or a doctor. Ask the telephone operator or a librarian about a nearby eating disorder clinic or a hot-line number. Or phone or write to one of the following national organizations. Your inquiry will be confidential, and they can recommend support programs, free self-help groups, clinics, or therapists in your area. If you write, include a large, stamped, self-addressed envelope.

National Association of Anorexia Nervosa
    and Associated Disorders (ANAD)
P.O. Box 271
Highland Park, Illinois 60035
(312) 831-3438

American Anorexia/Bulimia Association, Inc.
133 Cedar Lane
Teaneck, New Jersey 07666
(201) 836-1800

Bulimia America Self-Help (BASH)
% St. John's Mercy Medical Center
615 South New Ballas Road
St. Louis, Missouri 63141
(800) 222-2832

National Anorexic Aid Society
550 South Cleveland Avenue, Suite F
Westerville, Ohio 43081
(614) 895-2009

Anorexia Nervosa and Related Eating Disorders, Inc.
P.O. Box 5102
Eugene, Oregon 97405
(503) 344-1144

Treatment may include short-term individual therapy, hospitalization, family therapy, or behavior modification therapy. It will entail gaining back some weight, learning to eat a balanced diet, and readjusting emotionally to overcome the phobia of weight gain and begin to deal with underlying troubles. You can recover. Your periods will return. You'll look healthier and feel stronger and more confident. You will get to a point at which willful starvation no longer appeals to you.

Bulimia

Jessica is not underweight. Her friends don't even realize she has a problem. But Jessica knows she's a compulsive eater, and she feels disgusted and guilty. At times, that guilt sends her back to the kitchen, where she eats a box of cookies, a bag of doughnuts, half a pie, or a quart of ice cream. She scarcely pauses between bites because she doesn't want to acknowledge what she's doing. After a pig-out, Jessica goes straight to the bathroom and vomits.

At first, she thought throwing up was a great way to get to eat her favorite foods without gaining weight. That was back when she had to use her finger to make herself vomit. Unfortunately, her unhealthy whim led to frequent self-induced vomiting, and now when she bends over, the food comes up on its own. Her mouth hurts and sometimes bleeds, and lately Jessica has been depressed by her yo-yo feast-or-famine eating patterns. Her fixation with food has gotten in the way of her social life. It has also diverted her attention from her other real problems.

Jessica spends a lot of time in the kitchen and bathroom. She binges about a dozen times a week. Sometimes she gorges on spaghetti, crackers, and bread instead of sweets. Sometimes she gets rid of it by using a laxative, an enema, or a diuretic instead of vomiting. But her weight doesn't fluctuate much—which frustrates her all the more.

Her parents think she simply has a healthy appetite. No one suspects that Jessica has a problem, because she covers her tracks. She hides her food. When she wants ice cream, she doesn't go wild at Carvel. She has two cones there, then goes to Swensen's, Baskin Robbins, and Dairy Queen.

Her obsession is becoming expensive. Once she stole $15 from her father's wallet for food. That made her feel terrible, and *that* made her binge extra. She wishes she could stop, but sometimes she panics and is afraid she has forgotten how to eat normally.

Jessica suffers from bulimia. If she continues to binge and purge, she may cause permanent damage to her body.

Bulimia (literally, "ox hunger") is common among young women and more prevalent than anorexia. Some anorexics "recover" only to become bulimic, which means they haven't really faced the conflicts behind their eating disorder. Also, just as some anorexics may avoid facing their sexuality by regressing to an almost prepuberty state physically, some bulimics mask their curves in fat.

A bulimic's habits are harmful. By vomiting right after eating, the bulimic throws up not only calories but water and digestive fluids as well. This can cause dehydration and a serious imbalance of body chemicals. The stomach acids that come up the esophagus and pour into the mouth can cause bleeding, gum disease, and tooth decay. Fasting leads to malnutrition and kidney problems and may stunt growth. Abuse of laxatives and enemas can make the bulimic prone to constipation and bowel lesions. In severe cases, the bulimic's eyes may be bloodshot and the hands and feet may be numb. Often the bulimic feels out of control, isolated, and depressed.

If, like Jessica, you are bingeing and purging and are always eating because of emotional rather than physical cues, you need help. Talk to your family or doctor or contact one of the groups listed. You can learn to modify your eating behavior, to take responsibility for your body, to express tensions in more constructive ways, and to be nicer to yourself. You will get better and, with determination, you will stay well. But the longer you are bulimic, the harder it is to recover.

EXCITED ABOUT EXERCISE

Don't think exercise. Think making friends, feeling stronger, losing weight, and living longer.

I hate the idea of exercise. But I love to bicycle, ski, swim, hike, dance, and play Frisbee. My friend Judy and I used to jog almost every day in summer when we were neighbors. It was a great way to keep in shape and to have one-on-one visits. Jogging is perfect, too, for getting to know guys. I used to be timid about asking a guy out for Friday night, but I was brazen about inviting Brad or Neil or Roberto to go on a long, talkative jog.

My friend Jen doesn't jog. But when we get together, we talk and walk—for miles. My former roommate Ellen and I figured out how to blab even while swimming! We'd meet at the pool, grab kickboards, and do laps while we visited.

This year I joined an aerobics group. In three weeks, I had thinner thighs, a firmer fanny, and several new acquaintances.

If you're a solitude fan, exercise can provide a time to be alone. Bliss can be a solo bike ride. If you're alone but want distraction, do sit-ups in front of the television or jumping jacks by the radio.

Will exercise make you voraciously hungry? *Au contraire.* Exercise actually suppresses appetite. If you exercise just before a meal, you'll get a double benefit. You'll eat less, and you'll burn calories faster, because your circulation speeds up. Plus, if you've just worked out, it's easy to feel health-minded and forgo the sundae. My favorite times to exercise are before dinner (when I'm getting hungry and tempted to snack) or first thing in the morning (so I start my day awake).

You may be getting enough exercise in gym, but why not go out for a sport or enlist a friend with whom to run or play tennis regularly? A minimum of twenty minutes of aerobic exercise three times a week is a must for health and well-being.

Walk whenever possible. Even if you have your license, why bother with car keys and parking when you're only going half a mile? Same with elevators. Don't press the button—climb the stairs!

If you want to take up jogging, be sure to start slowly and walk when winded. Other precautions?

- Get a good pair of running shoes.
- Warm up and finish by stretching.
- Jog flat-footed or roll from heel to toe—don't run on tiptoe.
- Jog on grass, not concrete.
- Don't jog right after eating.
- Don't jog near traffic or at dusk.
- Breathe through your nose, not your mouth, especially in a polluted city.
- When you come up behind somebody, say "Excuse me" or "Good morning" or "On your left" so the person doesn't think he or she is about to be ax-murdered.

One thing I like about exercise is it makes me feel I've earned my daily shower. When I step in hot and sweaty, I feel extra-clean and fresh when I step out.

I even jogged on my wedding day, with Judy, my maid of honor. My mother, aghast, was afraid we'd fall and have to hobble down the aisle. Instead, jogging made us both feel less nervous. And our cheeks looked naturally rosy.

Anybody out there think exercise is unfeminine? Once upon a time, it may have been considered unladylike for a woman to catch a high fly or have a vicious backhand. Today, staying fit is sexy. Ask Jane Fonda and Victoria Principal.

Too tired to exercise? Nonsense! A twenty-minute walk invigorates you more than a twenty-minute nap. Regular exercise gives you energy rather than sapping it. And yes, you can and should exercise during your period.

Racquetball, running, ballet, swimming, yoga—they're all marvelous, but you can also burn calories and tone muscles by doing a private belly dance as you brush your teeth. Or by walking briskly instead of shuffling your feet. Or by scissoring your legs as you talk on the phone. Or by pressing your feet down while studying as though you alone are preventing the floor from rising.

Here ends my Physical Fitness Pep Talk. Start exercising, if you don't already. It'll lift your spirits, improve your complexion, firm flab, relieve stress, strengthen your heart, speed your circulation, and leave you full of vim and vigor.

BODY SWEAT, BODY SMELLS

A couple of years ago, you hardly perspired, let alone had body odor. Now some of your glands are working hard to keep you cool, and that may mean underarm wetness. Some say, "Horses sweat, men perspire, and women glow," but while *glowing* sounds pleasant, *smelling* is another story.

Fight back! Shower or bathe daily. If necessary, use antiperspirant (to stop the wetness) or deodorant (to stop the odor) or a combination product. I prefer roll-ons, since pressure sprays pollute the atmosphere. Change brands periodically, since each product loses some effectiveness once your body gets used to it. Try to wear cotton or well-ventilated clothes.

While we're talking body odors, is gas ever a problem? If so, avoid notorious foods such as beans, cabbage, radishes, and spicy foods; don't drink too much apple cider, apple juice, or soda; don't chew gum endlessly. And eat s-l-o-w-l-y.

Want to smell like lemons, flowers, or exotic essences? Don't take bubble baths, because some can cause vaginal or urinary irritations. Instead, wear cologne. To sample testers, spray a little on your forearm, wait a few moments, and sniff. Your nose gets confused after three or four fragrances, so it may take a week to decide which to buy. Don't go too sweet or heavy, and remember that a little goes a long way. The effect should be subtle as a whisper.

CLEARING THE WAY FOR SMOOTH SKIN

Do you have a peaches-and-cream complexion? Do you even know anybody who does? Often when you want to look your best, your skin may look its worst. (*Teen* is truly a four-letter word!) More than 95 percent of the population runs into some acne trouble at some time. Many girls find their hormones are going haywire and pimples are popping up on their faces with the dependability of dandelions on a spring lawn.

The good news? Proper care can improve your complexion, medicated makeup can hide your blemishes, girls' skin troubles are generally not as bad as guys', and your flare-ups are only temporary. Soon your angry skin will calm down—and you can start worrying about wrinkles!

My teen diary is loaded with skin worries, such as: *"My face is a pimple patch but not as bad as usual."* After a year or two of private battles, I went to a dermatologist.

"Help," said I.

This is what he said:

1   Don't eat chocolate, nuts, sharp cheeses, or shellfish. Don't drink coffee or colas. Don't use iodized salt. (Other dermatologists claim chocolate is okay and point out that different people's skin reacts to different foods, and that it is worth finding out what in particular makes you break out.)

2   Hands off! Don't rest your chin or forehead in your palms. Don't pick at blemishes or squeeze blackheads—you can end up squeezing them in instead of out.

3   Drink plenty of water and juices; get a little sunshine; get lots of exercise and sleep.

4   Wash your face gently but religiously twice a day, and wash your back and chest well when showering.

Then he wrote out a prescription for antibiotics and recommended a cleansing soap. I followed his orders, and my complexion improved.

If your skin is polka-dotted, consider seeing a dermatologist. The first visit may cost around $30, and follow-up visits might run about $20 each. Sure, you could wait to outgrow your acne, but that could take years and leave scars. Dermatologists also remove warts and help get rid of pockmarks. If a wart, mole, or scar changes, have a dermatologist or doctor look at it—today.

New antibiotics and effective soaps are constantly being developed. Benzoyl peroxide and retinoic acid (vitamin A acid) help reduce the plugs in pores. And many dermatologists prescribe antibiotics such as tetracycline and erythromycin for oral or topical use. Of course, pregnant women should not take most drugs, and whenever a doctor prescribes a treatment, it is essential to follow directions precisely.

Should you curb your diet according to my dermatologist's plan? Maybe. Some experts say diet has nothing to do with pimples. You know your skin best, so you be the expert. If you eat a Mounds bar, is your face soon covered with little mounds? Why not run an experiment? Eat a forbidden food one day and see if you break out the next. Or eat healthfully for a few days and see if your skin looks extra pretty. Try this after your period so you don't throw off the results. You may end up devising your own off-limits list to include foods that make your skin react most. (French fries? Pizza?)

But pimples do not live by food alone. No matter what you eat, you may be a craterface for a while. Acne outside is a sign that you're maturing inside. You may break out around your "time of the month," or when you are stressed or scared or excited—or for no reason at all. Acne is not affected by sex life. And acne is not a losing battle, because you win in the end.

Meanwhile, don't forget to wash (not scrub) your face. Many pimples despise soap and water and will pack up and flee if you wash regularly. Your best zit-zapping plan of attack is to wash with soap and warm water morning and night, and rinse well with cool water before patting dry with a clean towel. Keep your hair clean, because greasy hair means greasy skin. (A shower a day helps keep the dermatologist away.) Never apply makeup before washing your face.

If your skin is soap-sensitive, try Neutrogena or other mild soaps. If your skin is dry, use a gentle creamy soap and a moisturizer. You can also spritz your face with a plant mister before moisturizing. The mist will make your skin as happy as it makes your asparagus fern! If your room is overheated, you can buy a vaporizer or put a pan of water on the radiator for added moisture. Prone to chapped skin? Smear lotion on your elbows, knees, hands, and feet.

Okay. Let's say you've been eating tofu, wheat germ, and other wholesome foods; you're washing well; you're exercising; you don't *use* makeup let alone sleep with it on; you swab your skin with a good product at bedtime—yet you still wake up every once in a while with a pimple the size of a tepee at the end of your nose.

What should you do? Wear a Band-Aid to school? Say to friends, "Can you believe this horrendous zit? I'm so ugly! My face looks like a relief map of the Andes!" Stay home and watch *Ryan's Hope?* No! Your best bet is to dab on a little medicated makeup and forget about it. In high school, my handsome older brother Mark once told me he didn't mind when his date had a blemish or two because it made him less self-conscious about his own slight acne.

Hang in there. Your face will soon clear up, and I doubt there will be a single telltale scar. More questions? Call 1-800-235-ACNE.

Speaking of complexion complexes, consider for a minute that golden tan we all crave. True or false: you want a surfer's tan and you don't care if you look like a prune in thirty years.

If you answered *true,* I'm with you. Baking in the sun is a sensuous luxury, and a deep tan under a white dress is striking. But when you are forty-four pushing fifty and your skin is dry, leathery, and lined, and you've already had a cancerous cyst removed, you'll probably wish you could step into a time machine and throttle your former self.

What's more, you *can* tan without burning or inviting skin cancer. Here are a dozen tips.

   1   Always bring a T-shirt or long-sleeved blouse with you to the beach or pool. Buy a cute hat to protect your cute face.
   2   Start tanning gradually. If you lie out for a full hour on day one, you won't look stunning by nightfall, you'll look like a lobster in pain. And if you're indoors up North all year and suddenly vacation for a week in the tropics, your skin will not appreciate the surprise.
   3   Douse yourself with a sunscreen lotion before and during sunning and after swimming. If you pour on the baby oil, you'll burn to a crisp. But if you apply a product with PABA (para-aminobenzoic acid), you'll block the most harmful rays. Start with a product that has a high sun protection factor, such as 15, then later use a lower SPF, such as 8.
   4   Don't trust those clouds. Around 70 to 80 percent of the sun's ultraviolet rays shine through them.
   5   Don't broil at midday. The sun is strongest—and most harmful—from 10 A.M. until 2 P.M.
   6   Know thyself. If you're fair-skinned, you may burn easily.
   7   Don't use a sun reflector. The skin under your chin and earlobes is particularly sensitive.

8   Stay away from sun lamps. Why wither your skin without getting the fun of the sun?

9   Take extra precautions if you live in the Southwest, the mountains, or wherever sun rays are especially fierce.

10   Take extra care if you're skiing, because snow reflects the sun's rays.

11   Know that birth control pills and certain antibiotics can make your skin more susceptible to burning or blotching.

12   Use a moisturizer after catching rays, so your skin will stay smoother longer. For best benefits, apply after you wash or bathe, while your skin is still moist.

A NOSE IS A NOSE IS A NOSE
AND ALL ABOUT EARS

You've tackled your skin troubles. What about the rest of your face? To be thorough, I'm going to tell you about cosmetic surgery—but don't expect me to recommend it.

For starters, it's expensive, it hurts, and it won't guarantee you'll be elected class president or prom queen. Plus, by replacing your distinguished feature with an ordinary one, you're losing part of your individuality. Jimmy Durante or Barbra Streisand might never have made it if they'd each had an everyday nose. Who nose?

So think twice, then twice more before you decide on plastic surgery. Is your life really being ruined by your hook nose or big ears? Or is it your attitude that needs fixing? If you change your hairstyle, don flashy earrings, make up your eyes, apply lipstick, and smile—won't that do the job? Besides, your face may still be changing and growing, and most surgeons won't operate until you're at least seventeen.

Say you are seventeen and you're sure—really sure—you want to see a different face in the mirror. Talk to your parents and family doctor. Find a competent specialist or you could end up looking worse instead of better. Elective surgery may cost anywhere from $800 to $3000 and is not usually covered by insurance unless it is medically necessary.

Consider having the operation the summer before college or before a family move. And don't expect miracles.

I visited my friend Miriam after she had her nose reshaped. "I had local anesthesia, so I didn't feel much, but I'm sore now," she said, sounding as if she had a terrible cold. For several weeks after the rhinoplasty operation, she had to avoid sun and take care not to bump into anything. (No Eskimo kissing that summer!) But when she started college, instead of feeling like Pinocchio, Miriam felt pretty. Instead of wasting time worrying about her schnozz (boring!), she directed her energy elsewhere.

Are you all ears? Many big-eared women (like me) hide their ears under hair, scarves, or hats. But some opt for otoplasty. A good-looking friend of mine told me that when he was growing up, he endured several nicknames, such as Dumbo, Elephant Ears, and Mr. Spock.

"Kids are so mean!" I said. But when Ben showed me an adorable photo of a flappy-eared eight-year-old, I almost burst out laughing.

Fortunately, he laughed first. "They stuck straight out!" Ben admitted and told me about his operation. "It was June and I'd broken my leg playing football. My mother came up with the idea, and since I was laid up anyway, I figured why not. The doctors cut away a little cartilage and pinned my ears closer to my head. Then I wore a bandage for a week. That, with the cast, and I looked like a wounded soldier. Anyway, my leg healed and so did my ears."

Rather than protruding, Ben's ears now lie flat against his head.

Ear piercing is a kind of cosmetic surgery, too, although it's small potatoes next to the dramatic physical and psychological transformations associated with rhinoplasty and otoplasty.

If you want to pierce your ears, first be sure you can. Do you bleed more than most people? Are you unusually prone to allergies and infections? Do you have keloid skin or skin that scars easily? (I do.) If you answered no, no, no, no, then yes, you can get your ears pierced.

But don't have a friend do it. Go to a doctor or qualified jeweler. It's not expensive and it doesn't hurt much. Then keep your gold posts in for as long as possible before wearing other metals or wires. And at first always swab your ears with alcohol to minimize the risk of infection. If your ears become red or swollen, consult your school nurse or doctor.

EYE DEAL

Do you need glasses? One out of every two Americans does. Seeing your best is part of looking your best. Don't squint or let your grades sink or say a mere *hi* in the hall because you can't identify the friendly hunk approaching you.

In college, I went to the theater with my friend Gilbert and, feeling coy, tried on his glasses. What a shock! I could see the actors' expressions rather than just fuzzy features. I hadn't realized what I was missing. An optometrist confirmed that I needed glasses for plays, movies, and driving. So I got framed! Now I love seeing leaves on the trees, feathers on the birds, windows on the skyscrapers, faces in the crowds.

Do you get headaches after you read? Is your vision blurry? Do you have trouble making out road signs, small print, subtitles, or words on the blackboard? Get your eyes checked annually. If you need glasses or contact lenses, don't wait around.

Glasses come in all sorts of attractive shapes, colors, tints, and styles. Some people look better with them on than off. I know a graduate student who owns half a dozen frames and wears them to match her outfits and moods.

Contacts often cost more than glasses, require more care, and take some adjusting to. The payoff is that contacts don't change your appearance and do offer better peripheral and straight-ahead vision. Your eye doctor can help you decide if you want soft, hard, or extended-wear contacts, with tinted or clear lenses.

A MOUTHFUL ABOUT MOUTHS

My first dentist was a horrible bald man with a tic. He used to make me kiss him on the cheek each visit and he was stingy with the Novocaine. "Raise your hand if it hurts," he'd say, then ignore me as I waved wildly. His motto was probably: Drill, fill, and bill.

We changed dentists. My new one is friendly, painless, and capable. He doesn't hand me a headphone when he works, but, hey, you can't have everything. My only complaint is that sometimes he asks, "How have you been, Carol?" then pops a water-sucking gizmo under my tongue so all I can mumble is "Fffah, jjus ffahn."

This dentist always gives me sunny sermons about oral hygiene. Brush, floss, and use a water jet. Morning, noon, and night. Carry floss and a toothbrush in your purse for after lunch—the brush should have soft bristles and be replaced often. "At least rinse your mouth at the water fountain or in the bathroom," he pleads, "and avoid sticky sweets and sugar-coated gum." "Coffee, tea and cigarettes stain your teeth," he warns, "and cola rots them." I go to him every year, but none of his advice impresses me as much as the block-letter sign that hangs in his office: IGNORE YOUR TEETH AND THEY'LL GO AWAY.

Run your tongue over your teeth right now. Do they feel coated and grimy or slick and clean?

Does the tap water in your town contain fluoride? Fluoride helps strengthen teeth. That's why a fluoride toothpaste is the best cavity-fighter. Do your gums bleed every time you brush? You don't want to develop periodontal (gum) disease, so floss religiously.

Do you ever have halitosis? To prevent bad breath, use a mouthwash and brush your teeth and even your tongue and the roof of your mouth gently with toothpaste. If you're going out, don't eat onions or garlic bread. Carry mints with you. Your breath is still bad? You may have indigestion, an infection, or tooth decay, so see your dentist.

A college friend and I thought up a tactful way to inform each other when we had stale breath. We'd say "B^2" (for bad breath) just as many people say "XYZ" for "examine your zipper" (a less humiliating cue than "your fly is open").

What about braces? No one said they were fun. I was a Tinsel Teeth when I was fourteen. In ninth grade, I once wrapped my retainer in a napkin at lunchtime, bussed my tray, and accidentally threw my lumpy napkin away. I realized what I'd done in the middle of geometry and went racing to the lunchroom custodian. But the trash can had already been emptied into the huge garbage bin outside. Crestfallen, I returned to class. Twenty minutes later, the loudspeaker blared, "Will the girl who discarded her retainer please report to the cafeteria?" Talk about feeling mortified! The custodian and I were soon sifting through four garbage bags. I found my retainer, but had lost my cool!

Yet I am happy now that my bite is right. If you have braces, remember you're not the only one, and your teeth will soon look fabulous. Meanwhile, hold off on lipstick if you don't want to accent your mouth. But don't stop smiling.

By the way, you may want to ask your dentist or orthodontist about the new invisible or lingual braces (more expensive than hardware) and about bonding, which is a modern, less costly alternative to capping. Go to a pro—put your money where your mouth is!

Your wisdom teeth probably won't appear for several years. If you're lucky, they won't appear at all or they'll grow in straight. If not, welcome to the club. You may have to get them removed—which means, instead of getting money from the tooth fairy, you give it to the oral surgeon.

After your teens, you'll be less cavity prone. But the teeth you have should last a lifetime (that's 78 years for most women), so take care of them.

HAIR CARE

I hope you're happy with your hair. I'm pretty happy with mine. I wore it long in high school and I've had it short ever since. Mine is the wash-and-wear variety, but I understand the angst of those with less manageable hair. My college roommate got up hours before class to wash, dry, and straighten her hair. And my mother stayed up late at night to wash, dry, and curl hers.

Shall I tell you three dumb things I did with my hair when it was long? First and worst, I hunted in it for split ends—a waste of time and a good way to go cross-eyed. (Getting my mop chop broke that habit in a hurry.) Second, I sprayed a bleach product in it when I was ten. Months later, when the brown roots grew in, my half-and-half hair looked cheap and unattractive. Third, I didn't know about brushing tangles out *before* shampooing or about using a conditioner, so I often emerged from a shower with a head full of sailor's knots. End of confessions.

How about you? Are you shampooing as frequently as you need to? Meryl Streep told David Hartman that to be beautiful, "You hold in your stomach a lot, and you just wash your hair a lot." Shampoo short hair every day if necessary; shampoo long hair less often so you don't damage it.

Choose shampoo for dry, oily, regular, or damaged hair or for a dandruff problem. Then switch brands occasionally, because your hair may get used to a product and not come as clean the twentieth time as it did the first.

Why do the directions suggest you lather and rinse, then repeat the whole process? Because that way you'll use up the shampoo in a flash and quickly shell out another $2.99. Unless you let your hair get so greasy you could fry an egg in it (heaven forbid), one sudsing should suffice. Work up a lather in your hand before you apply it to your hair. If your hair is long or particularly dirty, go ahead and use a dab of shampoo for round two. Massage your scalp with fingertips, not nails. And be sure to get out all—*all*—the shampoo. Until your hair squeaks, don't hop out of the shower.

If you have dry, brittle, or damaged hair, you may want to use a conditioner. Combing your hair with a wide-tooth comb or brushing it with a straight brush with soft bristles and rounded tips will help, too, because that activates oil glands. Let your hair air-dry whenever possible.

When your hair is wet, don't brush it. Comb it with a wide-tooth comb. Keep combs and brushes clean by washing them with shampoo. Some hairs will fall out whenever you comb or brush. Don't worry unless you're losing lots of hair in chunks.

The following are foolproof ways to destroy your lovely locks: Braid strands so tightly they snap off at the hairline. Tug off curlers violently so hairs break. Blow-dry hair with high heat and no attachments between curls and red-hot wires. Get your hair permed or chemically straightened too often. Eat too much junk food.

I once asked a man who cuts hair, "Do you think women look best in long or short hair?"

His answer: "They look best in hair that is well styled and well kept up."

But whom can you trust with a pair of scissors? I've had my hair cut at barber schools for $4, at salons for $12 to $20, and at fancy New York shops for $40.

What's important is to look around until you find a stylist you like. If you admire a friend's cut, ask who did it and make an appointment. Once you're in the chair, trust the pro or speak your mind. Don't let anyone whack away a foot of hair while you save your tears for Mom. If you're happy with the job, remember the stylist's name and become a regular customer.

Don't hide behind your hair. Long hair needs to be trimmed every few months. Short hair, every six to eight weeks. Hair grows fastest in summer. Sounds expensive? Sometimes you can save money by shampooing at home or skipping the blow-dry. Call ahead and ask. Or have a competent friend do the job.

What about body hair?

About two years before your first period, your pubic hair probably started growing in, straight and fine at first, then coarser and darker. About six months before your first period, your underarm hair may have begun to appear. You may even have a few tiny hairs around your nipples.

Lots of young women don't get rid of the hair on their legs and underarms. If the hair doesn't bother you, don't bother it.

If you *do* want silky legs and smooth underarms in summer or all year long, you may want to start shaving. Once you begin, your hair won't grow back quite as fine as it was, so you may have to continue shaving.

Shaving is easy. Use a cream or soap and try not to nick yourself. I like disposable razors. If you're shaving in the tub, be sure to clean it afterward so you won't leave a ring for the next person.

You could try an electric razor. (Not with wet legs or the experience would be shocking!)

Waxing is another alternative. You can buy a do-it-yourself product, or go to a salon, where it hurts less and costs more. The effect of waxing is long-lasting, and the technique is popular in Europe.

Using a depilatory on your legs seems slow and messy to me, but that's another option.

Do you have a mustache? I do. Not a handlebar, but a noticeable nuisance nonetheless. Every so often, I have to cream the fine hairs off with a depilatory. That doesn't leave stubble or stimulate growth. And it beats five o'clock shadow!

Some women prefer bleach. I don't think much of white mustaches. You could wax it off (ouch) or, if the problem is serious, you might consider electrolysis. It's not cheap, but it is permanent because it destroys hair roots. Your physician can recommend an electrologist. Don't expect overnight wonders. I know someone who has had periodic appointments with an electrologist for four years now.

Ditto all the above for any other unwanted body hair: on your chin, belly button, thighs. If your eyebrows are very bushy, or if you have an almost-eyebrow between your eyes, you may want to tweeze or cream away those hairs. I knew a girl who looked as though she had one long eyebrow instead of two short ones. I didn't know her well enough to say so, but she would have looked prettier if she'd tweezed or dissolved the middle brow. I hope some close and gentle friend eventually made the suggestion, and I hope the girl was mature enough to say, not "Mind your own business," but "Thanks for letting me know."

NICE NAILS

Modesty is fine, but it's crazy not to recognize and enjoy your good qualities—particularly if you're going to feel awful about one puny pimple or one unwanted hair.

That said, I hope you won't slam your book shut if I tell you straight out that I have nice nails. I didn't always, but I do now and I show them off by painting them vivid colors from cherry blossom to spiced apple.

The thing is, I bit my nails to the quick in high school. The class creep once walked past me in the hall, jammed his hand upside down in his mouth, and pretended to gnaw—a cruel imitation of yours truly.

He made his point. Not only were my nails ugly, but the nibbling habit itself was ugly.

I tried to quit. I tried bad-tasting polish. I tried wearing gloves during scary movies. I tried nail hardener. I taped my mouth shut while doing homework. I wore Band-Aids on my stubs at night. But I didn't stop for good until my husband proposed.

Rob presented me with an antique diamond ring that had belonged to his grandmother. I couldn't wear such a beautiful ring on such an unsightly hand, so I dredged up all my willpower and kicked the habit.

If you're a biter, you don't have to get engaged to break the habit. When you're truly ready to quit, you'll quit.

Check your nails. Maybe you've never bitten, but are they looking their best? Are they ragged or uneven or dirty? Are they so long they look like claws? People *do* notice.

Use an emery board and file your nails in one direction only. If you want to polish them, start with a clear base coat. That strengthens them and keeps them from turning yellow if you use colored polish. Let each coat dry thoroughly before applying the next coat. And make sure the polish on all ten nails stays on. No bare spots! (I often carry the polish

I'm wearing tightly sealed in a plastic bag in my purse.) Remove all old polish before applying a new color, even if that means giving yourself a manicure every few days.

I don't think expensive polishes stay on any better than cheap ones. All polishes last longer if kept in the refrigerator.

If colorful nails don't appeal to you, skip the glass bottles and cotton balls. I think polish is fun; you may think it's frivolous or only for special occasions.

COSMETICS AND CLOTHES

A girl in my high school, Vivian, always stood tall, wore chic, pulled-together clothes, did her makeup just right, and carried herself confidently. She assumed she was beautiful, and no one questioned her.

Looking over my senior yearbook, I see that she was cute, but no cuter than Judy or Jen. Yet because Vivian made a point of looking her best, she glowed with self-assurance. She didn't come off as vain or affected. She came off as striking.

Attitude and self-esteem really are half the battle. Remember the song from *West Side Story?* "I feel pretty, oh so pretty . . ." Maria had the right idea. If you think pretty instead of mousy, others start thinking of you as pretty instead of mousy.

Positive thinking alone can't turn an ordinary girl into a Perfect Ten. But if you like yourself and play up your best features with makeup and clothes, you can go up several points on that infamous 1 to 10 scale. As Helena Rubenstein said, "There are no ugly women, only lazy ones."

Makeup is a remarkable option. Just consider the before/after faces of the Merle Norman ads, or how cosmetics made Julie Andrews look like a man in *Victor/Victoria* and Dustin Hoffman look like a woman in *Tootsie.* I didn't wear any makeup in my early teens and I rarely do now when I'm home writing. But I love putting it on when I go out. A little brown eyeshadow, dark mascara, eyeliner, blush, lipstick—and abracadabra, I look and feel more glamorous! Face-painting is fast, creative, and, for me, one of the pleasures of being female.

Inexpensive makeup often works as well as the expensive stuff. Experiment, and throw makeup out when it gets runny or flaky or old. Don't borrow a friend's makeup. If your eyes or skin get irritated, try hypoallergenic varieties. Also beware of free makeovers—the boutique beautician will encourage you to spend $39.50 on supplies afterward.

With makeup, less is more, and soft and subtle look prettiest, especially on girls and especially during the day. You want people to think "You look pretty," not "You do your makeup well." Study magazines and friends. And don't wear so much that you feel homely without it. If you don't wear any, that's A-okay, too.

What about clothes? Do you have a passion for fashion? I can't afford to update my wardrobe every season, and I couldn't get away with gold knickers or leather pants anyway. (Where would I wear them?) But I like keeping an eye on mannequins, models, and peers. I try to create new looks by playing up accessories—a shiny belt, round red earrings, a bracelet. Since I love flat comfortable Chinese shoes, I've bought them—at $6 or less a pair—in a rainbow of colors.

Keep your clothes clean and in good repair. Give things to charities each year (bonus: it may be tax deductible), and put summer clothes away in winter, and winter clothes away in summer.

Figure out what colors and styles are in vogue and look best on you, then try new combinations. Some clothes make me look dumpy, while others make me look slender. Dark colors flatter me, but pretty pastels wash me out. Accent your best figure feature with bright colors and downplay your worst with dull ones. Trade clothes with friends; give and accept hand-me-downs. As you get to know yourself, you'll create your own style.

You project your personality and interests through clothes. Are you artsy, preppy, sporty? Show it! If you're romantic, you may favor ruffles and lace. If you're athletic, you may prefer sweats and casuals. Don't give off conflicting messages by dressing trendily if you're super-conservative, wearing pink and green if you're down on preppies, or buttoning your shirt up to your chin, then acting like a vamp.

Looking like everybody else is fine, and safe, but why not learn to express yourself. With flair! With the right attitude, makeup, and wardrobe, you can sparkle.

EVEN BEAUTIFUL GIRLS GET THE BLUES

Yes, there have been times when I'd have swapped my mug for the face of a cover girl and my body for an actress's show-stopping curves. But those of us who haven't won any beauty pageants should remember that those who have don't necessarily lead happier lives.

One of my high school pals is a model, yet although black-haired green-eyed Danielle always looks terrific, she doesn't always feel terrific. She's not deluged by dates. (Are guys scared of her? Are her standards impossible? Do guys assume she's taken?) When they do call, Danielle wonders if they care about her or if they're after sex or just want to show her off like a trophy.

Meanwhile she's already worrying about what she'll do in five years when her face-based career could come to a thudding halt.

Danielle has few girlfriends with whom to discuss her insecurities. "When I meet a girl, I feel I have to bend over backward being nice or she'll think I'm conceited."

Her confession shamed me into realizing that when I meet a knockout, I'm not always my most amiable. Part of me feels threatened and almost wants to believe that although she's stunning, she's also shallow, boring, or quick-tempered.

You may be more magnanimous. You may have no trouble immediately liking a girl who is gorgeous, brilliant, talented, rich, happy, and seemingly picture-perfect. If so, you deserve a *Saint* before your name. Most of us want to glimpse a filling in that dazzling smile. We want our goddesses to be human.

Another pitfall of being beautiful is that beauties are often judged by ridiculously high standards. Have you ever seen a model in a magazine and instead of thinking, "She looks exquisite," thought, "She's looked better" or "She's not *that* amazing"? It must be tough knowing the pressure is on to look breathtaking day in and day out.

I'm not saying we should feel sorry for gorgeous women or assume *lovely* means *lonely*. But it's good to look at the flip side of beauty. Plus, like Avis, we fair-to-cuties try harder, and that usually means developing our personality and intelligence—traits that never fade.

SLEEP TIGHT

Are you sleeping too little or too much? If I sleep less than six hours, I'm grumpy. More than ten, I'm groggy. Sleep is essential to keep your resistance up. But if you're sleeping away half the day or napping constantly, you may be using sleep to escape. Insomnia, too, is often a sign that something is troubling you and needs to be talked out.

For most people, nodding off is not a problem. When it is? Skip the coffee, cola, tea, or chocolate at night because they contain caffeine, a stimulant. A cup of milk or chamomile tea accompanied by a warm bath or not-for-school book is a more soothing choice for the wide awake. Don't take sleeping pills; they're addictive. And try to think of occasional insomnia as an opportunity: to do schoolwork, write in a diary, or read a short story.

When you're ready for bed, take off socks and underwear and put on a comfortable gown or pajamas. Lie on your back on a firm mattress, ideally without a pillow or with a fairly flat pillow. In that position, your spine is aligned, none of your organs or limbs is squashed, and you won't wake up with a crick in your neck or your cheek all puckered with wrinkles from the sheets. Now breathe rhythmically from the bottom of your lungs through your nose. Imagine yourself floating. Tell your muscles to relax, one by one. Drift. Zzzzz. . . .

MONO: A TEEN DISEASE

Freshman year at college, my motto was: Work hard, play hard. For two months, I got up at 7:30, went full steam until dinner, studied until 9:30, partied until 1:30. Late to bed and early to rise proved unhealthy and unwise and was the start of my demise!

To put it more succinctly: I got mono.

It was a cold November, I was run-down, I hadn't been wearing my hat or gloves, and I'd been ignoring a sore throat. The lymph glands in my neck began to swell, and I remember watching somebody jog (my sport!) and thinking, "How can he have so much energy?" I went for a finger-puncture blood test, and my fear was confirmed.

My case of infectious mononucleosis was diagnosed early, but there are no magic-cure pills. "Get plenty of rest and sleep and eat a balanced diet," was all the doctors could recommend. "Avoid contact sports, because if you rupture your spleen, you're in big trouble."

I took it very easy for a week and felt better fast. But some cases of mono knock people out for months.

Mono is still a mysterious viral illness. Anybody can contract it, but teenagers are most susceptible. Although it's been called the kissing disease, you can get it without kissing, and it's not as contagious as you might suspect. It's more contagious in the incubation stage (before it's diagnosed) than afterward.

If you've had mono once, you are unlikely to get it again. Let's hope you don't get it at all.

Whenever you have bizarre symptoms, take them seriously. It's free to see the school nurse. It's easy to make a doctor's appointment. Don't let anyone call you a hypochondriac when *you're* the one who is hurting. Maybe the nurse will say "It's nothing, false alarm," but then your mind will be at ease. Or maybe you have a common cold and need to be reminded to rest, drink plenty of fluids, gargle with salt water, and take medication. Or maybe your stomach or head hurts due to stress and not physical factors. Fine. Psychosomatic bellyaches still ache, so it's important to know you may need not an antacid, but to start untying the knots.

I try to take as few pills as possible. When I do take them, I follow directions carefully. Don't just swallow a pill. Down it with plenty of water.

In the *Sex* chapter, I'll tell you all about sexually transmitted diseases. Illnesses not commonly associated with sex or teens aren't covered in this book. If you don't have diabetes, epilepsy, anemia, asthma, or any other disease, count your blessings. Really. If you do, follow your doctor's advice and take extra good care of yourself.

DISABILITIES

Given: We often take our youth and health for granted. Equally true: We often take our "normal" bodies and minds for granted.

Millions of people aren't so fortunate. Some have slight dyslexia, a treatable reading disability. Others have severe cerebral palsy. Others are paraplegic. Others are deaf or blind. Others . . . well, the list could go on and on.

I'm not suggesting we thank our stars each day for our twenty fingers and toes and our ability to wiggle them—although that's not a bad idea. I am saying we should remember to treat disabled people with respect, not with condescending courtesy, unwelcome pity, cruel teasing, or grudging avoidance. Too many people act as though disabilities were contagious and all disabled persons were also retarded or unfeeling.

As Ted Kennedy, Jr., whose right leg was amputated a dozen years ago, eloquently put it, "Disabled people are not unable people. . . . we are people first and disabled second."

If someone is deaf and can lip read, don't shout. Face the person, speak slowly, and enunciate well. If someone is blind and hesitating at an intersection, don't grab the person's arm. Offer help without insisting. If you're baby-sitting for a little girl and she points and says, "Why is that boy in a wheelchair?" don't scold the child. It's natural for her to be curious. Tell her it's impolite to point, but give her an answer. "Maybe because of an accident or an illness or because he was born with weak legs. He uses the wheelchair to get around." If you yank the child away and make her feel uncomfortable, you're reinforcing the idea that disabled people should be shunned.

Have you ever been with a friend who has parked in a space reserved for the handicapped, then gotten out limping and giggling? To someone else, the convenience of the space is not a laughing matter. I'm for finding another parking place and being glad you're able to walk the extra yards.

If you are or have recently become disabled, it's bound to be very hard at times to accept your limitations and society's prejudices. I hope you'll ultimately concentrate on what you *can* do and not get bogged down in what you can't. Counselors and rehabilitation centers can help you toward that aim. To quote Ted Kennedy, Jr., again, "It is not that people are handicapped. It's that they're physically and mentally challenged."

SPEAKING OF BODY LANGUAGE

Ever notice the ads that show before/after shots of women who have supposedly lost weight, increased their bust size, or gotten rid of pimples and varicose veins? In the before pose, they're slouching and frowning. In the after photo, they're standing tall and smiling. No wonder they look better! That's what body language is all about.

If you look around at an airport, you can make some fairly accurate guesses about people by "reading" their bodies. You can't know how they feel about a nuclear freeze, but you may be able to tell how they feel about each other.

Imagine that on one bench you see a man and a woman with two feet of space and two briefcases between them. They're reading with their legs crossed in opposite directions. Are they friends, business partners, siblings, strangers?

If you guessed strangers, you're probably right.

How about the couple on the next bench? They're talking, smiling, looking into each other's eyes. He brushes her hair with his fingers; she gives his arm a squeeze.

Chances are they started dating recently. If they'd just met, they'd be less forward; if they were married, they'd indulge in less PDA (public display of affection).

The twist is that if you can figure out facts about people just by tuning in to how they sit, stand, touch, or move, they can do the same about you.

Body language can speak louder than words. A wink can start a romance and a hug can stop a quarrel.

My mother always got after me to—ready?—stand up straight, pull back my shoulders, tuck my fanny in, not wrinkle my forehead, not swing my arms as I walked, look people squarely in the eye, and shake hands firmly without fracturing fingers. My response was usually an exasperated polysyllabic "Mah-ah-ahmmm!" but now I'm grateful. Because I learned to look confident, people started treating me as though I were confident, and I began to feel confident.

Do you have teachers who move and gesture while they lecture? You probably pay more attention to them than to the ones who sit behind the desk, arms folded, shoulders drooping. Teachers can tell if you're fascinated or bored by whether you're leaning forward attentively or slumping and drawing on your shoe. So sit up—your grades may go up, too.

Caution: You can't always read strangers correctly, because body language varies somewhat from person to person and culture to culture. For example, some people look down to show respect rather than maintaining eye contact. And European teens do more handshaking and cheek-kissing than we do.

Or consider the limp handshake. I used to tutor English to a charming Japanese woman who had just moved to America. Yoko bowed beautifully but shook hands about as energetically as an old Labrador. One day we worked on it. Now Yoko can shake as well as a politician—and I can bow!

No matter where you are, you probably want your body to show that you are warm, open, and amiable. Unless you insist on being center stage and gesticulating wildly, or on clinging to dark corners and standing tense and immobile, you probably aren't closing out anybody. If you think your body doesn't register as friendly, relax and smile so others feel welcome. You'll start meeting new people and making new friends. Speaking of which, let's move on to the *Friendship* chapter, shall we?

2
FRIENDSHIP

YOU DON'T LIKE EVERYBODY; WHY SHOULD EVERYBODY LIKE YOU?

The phrase "just friends" makes little sense to me: Friendship should never be trivialized.

It takes time and effort to make new friends and keep old ones. It's not easy to overcome shyness, listen to someone else's troubles, phone or write when you're busy, get together with the girls when you'd rather spend time with a guy. But it's worth it. I don't collect coins, stamps, or cat figurines, but I guess I collect people. Friends are one of the staples of my life.

Friends congratulate and console, heighten pleasure and ease pain. Judy sent a bouquet of flowers when Harper & Row offered me the chance to write this book. And I was matron of honor at her joyful wedding. Jen drove for miles to be with me after my father died. And we talked for days after she broke up with a man she loved.

You can get by without being popular; you can live without a boyfriend; you can survive without one particular best friend. But if you have no friends, you're missing out. After all, a friend who likes you teaches you to like yourself. Friends exchange the gift of self-confidence. This chapter is about making lasting friendships with girls and guys and, most vital, making friends with yourself.

GIRLFRIENDS LAST LONGER THAN BOYFRIENDS

I'm not knocking romance or saying that sweethearts never go platonic or high school honeys never marry. But chances are, in ten years, you'll still be in touch with some of the girls who are close to you now, whereas the guys in your life now will be in someone else's life.

In high school, I spent thousands of hours with a terrific green-eyed curly-haired boyfriend. Today we exchange Christmas cards every few years. I also spent endless afternoons with Judy and Jen. Today, though we live in different cities, they are still important to me and we keep in touch.

Same thing happened in college. I dated Chris, Walter, Steve, Ludo, Alger—lots of guys, lots of fun. But most of the Yale males I keep up with are the ones I never kissed. Meanwhile, the girls I knew in classes, dormitories, and dining rooms are still my buddies. When Helen, Ellen, Amy, Sonia, and I got together at a class reunion recently, we had a blast.

Don't turn down dates. But be aware that your summer loves may not last until fall, whereas the friendships you make with girls now may last a lifetime.

TEN WAYS TO MAKE FRIENDS

You'd like to make friends and widen your social circle? Don't just stand there—smile, laugh, talk, listen, ask, whisper, admire! As Ralph Waldo Emerson said, "The only way to have a friend is to be one."

1   **Figure out whom you want to be friends with and why.** If you want to be friends with Melodie because she's popular or Sandy because she's pretty, it will probably be more difficult and less rewarding than if you want to be friends with Sue because you both love to write or Barbara because you're both into hiking. Your future friends are the people with whom you share interests.

You can also learn by observing the people you want to know better. Why do you wish Lanie were your friend? If it's because she is always "up" or funny or considerate, then cultivate those traits in yourself.

2   **Get involved with after-school activities.** If you're interested in sports, join the field hockey or gymnastics team and meet the athletes. If you're interested in government, join the student council and meet the politicians. Stars in your eyes? Try out for the school play. If you don't make it, don't stay home. Help with sets or lights or props or programs.

When I joined the Byram Hills French Club, I met fellow francophiles. When I volunteered to work with handicapped kids at the Mount Kisco Boys' Club, I made friends with some popular older students who had never before lowered themselves to say hi to me in the halls. When I became timer and scorer for the Boys' Lacrosse Team, I got to know some great guys.

By being active and on the go, you keep meeting people, and you stay busy and interesting. Besides, someone who is enthusiastic about lots of projects usually makes better company than someone whose main extracurric is sitting around. So don't spread yourself too thin, but don't sit there like a blob of mayo.

3 Introduce yourself and remember names. Don't wait for someone to make formal introductions or for a person to decide he or she would like to meet you. March right up and say hello. When I say, "Hi, I'm Carol," to a girl I've never met, she doesn't look at me funny. She says hi back.

I wasn't born with a skill for remembering names. But I've learned to be good at it. It's easy. When someone introduces herself, listen to her name and repeat it: "Glad to meet you, Janice." A few sentences later, use her name again: "Janice, where are you from?" Make a point of catching the name the first time, and you won't forget it so quickly.

Some people try to remember names by associating them with the person. Blair is blond; Toby is tubby. Whether you remember names by paying attention on the first go-around or by using an elaborate mnemonic device, it's a knack you should acquire a.s.a.p.

What if you say "Hi, Tim" in the lunchroom, and Tim doesn't remember your name? He may feel embarrassed as he mumbles an unadorned hi. But he may also rush to ask his friends who that friendly girl is.

4 Master the art of conversation. Don't you hate when you're in the middle of telling a story and someone interrupts? You're describing your date to see the *Casablanca/Play It Again, Sam* double bill with Raleigh. "No sooner did the lady behind the counter hand me my popcorn," you say, "than I slipped and spilled it! Raleigh turned around and—" Then some loudmouth butts in, *"Play It Again, Sam? I saw that! Woody Allen is awesome! I was just reading this interview. . . ."*

You'll make friends faster if you let people finish their sentences and thoughts. Let them talk, and listen to what they're saying. If someone says she just got back from vacation, don't immediately chime in, "So did I." Ask, "How was it?" "Where'd you go?" If she says she went white-water canoeing down the Colorado River, don't say "Huh." Encourage her to tell you about it by nodding, looking her in the eye, asking questions requiring more than a yes/no answer, saying "Really?" and peppering her paragraph with "That's amazing" and "How incredible." What if that same loudmouth Woody Allen fan interrupts her story? Wait it out, then invite her to pick up where she left off by saying, "So what *did* you do when the boat toppled?"

People like to talk about themselves, and a good listener is always appreciated. Besides, you learn more by listening than by talking.

That doesn't mean you should give your tongue to the cat. But just as run-on sentences don't thrill your English teacher, nonstop chitchat won't win you instant pals. If you're sparing no details ("Last Friday, or maybe it was Thursday, I'm not sure, anyway, Robin and I went to that lake, you know, the one with the pier that's really long, anyway, so he goes, 'I like this place,' so I go, 'It is pretty,' and he goes, 'Yeah,' and we looked at the clouds—there was this one that looked exactly like a scoop of vanilla ice cream . . ."), you're boring somebody. Beware, too, of talking too much about yourself. (Have you heard the joke that defines an egotist as someone who is me-deep in conversation?)

The ideal conversation should run about half listening, half talking. If you tend to be too quiet, force yourself to speak up more in class and at meals. You don't have to expound on the politics of Latin America, but say something. Make a deal with yourself that every day you will hold a brief conversation with at least one girl, guy, teacher, librarian, or someone you hardly know. A little shyness can be endearing, but if you're *too* timid, some will misinterpret your shyness as snobbery. Worse, you aren't meeting people. Yet you have nothing to hide. You have as much to offer as the brazen kids—who sometimes feel anxious, too.

5   Develop charm. Is charm something you're born with? Not necessarily. If your father is a Boston-bred ambassador and your mother is a Southern belle actress, the odds are in your favor. But anyone can learn to be irresistibly charming, to guys and girls.

Charm is empathy with style. It's making sure no one feels left out. It's telling your friend's parents that their home looks like it belongs in *House & Garden* (if it is well decorated) or saying that you've never tasted such fabulous zucchini bread (if it is truly delicious). It's offering a hand when needed. It's being supportive instead of sarcastic. It's answering, "Are these pants too tight?" with, "I think your other pair is more flattering" rather than "God, you've gained weight!" It's helping someone get his foot out of his mouth instead of laughing at his faux pas. It's apologizing when it was your fault. And when it wasn't, it's saying, "I must not have explained this very well," instead of, "I can't believe you screwed up!" It's giving a guy the benefit of the doubt. It's making a girl feel good by tuning in, drawing her out, and showing with and without words that you are enjoying her company. It's listening to the end of a story when you realize no one else is. It's laughing at someone's joke even when it wasn't funny.

As you first practice charm, you may feel phony or manipulative or as though you're trying too hard. But soon it should feel more natural and become more genuine.

People like people who like them. So if you find someone you like, and you project that fondness or respect, you have a head start on turning a stranger into a friend.

6   Give and get compliments graciously. Flattery may not get you everywhere, but it won't hurt in your quest for friends. When you admire something, say so. Everybody loves a sincere compliment, so learn to praise generously. "What a great necklace!" "Your handwriting is so pretty." "Our basketball team would be nothing without you." "You drive really well." "You have the sunniest smile." Hardly anyone would greet a warm compliment with a cold shoulder.

If you want yours to have extra impact, pay tribute to something that usually goes unnoticed. If you ran into Paul Newman buying a ham on rye at a deli, you wouldn't make an impression with "You have the bluest eyes." Same principle with classmates. Yet you'd be surprised at how delighted the school quarterback would be if you told him he has a beautiful voice. (Don't be insincere. False flattery will endear you to nobody.)

You're not a compliment butcher, are you? Some people mean well but their compliments come out backhanded, so instead of sowing the seeds of friendship, they're paving the path of animosity. I once made the mistake of telling a girl, "You've lost a ton of weight!" instead of simply, "You look wonderful." My slim would-be friend looked more grim than grateful.

Other gems to avoid: "Your complexion looks clear today." "Your hair looks so shiny—you must have washed it." "This is really tasty; you didn't cook it yourself, did you?"

And when the tables turn? Do you accept compliments gracefully? If a guy says, "I like your shirt," do you immediately say, "I like yours, too"? Do you gasp, "You're kidding, I've had it for *eons*"? Do you explain, "I picked it up for $3.99 at a garage sale in Kansas City"? The best way to accept a compliment is to smile and say, "Thank you." If you like, you can add, "That's nice of you to say."

Beware of fishing for compliments—you might come up with a boot!

7   **Don't rush it.** Friendship at first sight? Could be shaky. You'll hit it off with some people instantly, and you'll click with others fairly fast, but friendships, like plants, take time to grow. Some friendships that are quickly made quickly fade.

If you try to hurry a friendship, you may come off as pushy or intense. If you ask dozens of questions, you may seem nosy instead of amiable. Don't be too modest, but if you toot your horn too loudly or launch into your life story, you'll sound like you're in a job interview instead of a social situation.

I remember having lunch in college with a friend named John. The subject was mountains, and he was telling our table about how he'd climbed Mount Kilimanjaro. I was so impressed I nearly fell off my chair. Not only had John scaled such heights, but he had never mentioned it before. If John had described the same feat when we'd first met, I would have been impressed, yes, but I might also have thought, "What a showoff" or "What a name-dropper" or "I bet he couldn't wait to get that in."

So take your time making friends.

8   Be willing to risk rejection. Just as you don't like everybody, everybody won't like you. Some people just aren't going to be as amicable as others. Their loss.

In the meantime, be known for your niceness. If you hide in a shell, you won't meet anybody, let alone cultivate friendships. Open up, be visible, take a chance. State your views, not what you think will make you accepted. Then if Brenda acts snooty, you wouldn't want to be her buddy anyway. (Who wants snooty buddies?) If she's sweet, it was worth the risk.

Is everybody gossiping about you behind your back? Probably not. When you get right down to it, it's egotistical to think your personality is a hot topic of debate. And what if the lunch table *does* discuss you the second you get up to bus your tray? Relax. If you're a warm, caring person, you have no reason to worry. What they're saying may be all good. As Oscar Wilde put it, "There is only one thing worse in the world than being talked about and that is not being talked about."

9   Arm yourself with zest and zeal. Ziggy is a lovable loser, but most of us gravitate to winners. When I ask an acquaintance, "How are you?" and she grunts about backaches, allergies, and fights with her sister, it doesn't make me want to join her for a bike ride. Snarls and complaints won't help you make friends.

If you are depressed, share it with your family and close friends, but try not to take it out on people you scarcely know. I remember one guy in high school who never smiled. I'd say, "How's it going?" and he'd shrug and murmur, "Ehhh." I'm not proud to admit it, but I never did make the effort to find out what was bugging him.

You don't want to come off as little Suzy Sunshine or Ms Pollyanna. But if you act happy and confident for two days and say an audible, positive "hello" to lots of new faces, you may be amazed to find they'll cheerfully greet you back. Next thing you know, you'll be *feeling* happier, and the smiles will come on their own.

10   Give parties. One way I made friends after moving to a new town was to give parties. When word is out that you're throwing a party, near-strangers start falling all over themselves to become your pre-party bosom buddies. Sure you see through them. But at least you are all taking the time to get to know each other.

What kind of party should you give, invitation only or open house? Find out what your parents will allow. How about a slumber party with eight or ten girls? It's fun to have séances, levitations, ghost stories, refrigerator raids, and time to talk. If everyone brings her own sleeping bag, it shouldn't be too much trouble. Or invite the guys. A pot-luck dinner or brunch is not much fuss. Tell one guest to bring the bread, another to bring dessert, another to bring hors d'oeuvres, and so on. You can provide the main course (inexpensive spaghetti? bake-ahead quiches?), and everyone can pitch in on the cleanup.

Other ideas include barbecues, picnics, and get-togethers that wind up at a movie or swimming pool or skating rink. How about playing charades or Trivial Pursuit? It may be easiest and least scary to invite people over without trying a theme, but theme parties are fun, too. That's when you're supposed to wear only black or white, or come in costume (or pajamas!); or when you give high tea and the guys appear in jackets and ties and the girls arrive in last year's prom dress or the bridesmaid gown they wore only once. If you have friends who like to bake, you could give a cookie party. Everyone brings a different kind of cookie, samples some of each, then takes home a small assortment.

Don't wait for someone else to give a party and then hope that Steve, Maggie, and Tony show up and talk to you. Draw up the invitation list yourself.

THE PURSUIT OF POPULARITY

The word *popularity* hardly exists in college. There are many groups of friends, and no one thinks about which is "cool" or in or right or best. Yet you're not in college, and being popular may matter to you now.

It mattered to me. For a long time, all I wanted was to be popular. No such luck. The twins and their chic circle did me the favor of talking to me, but I was never important to them. Wanting in and not getting in was lousy for my ego, but thank heavens Judy talked some sense into my head.

"What's so great about the twins?" she wanted to know.

"They're popular," seemed like a pretty feeble answer, but I ran it by her anyway.

"The masses look up to them. Big deal! They may be perfectly wonderful, but they've never been wonderful to you. With all the nice people out there, I can't believe you're hung up on them. Will it damage your reputation if you are seen with less popular people? Will it injure your image? I swear, Carol, sometimes your values make me ill."

At this point, I'd usually want to tell her to can it. But Judy was a genuine friend who knew me thoroughly and liked me anyway. And she had a point. Since the popular crowd wasn't spending time worrying about me, it was pretty crazy for me to spend time worrying about them.

If you are popular, congratulations. If not, relish your close friends and try not to care about the others. It may help to realize that popularity has a flip side. Sure it must be fun to be a trend-setting center of attention. But some popular girls feel cramped by their clique.

Melissa, a college friend, told me about the disadvantages of her high school popularity. She said she felt terrible when she won the class election because she knew her opponent cared more about school issues. "And I hated when my clique got into shoplifting. I didn't want to steal, but I felt I had to—like I'd lose popularity points if I didn't. There were sides of me the girls never knew. Since they liked me because I was funny, I felt I always had to be 'on.' If I was depressed, I couldn't cry. Sometimes it was as if I didn't have any friends." Melissa sighed. "I'd be lying if I said I didn't enjoy feeling liked and important. But it made the transition to college hard. No one here knew they were supposed to bow down to me. I was one more lowly freshman. Except I was full of myself."

A clique can be a crutch. Members feel secure, but they're taking their identity from the group and letting group values mold their characters rather than becoming unique individuals.

Although you may not be as popular as other girls in your class, your friendships may include a closeness that the popular girls have not found. And you are learning to be more self-reliant than girls who cling to a group for support.

YOUR FRIENDS DON'T ALL HAVE TO LIKE EACH OTHER

One advantage of not belonging to a clique or *the* clique is that you can have many diverse friends to suit your multifaceted personality. It used to bother me that Judy and Jen didn't like one another as much as I liked each of them. But they had friends whom I didn't take to, either. And why not?

It also struck me as odd that during vacation, I'd write such varied letters. Gossip about cute guys to Nancy. Pontification about the meaning of life to Norma. Was I being phony? Was I being the person each wanted me to be rather than the person I was? No; I had chosen several friends for my several selves. Different people bring out different sides of us.

So if your friends Seth and Emily are incompatible, see them separately. If Lynn doesn't understand what you see in Nancy, that's okay. If she puts you down for making plans with Nancy, examine her motives. Critical people are often insecure. Is she jealous or worried you'll stop being as close to her? Reassure her that you value her friendship as much as ever. Maybe Lynn's concern is that Nancy may be a bad influence—

she's fast or sells drugs. Decide for yourself whether she's right and whether to heed her warning.

When you have friends meet, up their odds of taking to each other by making introductions that lead into conversation. Say, "Morine, I'd like you to meet Norah—she's a nature lover, too." P.S.: Don't be so worried about whether everyone else is having a good time that you're not having a good time.

CAN A GUY BE A FRIEND?

Sure. It may be hard to be friends with an ex-boyfriend, yet it's easy to have other guys as friends. Your friendships with your lab partner Ed, your neighbor Norm, or your pal's brother Louis are probably fun in their own right, and they also help you feel comfortable with guys in general and give you inside insights into the male psyche.

My friend Gilbert and I went to movies, plays, meals, and parties together. We didn't flirt; we talked. We didn't worry about the impression we were making or if our hair was sticking up; we were at ease. I could discuss some subjects more easily with him than with girls, and I felt safer going to some places with him than with girls. I'm now married and Gilbert is engaged, but we're friends for good.

Some of the best romances start as platonic friendships, but if you suddenly find you're smitten by a friend, proceed with caution. Why? Because if the fling doesn't work out, it's hard to go back to the fraternal bond. (R.J. and I got along great until I had to go and kiss him. After that, we felt awkward and the friendship—maybe not as solid as I had imagined?—went down the tubes.) If a male buddy has a one-way crush on you, try to drop hints gently about your other romantic interests and don't make a big deal of his changing feelings. His crush may pass. His friendship can endure.

You may sometimes feel jealous of your guy friend's girlfriends, and he may envy your dates. Make time for each other. Your mutual friendship can outlast your separate romances.

FIGHTS AND FRIENDS

Even the best of friends argue. That's fine. It's better to express resentment openly than to let hostility build. But it's also better to lose an argument than to lose a friend. And no matter how solid a relationship is, it's still fragile if it's not handled with care.

If you get a D+ on a test you really studied for, you may be angry.

Don't take it out on your chums, thinking they'll love you no matter what. Don't say, "You really tick me off the way you flirt with every guy who comes by" if what you mean is "I'm so mad Mr. Pryor gave me a D+ on that stupid test." Instead, share your frustration. Too many people vent displaced anger. They blow up at friends and family when their rage stems from an entirely different source.

What if you are genuinely peeved at a friend? What if Jill made plans with you and canceled at the last minute, and it's not the first time she's been irresponsible?

You could proclaim, "You take me for granted." But Jill might say, "I do not." You could insist, "You always stand me up or come two hours late." But Jill might counter, "I've never once been two hours late." She'll be right, you'll be wrong; she'll have learned nothing, you'll be madder than ever.

A smarter approach would be to address the issue as specifically, tactfully, and rationally as possible. Don't diffuse your case with a generality and don't lose your case with an overstatement. Say, "Jill, next time we do something, I'd appreciate it if you showed up—on time. It hurts me that I seem to take our plans more seriously than you do."

Keep your voice down, talk slowly, say "I . . ." instead of "You . . ." (that sounds less accusatory) and mix positive with negative. Instead of lighting into her, say, "Your friendship means a lot to me; that's why I feel let down when you seem not to care. It's also why I was glad two weeks ago when you got to my piano recital on time."

At the end of an argument, give each other a hug. If you can't— you're still fuming—then keep hashing things out.

Whenever you're unleashing anger, less is more. A boyfriend and I once agreed to meet outside the door of a concert hall, but I ran into a pal and went ahead inside as he parked. It turned out by the time he'd found a space and looked for me, the concert had begun and he couldn't get in. When I met him later, I sheepishly asked, "You mad?" He could have blasted me nonstop for twenty minutes. Instead he simply said, "No. Disappointed." I felt like a first-class inchworm.

Are you and your friend disagreeing about which movie to see? Compromise. See her choice this week, yours next week. Are you becoming competitive? Talk it out; strive to outdo yourselves, not each other. Are you on opposite sides of the abortion issue? Don't shout, "I can't believe you think that!" Say, "I feel differently." You don't have to agree on everything; you're friends, not clones.

Do you give in too easily? Some girls back down and beg forgiveness when they have done nothing wrong. Don't be belligerent, but don't apologize for breathing or sob at the first sign of a confrontation. Assert yourself!

Before *you* start a fight, have your facts straight. Before you explode, "Why didn't you invite me to your bas mitzvah?" be sure your invitation isn't in the mail.

Eleanor Roosevelt said, "Nobody can make you feel inferior without your consent." When someone insults or teases you, don't fight or cry or raise your voice—that's his or her intent. Ignore the comment or ask, "Why do you need to put others down to bolster yourself?" It's usually best to fight fire with water. Later you can decide whether his or her "Your breath could kill a herd of hippos" was pure maliciousness or whether you should invest in a mouthwash.

What about when you're the one who's out of line? Did you spread a secret when you should have kept your trap shut? It's too late to clean up that mess, but don't make matters worse by starting a cold war. Have it out. Your friend has a right to be upset. Listen and accept the blame. You could protest, "I didn't know it was such a deep dark secret." But should you have known? Rather than be self-righteous, admit your mistake and apologize sincerely. (By the way, while you'll win an audience if you gossip, you'll win respect if you don't. And secret-keepers get a bonus: You wouldn't believe all the juicy gossip I hear since friends know I'm close-lipped.)

In college, some friends and I once talked and played music until five one morning. The next day the girl on the other side of the thin walls told me she'd slept terribly. She was about to launch into a tirade about how rude and selfish we'd been, but I disarmed her (saving her lungs, my ears, and our rapport) by pleading guilty. "It was rude and selfish of us. I apologize, and it won't happen again." I made sure it didn't.

Friendship means sometimes having to say you're sorry.

STAYING FRIENDS

Can you remain close when your friend moves or goes to college? Absolutely. Samuel Butler said, "Friendship is like money, easier made than kept." Yet with a little effort, friendship *can* be forever. My family moved when I was in the middle of sixth grade, so I could no longer sleep at Debbie's once a week, but I managed to keep up with her, and we still see each other often. When I left new high school friends to study in France, I made *amis* abroad but stayed in touch with buddies at home. In college, I made more friends, again without losing important old ones. Same thing in grad school and in the neighborhoods where I've lived since then.

Obviously I've let go of lots of peripheral pals over the years. And lots have let go of me. (Some people want to leave their past behind.)

But it's not that hard to stay friends for keeps if you want to.

How do you stay close? You show that you continue to care. You may someday run into a long-lost friend and simply pick up where you left off. But usually you'll want to keep up the communication while you're apart—and not just on birthdays.

Write letters. It's not a chore; it's fun. Scribble a note during study hall, or after a date when you're too wired to go to sleep. Tell your friend what you've been up to and how you've been feeling. Send photos and news of mutual pals. Keeping up a correspondence often strengthens friendships. Some people can express on paper what they repress in person. For instance, it can be easier to write "Sue, I miss you" than to say it. Plus, petty aggravations don't get in the way of long-distance friendships. So send a card every so often. It takes less time, money, and energy than you'd ordinarily be spending on each other. Writing may also help you sort out your feelings about the way things are going. Don't be super-rigid about who owes whom a letter. It won't hurt you to send an extra missive, but it could hurt your friendship if you both keep silent just because you've lost track of whose turn it is.

I have a few postcard pals. Writing a postcard takes three minutes and costs next to nothing. You don't have to fuss with an envelope, and you can pack in piles of news. Why not make a pact with a faraway friend to exchange frequent postcards? Liven up the deal by agreeing to send the artsiest, wackiest, or tackiest ones you can find.

Another alternative is to send a cassette tape. That takes longer and works only if you both have a tape recorder. But hearing your friend's voice is the heartwarming payoff.

Maybe you can visit each other during summer or vacation. Expect some changes—and late-night catching up.

And how about the telephone? You could call each other at set times, say every other Saturday morning or the first of every month. The danger is the bill. Call at night, on weekends, or during other not-too-expensive times, and keep it brief.

TELEPHONE TACTICS

How true is the stereotype? Do teenage girls and telephones really stick together like P.B. and J.? When I remember how Judy and I tied up the line for hours (we lived right next door to each other) and how Jen used to call me where I was baby-sitting and sometimes the Matusows wouldn't have left yet and Dr. Matusow would answer and Jen, the chicken, would hang up—well, I still blush to think of it.

You may be spending over a thousand hours on the telephone during the next few years alone. So follow these telephone tips. And use the phone book. Calling 411 gets expensive.

1   After you dial, let the phone ring at least eight times. The person may be in the bathroom or on another line. (Don't you hate when you skin your shin on the coffee table while lunging for the phone—only to hear the dial tone?)

2   Say, "Hello, may I please speak to Peggy?" or "Hello, Mrs. Whobrey. This is Carol Weston. May I speak with Peggy, please?" It's more polite than "Is Peggy there?" If Peggy answers and says, "This is she," don't laugh—that's what she's supposed to say.

3   Don't play guessing games. Introduce yourself immediately. Unless your name is unusual, give your last name, too. I know lots of Johns, and it is embarrassing when I'm not sure which one I'm talking to from the start. Even when I phone my aunt, I'll say my full name because she probably isn't expecting to hear from me and she may know other Carols. If I'm talking to an editor, I may even identify myself beyond my name. "Hello. This is Carol Weston. I sent you the article on were-wolves . . . ?"

4   If the person you called sounds rushed, ask, "Did I catch you in the middle of something?" or "Do you have a minute?"

5   In your lowest, least shrill voice, gab. Pretty voices are more pleasant than dull or squeaky ones. You're concerned with the way you look and smell; give equal time to the way you sound.

6   If you're talking on the phone, talk on the phone. Don't also watch t.v. or make chili. I hate it when someone phones me, then bangs around in the kitchen. I want to believe the person called to converse, not to make a chore go faster. At least I'd like the caller to be candid about it—then I can grab my nail polish or do my dishes. (And don't eat or chew gum on the phone, either. It sounds terrible on the other end.)

7   After you've talked, don't say, "I gotta go now." Say, "Well, it's been good talking to you; I'll see you Monday" or "I better let you go but thanks for the science assignment." (If the caller won't get off, say, "Well, Shirley, thanks for calling" or "I won't keep you" or "I'm glad you phoned, and I look forward to seeing you at Laura's.")

8   When you first answer a call, make your *hello* sound cheerful even if you're feeling grisly. If it's not for you, take the caller's number and message, and *write it down.* That way your family won't mind taking messages for you. (You *do* have pen and pad by the phone, don't you?)

9   Does your friend's family have an answering machine? Don't crack up or hang up. Just say, "This is Katie Goldstein at 444-4444. I'd like Deborah to return my call when she has a chance."

10   Does your family have call-waiting? It may be worth the few

dollars a month, because then your brother can't pace around screaming, "Get off, I'm expecting a call." When you hear the click-click, you might say, "Sorry, I better run, talk to you tomorrow." If you've barely got on with caller number 1, say, "Would you hang on half-a-sec?" then get on and off quickly with caller number 2. Say, "Mrs. Allen, I'm on the other line. I'll have my mother call you when she gets in." If it's important or long distance, ask the person to hold on and get off with caller number 1. (My apologies if this seems obvious, but more than once I've spent my long-distance money on static while the person I called is jabbering away with someone else. Or I've chatted on and on, then felt like a fool when the person finally mentioned, "Listen, I'm on call-waiting with Gene. . . .")

11   Don't let an unknown caller know when you're alone. Say, "My father can't come to the phone right now; may I take a message?"

12   When to call? When it's evening in California, it's past midnight in New York. And if you always call at dinnertime or after 10 P.M., you may be losing points with friends' parents.

13   Don't be caught in a lie. In the era of technology, if Gretchen says, "I called all weekend" to a person with an answering machine, or "Your line was busy all night" to a person with call-waiting, it could be discovered that Gretchen, however well-intentioned, is full-of-it.

14   When an operator says, "Operator Dorothy, may I help you?" say, "Yes, Dorothy." By using her name, you'll brighten her day.

15   If you ever get repeated obscene or phony phone calls, after the caller has spoken, calmly say, "Yes, Operator, this is the call I'd like you to trace."

16   If you want to play an off-key "Happy Birthday" to someone on a push-button phone, here's how: 886809, 8868#9, 88*7532, ##9568.

BEING A GOOD GUEST

I remember when my friend Debbie's mother invited me for dinner. "We're having liver," she said. I told you how I feel about liver in Chapter 1, and there was no way I was going to subject myself to such a meal. But did I have the guts or know-how to decline graciously? I did not.

Within earshot of Debbie's family, I called home and said, "Dad, the Kirks invited me to dinner, can I stay?"

"Sure," said my father.

"Oh c'mon, just for dinner."

"I said you could," my father replied.

"Pleeeease, Dad? . . . Well okay, then could you pick me right up?"

Fortunately my father figured out my ploy and within minutes was in front of Debbie's, tooting his horn. But there are easier ways to wriggle out of a dinner invitation.

A simple "I can't tonight, Mrs. Kirk, but thank you, I appreciate your asking—and I'd love a rain check" would have done nicely. Parents eat up that kind of courtesy.

Whether you are accepting or declining an invitation, always say thank you. And if you have spent the weekend at a friend's house, write a quick note afterward to her parents. The longer you put off writing the thank-you note, the better it has to be.

Other good-guest thoughts:

- If you'll be spending a few days with a family, bring a gift: homemade bread, a jar of fine jelly, pretty soaps, a plant or book. If you're good with a camera, you might take pictures and send them copies.
- Don't be too shy with your friend's parents. Try to start a conversation by complimenting the dinner or surroundings, or saying, "Hannah tells me you teach at the university; that must be interesting."
- Offer to help wash and dry dishes; pitch in.
- Make your bed and be as neat as possible in the bathroom.
- Mind your manners (napkin in your lap, don't start eating until the hostess does, use the outside fork first, break your bread and butter it piece by piece, don't slurp your hot soup or tea . . .).
- If you sense your friend or her family might want a moment alone, quietly read a book or magazine. Don't expect to be entertained every second.
- If your friend's family is taking you out to dinner, don't order until they do. You'd be embarrassed if you asked for shrimp cocktail if they were planning to go for just main courses.
- Leave when you planned to or you'll wear out your welcome. As Ben Franklin put it in *Poor Richard's Almanack,* "Fish and visitors smell in three days." And as Jane Austen wrote in *Emma,* "It was a delightful visit . . . perfect in being much too short."

WHEN FRIENDSHIPS CHANGE

What if you don't fit into your clique anymore? Maybe you got in with them when you felt insecure, but now you realize they aren't your type. Maybe all they care about is Saturday night keg parties and you think drinking is stupid. Whatever the reason, you want out. What do you do?

If it's your group's stealing, smoking, drinking, exclusivity, or wildness that makes you uncomfortable, you could say so. Without being judgmental, say that you feel rotten after you shoplift, or you don't see the joy in getting high all the time. (You may discover that some of them aren't as hyped about it as they had led you to believe.)

The best way to start moving away from a clique is to be extra thoughtful to girls outside it. That's what a friend of mine did. "I used to smoke pot with my friends all the time," she told me. "Then one weekend I went with my family to visit a college out East with my older brother. The campus was beautiful, and I realized I'd want to go away to school too and that I was blowing it. My grades were terrible—my whole group was totally unmotivated. Right then I understood that if I could just do better in school, more doors would be open to me. So when I got back home, instead of calling my buddies, I called this other girl, who was straight and a good student. I made plans with her and gradually got in with her friends. About two weeks later, one of my old buddies was stoned in the girls' room and sneered, 'God, you used to be so much fun.' It was rough. But I'm at a good college now and I love it here."

When friendships shift, it can ache as much as or more than breaking up with a guy. It'll hurt if your tomboy friend turns into a young lady overnight, or if your neighbor gets a boyfriend and discards you like scrap paper. You used to be able to think aloud together. Now you each worry that the other is taking everything wrong. Try to be patient, accepting, and open about the adjustments you're making. True friendship will survive.

I remember a heart-to-heart Jen and I once had. We'd both been quietly feeling smothered. Somehow the responsibility of being best friends in junior high had gotten to us. We each needed time for other people. After several uncomfortable weeks, we talked about our concerns. Imagine our relief when we discovered we'd both been upset about the same thing! Jen and I decided to be "bestest" friends instead of "best" friends. That left us feeling less possessive and obligated to each other, yet just as caring. Once we stopped feeling as though we *had* to spend every waking moment together, we had more fun when we *chose* to see each other.

I also remember a run-in with Judy. As I confessed to my diary, *"I feel like I don't have a best friend. Judy's changed. I'm sick of her telling me my faults. Her frankness is beginning to nauseate me."* Suffice it to say I'm awfully glad we made up, and Judy's candor is still one of the traits I most like in her. So don't let ordinary squabbles and moodiness damage extraordinary friendships.

Of course, just as you'll continually add friends to your life, you'll also let others go. It's natural to outgrow some pals or find you are growing in different directions. You'll want to stick by a friend who is going through a hard time (parents' divorce, problems at school), but what if there is no legitimate explanation for a friend's change or selfishness? Or what if you and a friend just don't click anymore? You could try clearing the air. You might say you've noticed things have cooled off between you but you'd like to work at staying close. Or you could decide to drift away with as few hard feelings as possible. (Always try to have more than one bosom buddy; you can't get it all from one friend.)

Grudges and hate are a waste of energy. I resented a friend-turned-bitch for almost six months until I realized that while I was practically developing an ulcer, this hot-and-cold girl was dating, partying, and not giving me a second thought.

Don't bother hating people because they don't accept you, or because they threaten you, or because you see in them some characteristic you don't like in yourself. Channel your feelings elsewhere; focus on your friends, not your enemies.

TEN WAYS TO LOSE FRIENDS

Friendships can be forever, but too often, they fall apart along the way. If you want to keep your friendships in good repair, don't sabotage them. Heed this what-*not*-to-do list.

1   Agree wholeheartedly when your friend says "I acted like such a jerk" or "My party was a total failure."
2   Neglect your friend whenever a guy comes into the room. Drop her whenever a guy comes into your life.
3   Stay on and on, leaving only when you're pushed out the door. Then, as soon as you get home, phone to talk.
4   Use your friend for her homework, car, hand-me-down clothes, or social status.
5   Become a bore: Constantly whine and complain, blab endlessly about your diet or boyfriend, or turn anything anyone says into a springboard for you to talk about yourself.
6   Become dependent and get jealous every time your friend talks to anyone else.
7   Be so envious of your friend's grades, clothes, looks, athletic abilities, relationships with guys, or whatever that you no longer enjoy her company or what *you* have.
8   Demand that your friend tell you everything. Promise not to tell. Spill the secrets.

9 Criticize and say "you should" a lot; try to change your friends and run their lives.

10 Notice when you need your friends but not when they need you. (For instance, call when you're upset but be impatient with their tears.)

BE YOUR OWN FRIEND

If you like yourself, others will like you, too. Even if the popular girls *don't* know you're alive, and Jimmy Harvey *doesn't* ask you to dance, you are still a good, worthwhile person with lots to offer. Believe in yourself!

Focus on your bright side. If you're speaking up in science class and a little voice inside you whispers that you sound like a nincompoop, tell it to shove it. Listen instead to the voice that's whispering, "Hey, you know your stuff." This is hard to pull off when you don't know a mollusk from a molecule. So try to be the smartest, warmest person you can, then give yourself the approval you deserve.

Some insecurity is normal. At times, I'll catch a glimpse of myself in the mirror and think, "Carol, you are the fattest thing that ever waddled." At other times, I'll think I'm so cute, I'll want to pinch my cheeks. So why not concentrate on pluses instead of minuses? I could sink into total despair if I thought about all the guys who didn't ask me out, all the articles I wrote that didn't sell, or all the skills (like singing or sewing) I haven't learned. Or I can bask for a moment recalling good times I have had, articles I have had published, skills I have acquired. I'm for basking; how about you?

When you consider your personality, give yourself credit for being energetic instead of clobbering yourself for being short-tempered. (Then work on lengthening your fuse.) When you look at your past, emphasize sunny-side-up periods; don't brood on scrambled ones. If you insist on recalling what a nerd you were last year, think about how you've grown since then. And how tough times help you appreciate happy ones.

Do you bad-mouth yourself? Stop. Don't discredit yourself by saying, "I'm a bitch; I can't help it," or "I'm a jinx; it's my fault we got a flat." When an unlucky thing happens, think "What a drag!" not "I'm unlucky." Be less hard on yourself. Measure yourself by reasonable—not impossible—standards.

Pretend you're a contortionist: Give yourself a pat on the back instead of a kick in the butt!

When you're in the absolute pits (and we all fall in occasionally), don't moan endlessly to your friends. Do something active you can be proud of and start pulling yourself out. Do a five-star job on an assignment.

Or astound your parents by cleaning the kitchen. Or go on a longer-than-usual bike ride. Or listen to upbeat music, see an absorbing movie, read a fun magazine, take a hot bath. Write in a journal. Start a scrapbook or look one over. Volunteer to help someone who needs you—doing something nice for someone else can lift your spirits, too. Tackling a project that isn't fun per se (sorting drawers, doing homework, working for a humanitarian or political cause) can also make you feel better. Do something you know you do well, or try something you've never tried. The course to take after you've struck out is to get back up at bat and hit one.

Believe me, I get the blues and the blahs too, and I can go off the deep end with the best of them. I'm not saying you should ignore anger or sorrow or let them build up inside you. But after you express negative energy, sit down, close your eyes, breathe deeply, and think "calm." Then do something to get back in gear.

You could stay bummed for ages, but what's the point? Why not strive to keep things in perspective? Why shoo happiness away? Whatever is upsetting you will probably pass. Things could probably be worse, but aren't.

One technique that has helped me is to keep a list for a few days of what I've done—not what I *have* to do. Tuesday might say nothing more than: "exercised, showered, dressed, read paper, looked up and read three articles on drunk driving, had a sandwich, wrote two pages, sent a postcard to Aunt Lisa, bought typing paper, cooked and ate dinner with Rob, called John and Linda, read a García Márquez story." For me, that's a fairly typical fine day. Yet when I'm down, that can feel like an I-didn't-get-anything-done day. Keeping a list helps me see straight.

Don't let yourself wallow too long. If you do call a friend, don't just unload your woes. Listen to her insights and advice. If you can't shake a long-term depression alone or with the help of friends and family, see a counselor or therapist. I once did, and the eight sessions were just what I needed to get over a loss.

Before you seek professional help, though, think about this: In some ways, *wholeness* is as important as happiness. Feeling down helps you grow up and become sensitive, wise, and empathetic. Feeling low is part of being human. And you can't always expect smooth sailing—especially if you're making waves.

If you're comfortable with yourself, you'll feel lonely less often. Everyone is alone from time to time (even on Saturday nights), but try to think of those hours as precious solitude, not painful loneliness. Depend on yourself. Learn to entertain yourself, whether by reading, cooking, bowling, exercising, gardening, thinking, or whatever.

As Abraham Lincoln put it, "Most folks are about as happy as they make up their minds to be." I won't quibble with honest Abe. Happiness doesn't just happen. You have to invite it over and welcome it in. Be true to yourself and do things that please you and things that please others. Even happiness can be a habit. Even depression can be habit-forming. You may have to work at being happy and you can't be happy all the time, but self-contentedness (which is how Aristotle defined happiness) is within your grasp. So seize the day! (Bonus: happy people tend to be healthy people.)

Since I'm ranting and raving about how you should like yourself, I'd better add: Don't go overboard. If you become conceited or smug or self-satisfied, you'll drive your near and dear ones away. A little modesty, please. There's room for improvement in everybody—in you, in me, even in the girls you envy and the guys you adore.

Speaking of guys (always one of my favorite pastimes), let's talk about that elusive stuff called love.

3
LOVE

Love is wonderful. And love is a mess.

Love is dopey smiles; giddy phone calls; deep talks on long walks; singing in a snowstorm; squooshing into the same section of a revolving door; identifying with every lyric on the radio—and feeling excruciatingly alive. Love is also dashed expectations; quarreling because you care; missing him the moment he says good-bye; aching when he flirts with someone else; longing for another letter; losing sleep over nighttime daydreams—and feeling blissfully deranged.

Love? I'm still trying to figure it out myself. It's the most complex emotion going. Heady, heartbreaking, poignant, breathtaking. And *I love you* means different things to different people at different times.

So while I can offer facts about menstruation and eating disorders, and while I can provide rights and wrongs about applying for a job or to college, I can't claim to have a hold on love. Love knows no facts, few rights, few wrongs. Love is full of contradictions.

Nonetheless, here's a chapter full of tips. How to let guys know you're interested, how to keep dates fun, how to let love last, and, sigh, how to survive a breakup.

Just keep in mind that love is something you have to learn the hard way—which, lucky you, also happens to be the fun way.

GETTING STARTED

The first love letter I ever received was in third grade, in Mrs. Gemunder's class. A blond named Billy passed a scribbled scrap of paper from the third row on the left, where he sat, to the second row on the right, where

I sat. It read, "Do you like me? ___ Yes ___ No."

This was exciting. I immediately checked Yes. But I wasn't going to make myself vulnerable for nothing. No fool I, in my brand new cursive handwriting, I added, "Do you like me?" I handed the note to my neighbor and watched as it passed from person to person to person to Billy. Billy read it. He looked up. He met my gaze. He smiled.

Ah, things were so simple then.

By junior high, they were complicated.

Why? Partly because I was love-hungry, desperate to be going with somebody. It scarcely mattered whom: I was in love with love. Here are some typical lines from my diary:

Tuesday: I don't think Jake likes me. But Nat (yuk!) told a kid he'd ask me to dance every dance at school. I'll say no!
Thursday: In dance class, Jake danced with me. He likes me!! I decided to change my future slumber party to a boy-girl party.
Wednesday: Jake doesn't like me. I bet he likes Danielle.
Thursday: Jake doesn't like me because I like him.
Friday: I'm not going to say hi or anything.
Thursday: I've given up on Jake. He doesn't like me. I like Evan a little.
Saturday: The dance was okay. Jake didn't dance with me and Nat did only once.
Wednesday: I got thrown in the lake by 9th grade boys. Fun!
Friday: My party was a success, but no boy likes me.
Monday: In Music, I wrote a note to Jen about boys and Mr. Parsons took it and said he'd read it aloud if I didn't behave. I behaved.
Friday: I don't know what boy to like.
Saturday: Dave is so cute and strong. So is Hugh. So is Walter.
Friday: The last dance of eighth grade wasn't that good because no good boys like me.
Sunday: I am so in love with everybody.
Thursday: I went in a rowboat with Walter.
Tuesday: Hugh Dalton may have seen a CW + HD on my French book. God!
Wednesday: I love three-ring pretzels.

Fortunately, I didn't permanently give up boys for pretzels. By age fourteen, I had a new curly-haired crush. According to my diary:

Jen and Judy prodded me and I mustered up all my courage and asked him, "Are you going to the concert tonight?"
"Why?"
"Oh, I don't know."
"Are you?"
"I was planning to . . ."
"I'll be there."

Then at 6:45, It happened. He called. He looked up my number and used his finger seven times for Me! . . .

Guess what? After that fateful concert, he and I ended up going out for three shining years.

So don't despair. There will be dry spells in your love life, times when you think, "It's not fair, even garbage gets taken out!" Fill those boyfriendless days with friends, family, work, sports, books, and yourself. And remember that it's A-okay not to always have a boyfriend. It certainly beats settling for someone scummy.

Be patient. There's enough love to go around. If you keep sending out signals, some is bound to come your way.

What signals? Keep reading!

SENDING OUT SIGNALS

You can't force a guy to like you. But you can stack the odds in your favor. How do you let the would-be Love of Your Life know you're interested without seeming too forward?

Easy. Sort of. Remember the *Body* and *Friendship* chapters? Wash your hair; watch your weight; dress to look your head-to-toe best. Be on the go; work on listening skills; project confidence even when your stomach is doing flipflops.

Well, all that advice applies whether you're looking for girlfriends or a boyfriend. Try not to be self-conscious. You have yak attacks with girls, so don't clam up with guys. Don't avert your eyes in the hall or stare at your shoelaces at the track meet. Even if he turns your knees to mush, try to be your attractive, easygoing, approachable self. (*Approachable:* that means not always being locked inside a group of eight girls.) You can even flirt a little.

Flirt? Yes. Flirting without being a flirt is an art. If you flirt with every guy in sight, girls will resent you and guys won't take you seriously. But if you never flirt, the guy you're wild about may consider you one of the crowd forever.

You don't like the word? Call it something else. Flirting is simply an informal way to let him know you enjoy his company, without your going out on a limb. It doesn't mean batting your lashes, giggling every time he breathes, or cooing, "Your cologne smells diivvviiiiine." And you don't have to wink or whisper. Just try a smiling, straightforward "Hello." Or pay him a sincere compliment. Ask questions and show interest in his thoughts and plans.

I used to worry that my mind would go blank fourth period in the library when I was about to run into my curly-haired crush. So I actually kept a hidden list of things to tell him. (He wasn't always able to play Mr. Cool as we talked, either. Once two of his friends flew a paper airplane at him that read, "How's your love life?")

Some girls like to drop hints to mutual friends to test the promise of romance. Third-party inquiries can work or can backfire, so use discretion. (Unless you're pretty sure he likes you back, I wouldn't make your crush public.)

Send out nonverbal signals, too. Look at the guy, look away, smile ever so slightly. Pull your chair closer to his. Touch his arm gently as you make a point. Whatever. It should feel relaxed and in the spirit of fun. It should communicate: "I'm friendly; I like you"; not "I'm lonely; I need you."

Tune in to what his eyes and body are saying. But don't jump to happy conclusions just because he's maintaining eye contact. However, if he's making small talk, encourage him. Guys get acute anxiety attacks, too, and many are reluctant to make the first move because they're scared of the big R. (Rejection!) If he says something tentative, like, "I'll see you at the game," say something positive, like, "I hope so." If you both adore the same group and he says, "We should catch one of their concerts," say, "I'd love to." (But don't pant, "Yes! Yes! Anytime! I'm always free.")

What if his eyes are lighting up, yet he's not issuing any invites or almost-invites? Are you bold enough to ask him out, or almost ask him out? If so, try something like, "Isn't it great that a pizza place opened on Main Street?" He'll put it together that if he invites you for pizza, you won't turn him down. Of course, if he's a victim of the "once burned, twice shy" syndrome, you'll have to be extra patient. Maybe you could suggest studying together or ask him to join you and a group of friends at a bowling alley.

I know a woman who flirted with a guy who flirted back, but made no plans. Finally she got up her nerve and oh-so-casually mentioned, "I'm having a party tomorrow night if you'd like to drop by." He said he would. And she? She ran home and frantically organized a get-together with all her friends. Know what? The couple is now happily married!

Warning: Keep your flirting low-key and ambiguous. If you're coming on like a steamroller, he may run for cover.

A date once told me, "Hey, I don't want to get married," to which I retorted, "I didn't propose." But perhaps I had been sending out I-sure-would-like-to-go-out-with-you-all-the-time signals instead of I'm-having-fun signals.

It's happened to me the other way around, too. Gordon wasn't eager, he was overeager, and that sent me packing. According to my diary: *"I really like Gordon, but at sentences like, 'You're good for me' and 'Do you realize you single-handedly got me out of a depression?' I withdraw. I'm also uncomfortable when he stares into my eyes, which he does a lot."*

So show him you're interested, but don't go overboard. Once in a while, especially if he's so-gorgeous-you-could-just-die, you may have to tell yourself, "Down, girl, down!"

ON YOUR MARK, GET SET—RELAX!

Will the real you please stand up? If your crush doesn't respond to the real you, he'd make you a lousy boyfriend and there's no point in longing for him. But if you are yourself—your best self—and he's smitten, what could be better? You can relax, say what's on your mind, and relish his fondness for the true you, shortcomings and all.

It may turn out *you're* the one who is not as interested as you once were. It's easier to fall for a stranger on whom you can project storybook qualities than for a human being with good and bad traits. If you find your crush doesn't have the fantasy personality you'd conjured for him and that you're on different wavelengths, okay. That's an important discovery.

If he's talking football and you hate football, you could pretend to be enthralled as he explains a strategy. But at best, you'd be dooming yourself to boring afternoons watching games on the tube or on the field. Molding yourself into the girl you think he wants will leave you stifled. Plus if Mr. Football finds out he's been feeling amorous about a nonexistent sports fan, he won't be too pleased, either.

Developing some of your sweetie's interests is a compliment. Pretending you already share them is not.

ICEBREAKERS: TWENTY-TWO WAYS TO LAUNCH A CONVERSATION

Flirt? Relax? Maybe you think you can't even strike up a conversation with a guy, let alone pull your chair closer and be your nice normal self. Fine. Let's backtrack.

You might be forgetting that lots of guys are as intimidated and tongue-tied as you. Most would welcome it if you took the first step. The shy guy in your choir group, the hunk jogging alone at the school track, the genius in your computer club—they may all have noticed you but not known what to say. So for Pete's sake (and Todd's and Jack's and your own), speak up!

Here are twenty-two conversation-starters. Don't memorize them, because they're not slick pickup lines. They're just natural ways to get a discussion rolling. Ready?

1   How did you figure out question number 12? (He's behind you in math, looking over his homework.)

2   What good movies have you seen lately? (You're side by side in a ticket line.)

3   Did you see who scored that goal? (He's in front of you at the lacrosse game.)

4   Why can't they ever serve lobster tails? (You're waiting for the lousy burgers the cafeteria has the gall to call lunch.)

5   What was your old neighborhood like? (He's new in town.)

6   What an adorable dog! (Or terrific boots or handsome sweater or great jeep.)

7   Do you have change for a dollar? (While he's checking, keep talking.)

8   Do you know where there's a bookstore near here? (Maybe you can walk toward it together.)

9   Hi. (He's bound to say hi back.)

10   Have you been here before? (You're at a tourist site, a baseball stadium, a doctor's office.)

11   So where are you from? (A tried-and-true standby to be used on trains, chair lifts, in lines, at parties, beaches, concerts, fairs—you name it.)

12   How far do you usually jog? (You've caught up to him and now maybe you'll do a mile or two together.)

13   What time is it? (When he answers, compliment him on his watch or say, "Phew! I thought it was later," and say why you're relieved.)

14   May I share your history book? (Don't forget yours on purpose, but if you left it in your locker, don't miss an opportunity!)

15   I know you from somewhere—did you ever go to Camp Sloane? (This age-old question lets you find out about each other's background and interests.)

16   Been here long? (You're in a long line, or you're at a subway or bus stop.)

17   Have you ever had Señor Véguez for Spanish? (You've both just received your course schedule for the next term.)

18   I can't believe it's raining again! (Cliché? Maybe. But discussing the sky gets conversations off the ground.)

19   Where did you learn to type so fast? (Or draw so well, take photographs, read palms, fix cars, dance, act, or play the guitar.)

20   Doesn't this remind you of a scene from *Dallas?* (Or any other pertinent television show, film, or book.)

21   You're Amy's brother, aren't you? (As if you had the slightest doubt—but that's his cue to ask who you are.)

22   Did you read about the senior lounge plans? (Or about any other school, local, or national news item.)

Think up your own questions, too, because breaking the ice is step one to melting his heart.

IS CUPID STUPID, OR DOES HE JUST HAVE POOR AIM?

You aren't breaking the ice and sending ask-me-out-ask-me-out-ask-me-out signals to the wrong guy, are you? Try not to fall for your sister's boyfriend, your art teacher, or the married letter carrier. Do you have tunnel vision for a famous basketball star or musician? No problem, so long as you don't care if he cares back. Is your heart sold on the popular guy every other girl is head-over-heels over? Swell—you may be the winning wooer. But brace yourself for the likelihood (alas) that he won't single you out. What if you've been flirting for months with the same guy and are convinced you could rock happily together as grandparents, yet he still scarcely knows you exist? You're inviting the blues.

Some girls subconsciously pick out-of-reach guys to drool over. Deep down, they don't feel ready for the possibility of sex, commitment, or connecting with someone who might argue with them or fall short of their impossible standards. It's safer to love from afar, and if unrequited passion doesn't daunt them, no harm done.

However, if *you* are ready for the real thing, why not shift your love energies? Give up gracefully on the movie idol. Focus on the sensitive and available, though less widely acclaimed, guys. Look again at the boy next door; stop writing off the foreign exchange student whose eye may be on you.

Maybe you think you can't help it. You want an honest-to-goodness relationship, but you've flipped for the Class Hunk who happens also to be your best friend's boyfriend. He's forbidden, but he's the only one who fuels your fantasies.

My dear, you'd be wise to take a deep breath, yank out Cupid's arrow, and find a more suitable object of your affections. Don't pine away, lovesick. Sometimes Cupid misses his mark.

My pragmatic advice may seem unromantic, but it'll probably make you happier in the long run. It's hard to avoid crazy crushes. It's hard to control desires and turn off dreamy thoughts. But you can do it. A crush is like a small flame. You can fan it into a forest fire or, if it's hopeless or off-limits, you can snuff it out.

If your love life, real or imagined, tends to be painful, look for a pattern. Are the guys you go for all the kind your mom hopes you'll marry? Good—if you like them as much as Mom does. Are they nice even though Mom wouldn't take to them? Okay. But if you're always aiming too high or too low, or if the guys are all handsome but shallow and oblivious to you, or if one after another is abusive, mean, taken, gay, faraway, unattainable, or your basic Mr. Wrong, try to be kinder to yourself. Try to end the destructive pattern. Don't keep thinking you'll be the one to reform a guy's character.

You're also not doing yourself any favors if the instant you get a guy, you tire of him and try to make another conquest. Or if you and your boyfriend are tight and going strong, yet you flirt suggestively with every other guy who is attracted to you.

The point isn't just to have a boyfriend. The point is to have a warm, wonderful relationship with a boyfriend. You deserve that, don't you?

SHOULD YOU DATE OLDER AND YOUNGER GUYS?

Sure, why not? My high school honey was a year older than I, and I'm a smidge older than my husband. My father was fourteen years older than my mom, and the age gap didn't keep them from having a solid marriage.

If you go out with a guy who is your age, give or take two years, great. Younger boys aren't all immature and older men aren't all lecherous. However (I bet you knew a *however* was coming), if your sweetheart is years younger or is in his mid-twenties or thirties, that does give me pause.

Let's say he's years younger. That may make you feel safer than you would if you were going out with a peer. Fine. But be sure you also feel secure with guys your own age who may challenge you more. If you think your ego needs a boost, make a list of your niftiest traits and commit them to memory.

Is your boyfriend not a boy but a man? Going out with an older man may give you status and prestige. The price? Growing up fast, ready or not. You'll be a woman for the rest of your life, but you're a teen for only a few precious years. A man may not be content to snuggle and kiss for hours (one of the finest features of teen romance) and may apply sexual pressure. He may also be bored by your tales of bombing a test or blowing up at your brother, yet you're entitled to share such stories.

One high school friend told me later that in the long run, she felt going out with Rick, who was in his late twenties, was not a smart move.

She couldn't take him to the prom or out with her friends. And she got so used to adult company that at college, she found the students childish and felt alienated. Plus as she got older, she stopped idealizing Rick, and that new attitude didn't always thrill him.

Although you may be proud to have won the attentions of an older guy, ask yourself why he isn't dating women his own age. Sure, it's because you're so terrific, but even *you* may be still more terrific when you have ten more years of maturity and experience behind you.

Some men love the intensity and enthusiasm of young girls—girls who supposedly aren't jaded and haven't "seen it all." But you want to be loved for yourself, not your sweet-young-thing innocence. Is your older man intimidated by marriageable career women? Does he revel in the hero worship you may be giving him? Are *you* using *him* because he has money, a car, sophistication? Your caring may be genuine, but it can't hurt to question his motives and your own.

Pretty soon, age gaps will hardly matter. Twenty-two? Twenty-eight? Thirty-three? Three adults. But the same gaps among twelve-, eighteen-, and twenty-three-year-olds can mean batting in different ballparks.

SHOULD YOU DATE SOMEONE FROM A DIFFERENT ETHNIC, RACIAL, OR RELIGIOUS BACKGROUND?

I went out with a philosophical Spaniard for nearly four years. The idea of a Madrid marriage did occur to Juan and me. But I wondered if it would be hard to teach our future kids Spanish and English. And would Spain's happy-go-lucky mañana mañana style drive me up a wall? Would I end up finding Spanish chivalry sexist? Would I get homesick for America? Would I be able to write well in English in Spain? (Hemingway did, but he was Hemingway!) Bottom line: Would our love truly be enough to make up for my leaving family and friends an ocean away?

Maybe. Maybe not. Juan and I broke up for other reasons—but that's another story. The point here is that keeping a relationship in top form isn't a breeze under any circumstances (witness the divorce rate), and marrying someone of a different nationality, race, religion, or background can make harmony even harder.

Yet who's talking marriage? As for dating (and friendship), yes, go out with whomever you want. Broaden your horizons. Gain insights from other people's perspectives. Expose yourself to other values and customs. I'm grateful for the years with my "Don Juan."

If your romance turns serious (or if your parents make life miserable), *then* ask yourself serious questions. Crossover couples usually do encounter extra friction and conflicts. Ask yourself whether you have substantial doubts about the rocky ride ahead. (Everybody has some doubts.)

Also be sure you love your guy for his personal qualities and not to prove to yourself and the world that you are open-minded or color-blind or tolerant or big-hearted.

My parents got married when crossover marriages were much more taboo. Mom is Texan and Dad was Russian-born and it worked for them. But love doesn't always conquer all.

Ask your heart and your head what is right for you.

SAYING NO NICELY

All right, so there you are, relaxing, laughing, asking questions, and hoping you're charming Rob. But no. You're charming Elmer. And Elmer asks you out. (Goons tend to have impeccable taste.)

What do you do?

If he says, "You wouldn't like to go with me to the school car wash, would you?" and indeed you wouldn't, say no. Say it nicely, but say it fast. "I'm sorry, thanks for asking," is sufficient. If you say, "I'm studying that day," then Elmer may ask you out another day, and it would be cruel to show up at the car wash with someone else. So don't tell a lie you'll be caught in. If Elmer is an out-of-towner who doesn't know your friends, you could say, "Thanks, but my boyfriend wouldn't like that!" That's a white lie, but it spares his ego. If he gives you the creeps, don't give him a mixed message; don't say, "Oh, I would have loved to—maybe another time?"

What if Elmer is persistent? What if he asks you out five Saturdays in a row, and every time you say you're busy, he asks about the following week? What if he invites you to the prom and it's only September?

Most guys can take a hint, but some need you to spell out the deflating truth or they won't get it. If you must break the news to Elmer that he's not your type, be gentle. Say something like, "Elm, you're a good guy and I'm flattered by your calling, but I want us to be friends, okay?" You could even tell him that you admire his fun-loving spirit but he's just not right for you. Use tact, but make sure he gets the picture because you don't want to give him false hopes.

What if—miracle of miracles—your Ideal Boyfriend calls and asks you out for Friday, but you've made plans you can't break? Don't give him the "I'm sorry, thanks for calling" line or he may interpret it as a polite brush-off. Be effusive. Say, "I'd adore seeing that movie with you but I can't miss my grandmother's eightieth birthday dinner. Could we go Saturday or another day?"

Perceptive guys learn to tell the difference between a don't-call-back no and a please-call-back no.

But why should they be the only ones to put their egos on the line? Even if you're too scared to ask him to a school play, you can still phone and ask about algebra homework. If he wonders whether you're more interested in him than in the assignment—so much the better.

TWENTY-EIGHT DATING IDEAS GUARANTEED TO STEAL HIS HEART

The good news is that sometimes, just sometimes, Mr. Wonderful asks you out, you're free, you accept, you start seeing each other, and presto— you're an item.

By now, you've gotten strikes and gutterballs at the bowling alley, shared popcorn at the movies, played video games, jogged side by side, munched pizza, wandered the mall, even beaten each other at miniature golf. Running out of rendezvous? No! The fun has just begun.

When your guy says, "What do you want to do?" don't shrug your shoulders and say, "I dunno." That's not being pleasantly agreeable— that's boring! Whether you live downtown or in the country, have spending money or are broke, there are plenty of plans to make. (P.S.: Many of these would be fun to do with girls, too.)

1 Greet the dinosaurs at a natural history museum, or check out other museums. You may find exhibits of antique autos, jukeboxes, wax figures, cartoon art, costumes, or arrowheads.

2 Call your county's agricultural office to find out if a nearby farm offers an all-the-fruit-you-can-pick deal.

3 Explore a college campus, then attend a concert, film, or lecture there.

4 Put on albums and aprons and bake bread. Give him some to take home.

5 Listen in on an interesting case at the courthouse, then discuss how you would vote if you were jury members.

6 Pack croissants and jam in a basket and head east to a hilltop to witness the sunrise. Or meet just before sunset with a picnic, Frisbee, poetry book, or sketch pad.

7 Go to the races and watch cars, horses, sailboats, or runners speed to the finish line.

8 Who cares if you're uncoordinated? Sign up for a free introductory dance class at a studio. Or go roller-skating or ice-skating—try holding hands without losing balance.

9   Browse at an antique store or rummage sale. Pick out one-of-a-kind gifts for each other.

10   Take karate or cooking lessons.

11   Visit a pet shop and fall for the kittens, puppies, turtles, and guppies.

12   Check newspapers and store bulletin boards to find out about concerts, country fairs, auctions, outdoor art shows, church bazaars, car shows, boat shows.

13   Plant an outdoor garden or a windowsill of potted herbs.

14   Have tea and crumpets at a fancy hotel restaurant.

15   Play tourist in the metropolis nearest you. Go to a skyscraper's observation deck and locate the landmarks below. If possible, take an architectural tour, a horse-and-buggy ride, or a boat tour. Or walk, walk, walk.

16   It's windy? Go fly a kite!

17   Raining? Stroll under one big umbrella, then head inside to play Monopoly, rummy, or Scrabble.

18   Go to a zoo and pause at the aviary, snake pit, and monkey house. Or go to an aquarium, watch the sharks get fed, then figure out how the lionfish, ghostfish, and unicorn fish got their names.

19   Rent a bicycle built for two and head to the hidden waterfall only you know how to find.

20   Splurge on a play—matinée or evening.

21   Many health clubs offer free classes to prospective members. Work up a sweat together!

22   Attend a professional football, baseball, soccer, hockey, basketball, tennis, or other sports game.

23   Is there a river or stream near you? Rent a canoe or rowboat, take along poles and bait, and go fishing.

24   Take advantage of a local business that offers free tours: from newspaper plant or television station to test kitchen, paper mill, or stock exchange.

25   Feed the ducks and geese at a pond. Feed the sparrows and pigeons at a park.

26   Is it true that truck stops offer great food? Find out! Order different dinners and split them. Or start the day right by meeting for breakfast.

27   Take a walk at a botanical garden, conservatory, or arboretum and see how many trees and plants you can identify.

28   You live near a planetarium? Study the exhibit on constellations, and that night, grab a blanket and star-gaze.

THE WAY TO A GUY'S HEART
JUST MIGHT BE MY CHEESECAKE

I can't promise that. But I *can* promise you that this recipe makes a mean cheesecake. So if all else fails. . . .

First of all, take the cream cheese (all 1½ pounds of it) out of the fridge to let it soften.

Start by making a big graham cracker crust pie shell. Recipes are on graham cracker crumb bags, but here's what I do: Take 2 cups of crumbs plus ¼ pound (1 stick) of melted butter plus ⅓ cup of sugar and 1 large tablespoon of cinnamon. Mix together. Pour into a 9-inch pie pan, pat down the mixture hard and evenly to form a crust, and chill in freezer for a short while (about 10 minutes) or bake at 375 degrees for 6 to 8 minutes. (You could buy a ready-made crust, but it's not as tasty or as big.)

Preheat oven to 375 degrees.

Now make the filling: With a beater, blend 1½ pounds (that's 3 8-ounce packages) of softened cream cheese (a little less is okay) with 1 cup of sugar. Mix in 3 eggs, one at a time. Add 1 teaspoon of vanilla and 1 tablespoon of lemon juice. Blend until smooth. Insert index finger and taste. Mmmmm. Pour into prepared crust.

Bake in preheated oven for 35 minutes.

While you're waiting, mix 1 pint (a little less is okay) of sour cream with 2 tablespoons of sugar and 1 teaspoon of vanilla. When your kitchen timer (you have one, don't you?) rings, take out the cheesecake, turn the oven up to 475 degrees, spread the sour cream mixture right on top of the hot cheesecake.

Return it to the 475-degree oven for 5 minutes.

Take it out, let it cool for 15 minutes or so, then pop it into your fridge to chill for at least 3-½ hours before serving.

The cheesecake can be garnished with chocolate shavings, fresh strawberries or blueberries, or eaten as is. *Bon appétit!*

NINE AWKWARD DATING SITUATIONS
AND HOW TO HANDLE THEM

No one would play the dating game if it weren't fun, but sometimes even the best evenings go awry.

Of course, some girls turn purple over nothing. If they need to go to the bathroom during intermission, they ignore nature's call, twist their legs, wriggle in the lobby, suffer through Act II, and finally bolt from their date's car without so much as a good-night kiss. That's silly. Instead, they could have simply said, "Excuse me, I'm going to the bathroom. I'll be right back." A guy won't be put off—he'll probably say "Good idea," and check out the men's room.

Then there are the girls who are too flustered to eat in front of guys. They fear the guy will think they're little piglets or will laugh if they spill gravy on their sleeves. Question: Are you appalled that boys eat to stay alive? Question: Would you crack up uncontrollably if a boy smeared ketchup on his cuff?

When you're dealing with guys, it sometimes helps to ask yourself what you'd do if you were with your best friend. If you had to go to the bathroom or were sloppy with the soy sauce, you'd pull through. You'd take it in stride. So listen, if your package of Goobers flips upside down at the movie theater and they all go clattering down the aisle, don't let it destroy the rest of the evening.

Here are nine sticky predicaments, complete with ways out.

1   You came to the game with a guy who likes you a lot but whom you consider a friend. During half-time, you go alone to buy popcorn, and the guy you've quietly adored for months appears, strikes up a conversation, and says, "Come watch the rest of the game with me." What do you do?

• Flirt, talk, offer him some popcorn, and tell him you'd love to watch the game with him, but that you can't today because you came with your pal Matt. If you sparkle, he won't be discouraged. Who knows? His interest may even double: You're not only attractive and popular, but you're considerate, too. Feeling bold? Suggest you sit together next week.

2   Watching fireworks at the amusement park was fun, but now you feel as if you're battling an octopus. You don't want to put him off entirely, but you don't want to go any further yet, either. And struggling to hold down his roaming hands has taken the fun out of kissing. What do you do?

• You could fiddle with the radio, apply fresh lipstick, ask about his childhood, announce that you're starving—but why not speak your mind? Tell him straight out that you like him and look forward to getting to know him better, but that you don't enjoy feeling so pushed. If he's a decent person who cares about you, he'll adjust his pace to yours. If he continues the passion play, ask to be taken home and don't go out with him again. His loss.

3   You've had a crush on him for weeks and this is your first date, a double with a pair of his friends. After the movie, you all get in your guy's car, which is parked on a side road. Suddenly the couple in the

backseat grows quiet and the windows start steaming up. Your guy drapes his arm over your shoulders. You're torn: You feel attracted to him, but also self-conscious and rushed. What do you do?

• Realize that he, too, may be ill at ease. Perhaps he's feeling pressured by his backseat buddies. Suggest taking a walk or going for a bite to eat nearby. That way you can get to know each other better before deciding to cuddle up.

4   All week you've been psyched for your blind date. Your aunt gave you such a buildup about her colleague's son, you were expecting a cross between Adonis and your favorite rock star. But when the doorbell rings, you find yourself shaking the sweaty hand of a 250-pound boy with bifocals and braces. "Ready to go dancing?" he lisps, and your heart sinks to your toes. What do you do?

• Make the best of it. Stay open-minded, and the evening will be more fun. You're learning more about guys in general. Besides, he might be charming or witty or introduce you to a guy more your type. If you're friendly without leading him on, you'll feel good about yourself. Later, thank him and shake his clammy hand before he has a chance to try to kiss you. If he's already puckered up and lunging forward, turn your head so his lips land on your cheek. (P.S.: Tomorrow you can rant at your aunt.)

5   He obviously likes you because he's asked you out every weekend for a month. But each date ends the same way: You talk until midnight, then he leaves without even a good-night kiss. The anticipation is driving you crazy! You've considered making the first move, but you're shy and fear that if you're the aggressor, it might threaten him. Still, you can't go on meeting like this! What do you do?

• If you think he likes you only as a friend, try to appreciate the friendship for what it is. But if you're pretty sure he's just too timid to take action, subtly let him know you'd welcome his advances. Sit close to him, or if you're walking, brush against him gently. Leave your hand near his. Linger before getting out of the car or at the doorway. Look into his eyes. You could even let your gaze wander briefly to his lips. Or give him a peck on the cheek. He'll take it as a go-ahead.

6   He's being so quiet you could scream. It's a twenty-minute drive back to your home, and you know you can't single-handedly keep the conversation going that long. Usually he's talkative, but tonight it's Monosyllable City. What do you do?

• Is he silent because he's angry or upset? Ask him what's on his mind. Say, "You seem a little quiet. Is anything getting you down?" He might want to open up.

If you think he's just feeling shy, realize that he probably appreciates your breezy efforts to keep the conversation rolling. Try asking "why" and "how" questions. What *would* you really like to know about him? Remember, too, that you don't have to be "on" all the time or fill up all the airwaves. Is silence golden? Well, silver at least, and it is natural.

7   Your parents don't like the guy you're going out with, and he senses it. The one time you invited him to dinner, the tension was thicker than your mom's homemade chowder. Now, at a concert, he suddenly asks, "Your folks don't like me, do they?" What do you do?

• Let him know your parents criticize *all* your friends because they feel protective. (Then ask yourself if your polite explanation is true, or if there are legitimate reasons behind their coolness.) It's also possible that your folks wish you'd spend more time with them or worry that you've been slipping in school, and they are unfairly using your guy as a scapegoat for other concerns.

To help everyone get along, remind your parents of your friend's strengths and accomplishments. And tell him about their interests. If he can get your dad talking about mystery novels and your mom talking about music, they may establish a rapport after all.

Before you meet *his* parents, make sure he smooths the way for you. It's better to ask his mother, "Do you enjoy being a realtor?" than to have to start from square one with the awkward "Do you work?" First parental meetings usually go best when they are brief and informal.

8   You're having dinner together at an Italian restaurant. You've just taken a bite of linguini when your old boyfriend—and his entire family—stroll in and plunk down at the next table. Suddenly you can hardly keep track of what your guy is saying. What do you do?

• You could shovel down your noodles and make a run for it. Instead, just explain the situation, excuse yourself, and say a quick and gracious hello to your old beau and his family. Get it over with. Your date shouldn't object. Greeting your ex shows you're mature enough to remain on speaking terms with someone who meant a lot to you.

And if you're *not* on speaking terms? Explain your uneasiness, and say you're going to shift your chair so you won't be facing that table: You want to concentrate on the him-and-now. If you still feel awkward, later you could suggest having ice cream cones elsewhere for dessert—your treat.

9   A guy you really like takes you to a boring party twenty miles from your home. After a few hours you want to leave. He doesn't. You feel stuck because you came in his car, you don't know anyone else who

could drive you home, and you don't want him to think you're a jerk for wanting to go already. What do you do?

•   Since you like him, it might be worthwhile to stick it out a little longer. Summon your second wind and introduce yourself to two strangers; or start a new discussion with your guy about sports, family, movies, pets, school, current events. Yet your needs are important, too, so whether you have an official curfew or not, don't be shy about reminding Mr. Rowdy that it's getting late. (You might even whisper that you'd hoped you two would have a moment alone before saying good-bye.)

If he wants to stay another hour and you want to leave now, agree to exit in thirty minutes. If thirty minutes comes and goes and he still refuses to budge—or if he's not willing to compromise in the first place—consider telling him that you're going to find a safe way to leave. Call home. Call a cab. You're going out to enjoy yourselves, and you don't have to put up with a bad situation any more than he would.

ELEVEN SUREFIRE WAYS TO RUIN A ROMANCE

(No, silly, I don't recommend them.)

1   Be a policewoman: Now that he's your possession, don't let any female thieves near him.

•   Wrong! Just because you want him doesn't mean everyone else does. Your heartthrob might be another girl's Elmer, and vice versa. Besides, if you play the smothering policewoman, your guy may bristle and play criminal—running in the opposite direction. Stop worrying. Relationships that are trusting and sturdy can withstand a few external distractions.

2   Play hard-to-get and other games.

•   If you've been doing all the giving, calling, and caring, you may want to lean back to see if he'll lean forward. I won't argue. But if you get in the habit of trying to arouse jealousy, play mind games, or second-guess each other, conflicting messages will shoot back and forth, and your romance may become a jumble instead of a joy.

3   Talk about commitment on the first date.

•   Bad idea. Don't worry so much about tomorrow that you hardly enjoy today. Neither of you should swear eternal loyalty to each other, anyway. Love is not a trap. If you start making him feel bad for not spending every second with you, you may end up with even more time on your hands. Remember: Pushy people push people away. As folk wisdom dictates: If you love someone, let him go. If he comes back, he's yours. If he doesn't, he never was.

4   Worry about his ex.
• She's his *ex*, remember? You're his now. Everybody is entitled to a past. Work on making this current romance as mutually satisfying as possible.

5   Be dependent: Now that you've paired off, you don't need anyone or anything else.
• Boring! A guy and girl can't be everything to each other. Don't let your love life become your whole life. Don't let it eclipse your other friends and activities. Besides, if you spend time apart, you'll have more to talk about when you're together.

You'll also be less broken up if you two ever break up. Going out with someone should add to your self-esteem, yet a girl who always depends on a guy may wind up feeling like a half-person.

6   Take him for granted.
• Some girls forget that relationships, like potted flowers, need to be taken care of. Other girls take their guys for granted because they figure, "If he likes me, he mustn't be as neat as I'd thought." No matter how long you've been seeing a guy, if you still care, let him know.

7   Open old wounds.
• Suppose he did go out once with the class tease while you were away. You've rehashed the episode nineteen times since then and he's begged your forgiveness. Now what?

Let it go. Get on with the present. Going over and over past bruises just prolongs the hurt.

8   Love him only when he's feeling cheerful and strong.
• That's not nice. You may be most drawn to him when he's up and confident, but he needs you most when he's down and out. Don't be a fair-weather girlfriend.

9   Get hung up on three little words.
• If one of you whispers "I love you" and the other isn't ready to echo the phrase, it doesn't have to be a problem. Some people are afraid of the words but not the feeling. Others drink two beers, get horny, and say "I love you" when they mean "I want you."

It's good to try to recognize the differences between "in love," "in like," and "in lust." However, as my poetic mother put it, it's not always necessary to "label it love or libel it lust." When my high school boyfriend and I were first going out, I wasn't ready to verbalize my emotions. I told my diary: *"We concluded that we have very strong affectionate feeling for each other. He calls it love. I call it nothing."* (By the way, I finally came around!)

If you declare love before your relationship has had a chance to develop naturally, your guy may panic or question the depth of your emotion. If you both profess love prematurely, then break up a month later, you may both feel more confused and distraught than if you hadn't given a name to your feelings.

10   Analyze the relationship to death.
• If you spend most of your togetherness time monitoring the progress of your relationship rather than enjoying it, you'll sour it. Sometimes one evening of fun can do more to recharge a romance than three of heavy discussion.

11   Harbor unrealistic expectations.
• You're infatuated. Lo and behold, just as the music, movies, and magazines promised, it's heaven—for about two weeks. Then he criticizes your dear friend. And you blurt that he's a snob. It turns out your Superman has a Clark Kent flip side, and his Wonder Woman is touchy. Should you scrap the relationship, figuring it has run its course?

No! Once you get past all the grand, magical stuff, you find the nitty-gritty of two imperfect individuals trying to deal with each other.

So don't set yourself up for disappointment. Don't put your guy on a pedestal, then frown when he falls off. Don't count on transforming him. No one is or will become too good to be true. If you want your "main squeeze" to be thoughtful, funny, smart, athletic, and so cute that everyone does a double take, you're asking too much. (Do *you* meet those standards?) And if you're asking too much, you're like the wide-eyed child who blows up a balloon until it gets bigger and bigger and bigger— and pops.

I'm not saying you should settle for whatever guy comes down the pike. You should expect to go out with a good guy who treats you well. But your love won't stay super-intense every day. And it's okay for Prince Charming to muddy his white horse once in a while.

I could go on, but the point is: Once you get a romance flying high, don't force it into a crash landing!

BREAKING UP WITHOUT BREAKING DOWN

Breaking up? Maybe you and your boyfriend can turn things around. Love is moody and goes through growing pains. Have several heart-to-hearts before you accept heartbreak and heartache.

Maybe, sigh, your waxing love has waned for good, and no one is to blame. Or you both realize that as much as you care, you just aren't each other's soulmate or future spouse. Not everybody you go out with is someone you'll hope to go out with forever. Which means you'll probably survive more than one breakup in your life.

Bummer. Breakups are hell. In college, I remember looking out my third-story window onto the courtyard below and seeing the guy who'd just suggested we "cool things" flirting merrily with another girl. In grad school, breaking up with Juan hurt terribly because I simultaneously lost boyfriend and best friend. Plus we both still harbored leftover love.

My high school honey and I? We broke up more than once. You've heard of false starts at track meets, right? Well, we had a few false ends. From my diary when I was sixteen:

> *I guess I was having my doubts. Apparently he was, too. He said he wanted to talk. He said the world is too big not to see other people. He was afraid of getting so serious.*
>
> *"Face it, our lives and friends are completely different."*
>
> *"But it hasn't mattered."*
>
> *"But it has."*
>
> *He asked if I wanted to give breaking up a try.*
>
> *"No, but I don't want you to feel obligated." By now, I was crying.*
>
> *"You really do care, don't you?" We kissed. "I love you; maybe I love you too much."*
>
> *We said good-bye.*
>
> *He stood in front of his car for a while, looking down and at me. Then he left. I sat on the grass in front of our house. Ten minutes later, I heard his rumbling Saab coming back!*
>
> *He said, "I was driving away and I said to myself, 'You stupid ass— what did you do that for?' "*
>
> *I smiled. "We gave it a try."*

Should we have broken up then and there? Maybe. False ends are usually indicative of problems, and we eventually did part ways. Of course, reconciliation can be fun. (*"I'm falling in love all over again. Like when we first met. . . ."*) But dragging out pain is a drag.

Can *your* relationship be saved? Is it worth saving? Deep inside, you and your guy probably know when it's sayonara time. When the relationship is more exhausting than exciting. When costs outweigh pleasures.

If you ever break up with a guy because he is abusive or alcoholic, don't feel guilty. In many ways, you're doing him a favor, because he may then have to confront his problems. Don't ever give a guy an ultimatum ("I'll break up with you if you don't . . .") unless you are prepared to follow through.

How do you go about breaking up? Gingerly. The process can be likened to removing a Band-Aid. You can do it gradually, pulling each fine hair as you go. (Oooooouuuuuch!) Or you can yank it off. (OUCH!!!) It hurts either way. Falling out of love is harder than falling in.

As painful as breaking up is, however, remember that the end of one thing is the beginning of something else. And breaking up beats clinging to a threadbare, one-sided, or mismatched relationship.

Sometimes these insights come fast, sometimes not. Do tell yourself: if your love was meant to last, it would have. And that freedom has its frills: you've been missing out on the fun of flirting, playing the field, and spending time with your pals and yourself.

Among the other fish out there are sharks and minnows, but also lots of good catches. What initially charmed your ex will charm your next. Or who knows? What *irked* your ex may charm your next.

If you've been given your walking papers, remember the bad times. After a breakup, we have a tendency to recall long talks and long kisses and to forget fights and not-so-hot feelings. His smoking irritated you? He was a tightwad? Great. Write down all the reasons behind your breakup and remember them as you grieve.

But do grieve. Tears help you heal, and you can't expect to be over him instantly. In fact, the hurt you feel now is a tribute to your love and your ability to love.

Breakups don't always come complete with explanations, and that can add to the confusion. If you and your guy can be gentle and honest with each other about why the curtain is closing, it may help your mutual growth and recovery. But too often, it doesn't work that way, and you're both left to puzzle it out on your own. Sometimes you get the shaft so suddenly you feel as though you were watching a movie and somehow missed the last scene.

Stay busy! You could feel sorry for yourself for weeks, but you have better things to do. Dress up and see your friends. (Remember—the ones you didn't neglect just because love entered your life?) Don't bicycle past places where you used to park. Don't listen to Your Song. Put away his photograph. Jog. Get your hair cut. Buy a blouse. Take up a new extracurric. Read a novel. Write your grandmom. Cuddle your cat. It's okay to stay in bed for one whole day if you want—but then get up and at 'em.

At first, you'll see flashbacks and mull over your last conversations, but fill your time so you don't sink into too much self-pity, guilt, rage, or remorse. (A little is natural.) Try not to suffer from withdrawal for too long.

If you meet someone else right away, he'll lift your spirits. Yet it's best not to race into romance on the rebound (or to get involved with a guy who's doing that). Give yourself time alone first. Patch your broken heart before you give it away again. It's only fair to both of you. Sometimes relationships overlap, but that makes healing harder.

Can you two remain friends? Some former couples pull off that stunt, though I've never quite managed to. If you can swing it, more power to you!

I do recommend trying to end things in a peaceful, dignified way. Don't threaten, beg, bitch, or scream at him. Don't bad-mouth last week's Mr. Wonderful to your pals. Don't hope he'll see the light and come crawling back. (Or if *you* instigated the breakup, don't try to get back together if you know you'll just be ending things further down the road.) You'll retain more self-respect if you can thank your guy for the good times, wish him the best, and move on.

(Then again, if he was a two-timing, double-crossing, total jerk about the whole thing and you want to blast him, I won't stop you. A loud breakup may help you deal with your anger. Or wait until you're alone, then punch pillows or tell him off in front of your mirror.)

Above all, don't conclude that love isn't worth it. Your broken relationship was not a waste of time. You enjoyed it and learned from it. Even if you got burned, weren't the sparks and toasty glow great while they lasted?

After you begin to feel stronger, get back into the ring. Not that there's anything wrong with going a long time without a boyfriend. But do check out the smorgasbord: Mario, Jeff, Bryson, Drew, Terrance, Ken, Joe. . . . Variety is spicy. And trial and error isn't such a bad way to go.

LASTING LOVE

Some romances take nosedives, others wind down and die natural deaths, and a few last a lifetime.

Tonight over dinner, a woman told me about her high school reunion. She described a bunch of adults milling around a gym wearing name tags attached to photos of their former selves. "I saw three old boyfriends," she said. "Dull! Dull! Dull! Neither Jay nor Karl nor Danny appealed to me. Boy, I'm lucky I made it to Jeremy."

I tell you this because back in high school, she never imagined that being dumped by Jay, Karl, and Danny would be something she'd be thankful for one day. Yet love isn't always supposed to be forever.

Summer romances are especially notorious for being intense, wonderful, and short-lived. Why do so many sunny romances chill in the fall? Because you and your guy have less free time, you're back under the student-body microscope, you may live miles apart, and the starry infatuation stage may be about up by September anyway. If you want to try to keep the romance going, by all means do. Write letters, phone, plan meetings. A fling *can* last a lifetime. But if you realize that you may have to let each other go someday, you may feel less devastated if that day comes.

People change and drift in different directions. And great boyfriends don't always make great husbands or fathers, anyway. Be aware, too, that to a certain degree, you may now be bewitched by love in general and not by Charlie in particular. Do you mostly adore Charlie or do you mostly adore adoring and being adored?

There's no way to control how long a relationship lasts. For now, if you want your current love to continue, try to be friends first and foremost. Give each other room to grow—none of this yearbook signing "stay just the way you are" nonsense! Keep your cards on the table. Keep your humor about you. If the magnetism lasts, and you remain compatible as you mature—if you grow up without growing apart—your love just may endure.

Getting married while you're a teen, however, is usually shortsighted. Teen girls often envision the rosy side of marriage (a permanent date, a kitchen, your very own bed-for-two) and forget about the added responsibilities of playing house (laundry, vacuuming, checkbook balancing). If you have superhigh expectations of what a marriage is, look around at the married couples you know—your parents, relatives, neighbors, friends' parents. That's marriage: for better and for worse. Marriage can be marvelous, but it doesn't make other troubles go away. And marrying to escape problems often just causes more problems.

The younger a couple marries, the higher the chances of divorce. Get this: Nine out of ten sweethearts who marry when one or both are under eighteen end up divorced.

How can you know now whom you'll want to eat breakfast with when you're fifty-nine? Take your time before choosing a life partner! And why jump from life-with-parents to life-with-husband anyway, without first testing the waters alone or with roommates your age?

My sister-in-law Lisa and her husband Andy were high school honeys who then dated around for several years. When they finally got engaged, they did so with open eyes. They'll never have to wonder what other loves could offer.

Another friend called off her wedding at the last minute. I admired her guts. As she put it, "Better to be mortified this month than miserable for years."

Before you marry anybody, soon or someday, make sure you thoroughly (thoroughly!) discuss your attitudes about money, children, sex, housework, education, religion, where to live, personal goals, and just about everything else under the moon. You're not both going to live with one of your parents, are you? (Their roof, their rules.)

Should you live together someday? It's up to you. If you do, may I suggest a one- or two-year limit to the arrangement? When time's up, marry or set each other free.

True love *can* last. But if your high school romance fizzles, don't languish forever. Another romance will blossom. And fade. Do you want to get married someday? A love that can stand the test of time will come along. Mature love grows and will wait until you're ready for the security and sacrifices that come with saying *I do*.

LOVE NOTES

Love at First Sight or When the Chemistry Is Right:

I could tell you Rob and I fell in love at first sight because an instant zing did flash between us. But then love at first sight only holds up if it survives a second glance, a third stare, and a fourth cross-examination. Intrigue at first sight? *That* I'll buy. Falling in love is lovely, but so is stepping in, and it's okay if you and your guy didn't feel immediate thunder.

He Said He'd Call and He Didn't:

Guys do that. They say, "I'll call you" at the end of a date even when they won't. It's not to string you along. It's their way of being polite. Like when we say, "Thanks, I had a good time" even though the evening turned out so awful, it would have been better to have stayed home, polished shoes, and changed the kitty litter. Of course, your guy might be shy. Or he might call in a few weeks. Don't park at the phone. If you can't stand the waiting game, call *him*. And remember that if he didn't call because he didn't like you, you wouldn't want to go out with him anyway.

There's No Such Thing As a Free Dinner:

If he wants to pay, I won't quibble. Just don't order the most or least expensive entrée on the menu. But why not offer to share expenses or invite him out once in a while? Say, "My treat." (That's more graceful than "Let me pay.") Don't let a guy spend big bucks on you if afterward one of you is going to feel you owe him $24.99 of hot-and-heavy smooching. If you invite *him* to the theater or a prom, let him know ahead of time that you plan to treat (or that you hope it's okay to split expenses).

Even if You Find Mr. Right, Things Will Go Wrong:

Not such bad news, really. Keeps you on your toes.

Chivalry Is Alive and Kicking:

Feminism is great, but I also like when a man holds a door open for me, and I make a point of holding doors open for men—and women. If a guy helps you on with your coat, don't lecture him on women's rights. If he opens the car door for you, don't get on a soapbox; get in, lean over, and unlock his door for him. I'm all for male gallantry and female courtesy.

Love and Looks:

If you run into your crush when you're wearing sweats, don't cringe. Smile. He looks cute in *his* sweats, doesn't he? On the other hand, do always try to look presentable. And if you know you'll be seeing him, make an extra effort to look decent. Love makes girls blossom, but then many take their guys for granted and go to seed. Beware: Love is blind, but not for long!

Guys Get Nervous, Too:

Once my brother Eric had an 8 P.M. date with a neighbor. He came into my room at 7:55 to ask, "Do you think I should be a little early, right on time, or a little late?" I said I didn't think it mattered. But that exchange mattered to me—it taught me to relax, because guys quake, too.

There Is Such a Thing As Being Too Honest:

Yes, you should keep the lines of communication open, speak your mind, and not lie. But no, you don't have to tell your boyfriend how far you went with each of your former honeys. Don't unburden yourself by lumping the burden on him. You also don't need to share every little thought that pops into your head, or tell him how you hate your fat thighs. *You* decide where to draw the honesty line. Love is sometimes saying what you think the other person wants to hear instead of the truth, and sometimes saying the truth instead of what you think the other person wants to hear.

Whoever Said a Girl Can't Give a Guy a Flower?

Not me.

Long-Distance Love:

I've been there. It can work. But exchanging eloquent love letters that skim above daily strife makes it easy for you both to romanticize the relationship. When you're actually about to see each other again, allow for an awkward period of getting reacquainted.

Going Out with More Than One Guy at One Time:

I've been there, too, and it's not as much fun as you'd imagine. It takes a lot of psychic energy to care a lot about two guys—and I for one never have been a fan of roller-coaster rides. If you think you and your guys can handle a triangle, okay. But if you sneak around, you may get caught, and you'll probably feel guilty. What about just casually dating more than one guy? Sure, why not?

Life Can Be Exhilarating Even When You're Not in Love:

Absolutely!

KISSING, ETC.

I'll keep this brief because I bet you have your kissing style down pat. Just take off your glasses and be soft, sensual, and creative. Kissing expresses caring. Don't feel compelled to break any kissing-without-breathing records or to jam your tongue into the guy's mouth if you don't want to. Beware of beard burn. And (uh oh, here comes a dumb joke) don't ever say to a vampire, "Wanna neck?"

My high school boyfriend and I sometimes argued about P.D.A. He took offense because I didn't like playing kissy-face in public. Once he even asked, "What are you going to do on your wedding day in front of all those people?" But I stuck to my guns and we did our smooching in private. When he told me to stop breaking our kisses, however, I was glad to comply—I hadn't realized I was cutting kisses short.

Decide how you feel about the *whos*, *hows*, *wheres*, and *whens* of kissing. Kissing and cuddling go a long way. Sex doesn't have to enter the picture for a long time.

From television and movies, you may have surmised that some adults rush through the preliminaries. Yet instant sex is often sound and fury signifying nothing. And many adults miss the kissing, hugging, back-rubbing, freckle-hunting, and hand-holding.

How did *you* first find out about intercourse? Did Missy Field tell your whole table one day at lunch? Did you stumble on a racy book when baby-sitting or at a slumber party? Did your mother sit you down to discuss The Facts of Life?

Now that the secret's out. . . .

4
SEX

WHAT YOU SHOULD KNOW BEFORE SAYING YES

If you're not yet having sex—three cheers. If you are, I hope that you don't have sex for the wrong reasons: Your friend is involved in an X-rated romance; or your sister has gone all the way; or your boyfriend is putting on the pressure; or you think you gain points if you score.

Sex should someday become a pleasurable, meaningful, guilt-free part of your life. But sex before you're ready or sex with the wrong guy is no fun. So proceed with caution. There are good reasons why you should wait.

This chapter is for those who are already sexually active and for those who intend to be virgins until their wedding night. It gives the lowdown on contraception, pregnancy, abortion, self-stimulation, sexually transmitted disease, homosexuality, rape, incest, and other topics you may wonder about.

TO DO IT OR NOT TO DO IT:
THAT IS THE QUESTION

Once upon a time, unless you were married, you didn't want anybody to think you'd gone all the way. Now lots of teens don't want anyone to think they haven't. Years ago, girls couldn't say yes. Now many can't say no. Back then, some dreaded the thought of being sweet-sixteen-and-never-been-kissed. Now some fear they'll be sweet-sixteen-and-never-been-_____ .

Let's just say too many girls are forgetting that virginity is not something to get rid of or feel ashamed of. Too many are feeling rushed into sex before they are ready.

If you are a virgin, you may be asking yourself if you are ready. Yes? No? Maybe so? It's a tricky question because it brings up many other questions.

- Are you responsible enough to use birth control every time and mature enough to have a baby or an abortion if it fails?
- Do you feel free to say no?
- If having sex goes against your parents' values, can you handle doing something they (or you) consider wrong?
- Do you love the guy, and does he love you?
- Are you two friends and not just partners in passion?
- Will you feel good about the decision the next day?
- Have you weighed the pros and cons?
- Will it mean as much to him as it will to you?
- Do you truly desire him physically? (Most girls don't feel intense sexual desire in their early teens.)

I'd want to answer all yeses on that miniquiz before saying yes to any guy. Sex at any age before you're ready is a bad idea. Better to let sex be something to look forward to. The suspense and wanting and anticipation make the eventual act more special.

If you can wait, wait. If you have doubts or think you would have regrets, wait. If you think being fast is the way to get or keep a boyfriend, wait. If you think you might lose any self-esteem if you say yes, wait. If you think your decision is based on wanting to rebel or wanting to conform, wait. If you can wait, wait.

What if your boyfriend is pressuring you? You're both in love and have been petting for months, and he says he's frustrated out of his mind? What if *he's* ready but you're not?

First of all, heartless though this may sound, nobody ever died of "blue balls." It doesn't maim a guy to have an erection and then not come (have an orgasm). That happens to him when he sees a sexy movie or thinks about bikinis during class. (I was 16 when I wrote in my diary, *"Judy and I were discussing erections. Can boys calm down or do they have to let it out? Eric* [my brother] *enlightened me that they could calm down."*) Second, lots of guys would prefer the frustration of not making love to the frustration of not kissing, so it's unfair for them to make you feel so guilty. Third, if you have sex for his sake, you're shortchanging yourself; you should be making love *with* him—not *to* him or *for* him. Sex goes both ways. It's not one person letting the other do things or one owing the other something. Fourth, many guys feel it's their duty to play offense while you play defense. Your boyfriend may be no more experienced than you and may even be relieved when you set limits.

Lines? Some guys use a variation of the ancient "You would if you loved me." You can reply, "You wouldn't insist if you loved me." A guy who doesn't care enough to be patient and respect your point of view doesn't care enough. Or he might argue, "Everyone else is." Fine. Why isn't he with everyone else? Or he might try the old, "We might die tomorrow." True. But we probably won't. And the only way to stay sane is to have hope and confidence about the future: your own and the world's.

Having intercourse means literally and figuratively opening yourself up to someone else. That's a Big Deal. Even if you're not a virgin, it's still a Big Deal—it's always a Big Deal. If you went all the way once with Ryan, you don't have to do it again with him or anyone else until you know you're ready.

Are you concerned about what you think your friends think? Believe it or not, virgins in your school are probably the silent majority. Recent statistics say that one out of three girls aged fifteen to seventeen has had sex. That means the other two haven't.

Once you've said yes to someone, it is harder to say no the next time. It also becomes harder to sort out how you feel about the guy. And if you and he do break up, the split may become more painful. Also consider this: Some couples aren't as sexually compatible as others. What if sex isn't so great with you and Ned? Will your relationship deteriorate?

Girls who do have sex should be discreet. To kiss and tell is all very well, but it's wiser to kiss and shut up. I'm amazed at how much I knew in high school about people I shouldn't have known anything about. My diary is peppered with tidbits (names changed) such as: *"Lance Harmon and Polly Shoor screwed when she was superdrunk"* and *"Mike is very upset with Diane for telling that they went to second. He found it 'intimate and personal.' Diane did, too, but she told Jen who told Carol who told Judy who told Steve who is best friends with Mike and mentioned it to him."*

So if you aren't going to keep your legs crossed, at least keep your mouth shut! Then if gossips gossip, tune them out. "Tease"? "Slut"? "Prude"? Labels are idiotic. Try not to use them or listen to them. Some nice girls do and some nice girls don't.

TRUE CONFESSIONS: MY FIRST TIME

Your first time is important. You remember it forever. Not that times two and three are run of the mill or that sex should ever be less than memorable. But there's only one first time, and the moment stays with you, for better and for worse. Are you expecting instant ecstasy? Don't.

Many guys and girls find the first go-around is awkward and clumsy, no matter how meaningful and poignant.

I hope your first time is with a steady, caring partner. That's how it is for most women. Others give away their virginity to someone who hardly appreciates the gift: the old everyone-else-is-doing-it-so-I-might-as-well-get-it-over-with-approach.

My first time was also my boyfriend's first time. We were in love and we'd waited and postponed and planned and were responsible enough not to insist on spontaneity. Nor did we want to be high or drunk; we wanted to be *there*. So we discussed the logistics, got birth control, and finally tried to do it. And tried and tried. I was tense and scared and, as I confessed afterward to my diary, *"It took an hour of true struggling."* Then the condom broke and so did the mood as I rushed to the phone to call Planned Parenthood. (The phone call was eventually followed by a test, but I was lucky and wasn't pregnant.)

To be honest, making love that first time was neither painful nor particularly enjoyable. I didn't bleed (many women do) and I didn't come (most women don't).

In my diary, I reported the lack of blood and commented, *"Maybe my hymen isn't even broken,"* and *"Maybe I'm still a technical virgin."* Right, and maybe the Pope is really a Moonie. Perhaps my wonderings were part ignorance, part wistful thinking. It isn't easy to say good-bye to girlhood.

IT'S EASY TO GET PREGNANT; IT'S EASY NOT TO

You can skip every other section in this book if you want, but read these next few pages. Maybe not this year, maybe not next year, but before you get involved in a sexual relationship. I've never made love without contraception. When my husband and I decide to try to have children, I'll put away the protection. But not until then.

It doesn't shock me that so many teens are having intercourse. But I am appalled that so many are doing so without birth control.

If you are sexually active, I won't stand in front of you waving a chastity belt. But if I could, I might show up waving a diaphragm. Sex without contraception is like skydiving without a parachute.

These are the widely published but hard-to-believe recent statistics:

- About 1,200,000 teen girls get pregnant each year (over 3000 each day); three-fourths of them did not want to, and 30,000 of them are under fifteen.

- Three out of five sexually active teens do not use birth control regularly.
- One out of five teenage pregnancies happen in the first month after a girl begins to have intercourse.
- One-half of teenage pregnancies happen within the first six months of sexual activity.
- Two out of every five girls who are fourteen this year will become pregnant at least once before turning twenty.
- Forty percent of sexually active teens get pregnant each year.
- Teen girls account for one-third of all abortions in the United States.
- Teen girls account for nearly half of all out-of-wedlock births in the United States.
- Three out of five teenage pregnancies are second pregnancies.

Stupefying, isn't it? If teens were better informed, these statistics could change. But too many parents and daughters get flustered when the topic of sex comes up. Too many schools don't teach sex education or teach it poorly or teach it at the wrong time. Too many students don't know the facts and spread misinformation. And too many sexy songs and steamy movies make everybody horny but offer no clues about how to keep from getting pregnant. (Does James Bond ever ask the babe in his arms if she's protected?)

It's your responsibility to protect yourself. We can get huffy about that. Why *hasn't* a contraceptive pill been invented for guys? Why don't males play a bigger role in birth control? Meantime, though, we're the ones with wombs, so *we* need to know how to avoid unwanted pregnancy.

Some girls (and this kills me) hesitate to get contraceptives because that's consciously admitting that they're having sex and they're not ready to face the fact. They figure, "Since I'm not using birth control, I'm not really having sex." Listen, if you're not ready to be responsible about intercourse, you're not ready for it. Which is fine. What's not fine is to deny what you're doing and wind up another pregnancy statistic. Don't ignore the cause-and-effect nature of sex and pregnancy. If you're adult enough to have sex, be adult enough to protect yourself.

Other girls feel contraceptives take the romance and spontaneity out of lovemaking. Pregnancy and babies don't do much for romance and spontaneity, either. The idea of reckless sex is all very nice during those minutes of heavy breathing. But it's not worth the weeks of worry as you pray for your period. If you're prepared, you're smart.

Still other girls don't use contraceptives because they are afraid their parents would find out. First of all, pregnancy is scarier than upset parents and harder to hide than a packet of pills. Second, the government gave sexually active teens a Valentine's Day gift on February 14, 1983: A federal judge barred the "Squeal Rule." That means that in most states, you can go to Planned Parenthood or any other family planning clinic for prescription contraceptives, and the clinic will *not* notify your parents. Finally, if your mother did find your pills, who knows? She may be more relieved than outraged.

Some girls have sex without contraception because they think they want a baby. They imagine sweet smiles and booties and aren't aware that babies get screaming hungry at 4 A.M. and usually aren't toilet-trained for two or three years. Babies require work, attention, and money. If you think a baby will bind you happily ever after to a guy, you haven't met any of the thousands of unwed mothers whose former boyfriends deny paternity and refuse to pay child support. Too many babies are born out of wedlock and into welfare.

It's dangerous to be naive. I know lots of intelligent girls and women who were unhappily surprised by pregnancy. One had a baby daughter, gave her up for adoption, and still thinks and wonders about her. Several had abortions and felt sad for months afterward. Two got married, and if you ask me (I know you didn't, but I'll tell you anyway), I don't think either marriage will last. In couple number one, the husband feels trapped and resentful. And couple number two's baby boy was born severely handicapped, and so far it seems neither groom nor bride is mature enough to cope with the responsibility.

Sure, some unexpected pregnancies lead to happy endings, but lots don't.

Once you realize that using contraceptives makes sense, you need to determine which kind is best for you. The following section can help you decide. You may be interested to learn that of the five million or so sexually active American teen girls, many of whom are married, approximately:

60 percent went to a clinic and use the Pill, diaphragm, or IUD
12 percent use foam and/or their partners use condoms
12 percent try unreliable methods like rhythm, withdrawal, and douching
16 percent hope for the best (heaven help them!)

The unfortunate P.S. is that many girls using contraception are not using it carefully enough to ensure maximum protection.

Please promise yourself that until you are ready to be a mother, you will make the effort to use contraception correctly and responsibly every single time you make love.

BIRTH CONTROL METHODS

The Pill

The pill has some real advantages if taken without fail at about the same time each day. The doctor may prescribe a twenty-eight-pill packet (a pill a day keeps the stork away) or a twenty-one-pill packet (take one each day for three weeks, then skip the week of your period before starting again). Once the first ten (some say fourteen) pills are taken, one can make love with complete spontaneity and without fear of pregnancy. (Borrowing one of your friend's pills, however, does no good at all—for you or her.)

The Pill, a combination of synthetic hormones similar to progesterone and estrogen, works by suppressing ovulation. With no ripe-and-ready egg present, a woman can't become pregnant. Used properly, it's almost 100 percent effective. No muss, no fuss.

Sound too good to be true? Some say it is and fear the Pill may be linked to increased risk of blood clots or heart problems. But most experts now agree that the new low-dosage Pill poses no serious health hazards for young women. Many say its benefits outweigh its risks: Not only is the Pill safer than childbirth, but it may prevent ovarian cancer in young women.

Who should think twice before going on the Pill? Girls who are quite underweight or who do not yet have well-established periods, girls who smoke, girls with certain medical problems (such as high blood pressure), girls who are forgetful and might miss a day, and women over twenty-five. No one should stay on it for years without a break. But for most sexually active girls, the Pill may be an ideal method of birth control.

Does it make you gain weight? When I was briefly on the Pill, I didn't get puffy. Nor did the Pill cause me nausea, spotting, depression, or headaches. But some girls do suffer these side effects. Pluses? The Pill makes one's periods regular, shorter, and less painful. If you suffer severe cramps, you may want to ask a doctor to consider prescribing the Pill for you.

I must admit I'm not comfortable with the fact that the Pill alters you internally. But then I'm not big on pill taking in general. Unless you are engaging in regular, frequent sex, I don't think it's worth it to fool with your body chemistry.

Are you on the Pill and not having sex? That's silly. Are you having sex because you're on the Pill? That's nuts.

Diaphragm with Jelly or Cream

Have you ever seen a diaphragm? Picture a flexible beige mini-Frisbee with a rubber ring around the edge and you've got the idea. A doctor measures you to determine what size you need before prescribing the diaphragm. He or she should check you again yearly to make sure the size is right, and more often if you gain or lose more than ten pounds or are a newcomer to sex or have a baby or an abortion. The diaphragm is not effective if it doesn't fit properly or if it has a hole or tear in it. So replace it at least every two years and make a habit of holding it up to bright light to check for a rip or filling it with water to check for a leak. (Heard the one about the dumb lady who kept her diaphragm near the bed—tacked to the bedpost?)

Diaphragms are not much more complicated to put in or take out than tampons, and a doctor or nurse will show you how. Once it's inside, you shouldn't be able to feel it.

Anywhere from six hours to six seconds before intercourse, you should prepare the diaphragm by squeezing at least a teaspoonful of spermicidal jelly or cream into the bowl of the dome and around the rim. Before inserting the diaphragm, pee and wash your hands. After intercourse, leave it in for at least six hours but never over twenty-four. If you make love again during this time, insert more jelly or cream with a plastic applicator without removing the diaphragm. Later, after removing the diaphragm, wash it gently with warm water, dry it, and store it away from heat in its container.

The diaphragm prevents pregnancy because the rubber barrier in front of your cervix physically blocks the speeding sperm, and the jelly or cream chemically kills them. Used properly, it works 97 percent of the time, but because some girls and women occasionally put it in incorrectly, forget to use it, run out of jelly, or lose or gain weight but don't get remeasured for size, the effectiveness statistic is about 83 percent.

The diaphragm has become more popular recently. It's convenient if you want to have sex during your period because it catches the menstrual flow. I'd especially recommend it if you only have sex once in a while and don't want full-time birth control for part-time sex.

IUD

IUDs are not recommended for young women. They're better for women who have already had kids and cannot use other methods of birth control. The reason?

Side effects. Some users get heavy periods and cramping. All users risk perforation of the uterus, tubal pregnancy, spontaneous abortion, and increased chance of pelvic inflammatory infection, which, in severe cases, could lead to sterility.

On the positive side, IUDs are about 98 percent effective and are the easiest method of birth control around. Once the doctor has inserted one into your uterus, you're all set for a year or so. You simply check monthly to make sure you can feel the nylon string attached to your plastic or plastic-with-copper intrauterine device. And you go for annual checkups to replace the IUD (especially if it's the hormone-releasing type) or make sure the loop or coil hasn't been dislodged or expelled. Most IUDs work by preventing a fertilized egg from implanting itself into the wall of the uterus.

Condom and Foam

I'm wary of depending solely on condoms. But if your partner uses a prophylactic and you use a contraceptive foam, you have nearly a 99 percent chance of not getting pregnant.

Condoms and foam are an easy and effective method. You can buy them without a prescription at any pharmacy. (Remember: being adolescent and pregnant can be more embarrassing than buying Trojans or Conceptrol.)

Just before intercourse, he unrolls the condom onto his erect penis (leaving a ½-inch space for the sperm-filled semen) and you insert the foam into your vagina. If penetration isn't easy, use prelubricated condoms. (Don't use Vaseline or petroleum jelly, which can weaken the rubber.) For extra protection, buy condoms that have a reservoir tip in which the semen can collect. After intercourse, as your partner withdraws, he should hold on to the rim of the condom so it doesn't slip off. Use a new condom each time, and never use a condom that is more than two years old.

Foam products vary, so follow directions. Many foams come premeasured and are inserted before intercourse.

The condom-foam combination protects from pregnancy because sperm are trapped in the thin rubber sheath, and if the condom does break (accidents happen), the sperm-killing foam acts as a backup and immobilizes the sperm.

There are virtually no nasty side effects associated with condoms or foam. Condoms actually protect against sexually transmitted diseases. Some guys complain that condoms cut down on pleasure and some girls say that foam is messy, but I think condoms and foam make for good contraception because they are accessible and safe: no doctors, no dangers.

And with this method, the couple is sharing the responsibility of birth control.

Don't rely on condoms alone, because 10 out of 100 girls who do wind up pregnant. If you rely on foam alone, you have a 22 percent chance of pregnancy. Use both—this is no time to save money or bother!

Vaginal Inserts

Cheap, easy to use, and easy to get (no prescription necessary). The trouble with the spermicidal tablets, capsules, and suppositories you place in your vagina is that they aren't terribly effective. And if you don't allow a good ten minutes before intercourse for the suppository to melt and foam, you're asking for trouble. So I'll pass on inserts, thanks.

Then again, when used *with* a condom, the insert is comparable in effectiveness to the foam-condom combo.

Rhythm

I bet the guy who sings, "I got rhythm, I got music, I got my girl, who could ask for anything more?" ends up with more: a houseful of babies! While it's wise to know how the rhythm method works so you know when you are most and least fertile, it's risky to rely on rhythm as a means of birth control, because your cycle changes. In theory, rhythm is only 87 percent effective, and in practice, it's only 79 percent effective. That means each year, out of every 100 women who rely on rhythm, 21 get pregnant. We're talking a lot of upset ladies.

You should know that you are most fertile at about the midpoint of your menstrual cycle (about two weeks after your period starts) and are least likely to get pregnant during menstruation. In other words, assuming you have a regular twenty-eight-day cycle (and for most women, that's a false assumption), if your period begins on January 1, you will ovulate sometime around January 14. One of your ovaries will release a single egg into one of your fallopian tubes, and that egg will travel toward your uterus. Your egg can be fertilized anytime during the next two days, and sperm can live inside you for up to four days. So if sperm meets and fertilizes egg anytime that week—presto, you're pregnant. The rhythm system therefore says: no sex before, during, or after ovulation. So you would abstain (or use other contraception) at least from January 11 through January 17 in that hypothetical cycle.

Many conscientious women do more than mark their calendars. They check for variations in their cervical mucus and body temperature and note conditions (stress, travel, sickness) that could cause an irregularity in their cycle. Such precautions make rhythm a little more effective.

The problem with rhythm for girls who don't have regular cycles is that they can't predict when they are ovulating. If you have a period the first week in January and not again until the second week in March, it's hard to know when you were most fertile. Other girls may be absentminded and have trouble remembering which days are safest.

Still others might feel passionate on a "dangerous" day and not have the self-restraint to say no.

Rhythm is safe and is sanctioned by the Roman Catholic Church. Although I do *not* advise it as your sole method of birth control, I do recommend that you learn when you are most fertile. Why? So that now you never ever take a chance during those times, and later, when you may want to start a family, you'll know when you'll be most likely to conceive. Remember that rhythm or no rhythm, you can get pregnant anytime—even during your period.

Withdrawal

Don't count on it. It takes a whole lot of willpower for a guy to pull out the very second his pleasure is most intense. Even if he means to withdraw before ejaculating, he might slip up, and that means millions of sperm racing in search of your egg. A drag if pregnancy is not your intention. Besides, I know I couldn't relax if I were depending on someone else's self-control to keep me from getting pregnant.

Even if your partner does withdraw in time, it may still be too late. A few drops of clear, lubricating, sperm-filled liquid may be secreted even before he ejaculates, and all it takes is one sperm (and one egg) to make a baby. Men may produce as many as 80 million sperm daily.

Withdrawal and rhythm are better than nothing, but why take chances and end up worrying? In actual use, withdrawal is only 70 to 75 percent effective. Not enough in my book.

Douching

Who told you douching worked as birth control? Not me. In less than a minute, his sperm may have swum beyond reach, and in a mere 90 seconds, one may have found your egg. Even if you bounce from bed to bathroom with Olympic speed, you're probably out of luck. Douching can even force some of the sperm higher into your uterus. I nix the method.

Contraceptive Sponge

Sounds great, although I'm still taking a wait-and-see attitude toward this new over-the-counter, one-size-fits-all doodad. The sponge, made of soft polyurethane, is less than two inches in diameter and is saturated with spermicide. You moisten it, insert it with your finger, and leave it in for at least six hours after intercourse. It remains effective for twenty-four hours, even if you make love more than once. To pull it out, tug on the ribbon loop, much as you would remove a tampon. It works as a physical and chemical barrier to sperm and seems to be up to 90 percent effective. It is not recommended for use when you are having your period. The Food and Drug Administration approved the sponge contraceptive on April 1, 1983, but some critics said their approval was premature and link the sponge to new cases of toxic shock syndrome. (Keep your ears perked for other new methods, such as the thimblelike cervical cap, but I wouldn't advise being first in line to try them out.)

Abortion

Wrong. Abortion is not a method of birth control; it's a too-late last resort. Read on.

WHAT IF YOU ARE PREGNANT?

I hope you're dipping into this section out of idle curiosity. I hope you're a virgin or have used birth control whenever you have made love.

But you may be reading this because you're pregnant.

Pregnant. It may not seem fair. Perhaps you've only had intercourse one measly time in your whole life. Or maybe you and your boyfriend were always careful about contraception—except once. Or maybe you mistakenly believed a myth like you can't get pregnant the first time or you can't get pregnant if you don't come. Some teens consider it cool to have sex but treat pregnant girls like social outcasts. Fair? No.

So you missed a period, were feeling tired and occasionally nauseated, had to urinate often, and noticed your breasts and belly beginning to swell. Did you wait around to see if your next period would come? No. You gave yourself a home-pregnancy urine test or, even wiser, went to a clinic (in your town or nearby), dropped off a jar of fresh-morning pee (or had a blood test), and waited for their call. They called. You're pregnant.

Now what? For a short time, you're a basket case. You deny it. You cry a lot. Then you talk to the counselors at Planned Parenthood or some other clinic, your boyfriend, and maybe even your parents. (They may be disappointed, but they may come through for you.) Telling a friend may be a comfort, but if your friend tells a friend, your news could become public.

Start considering your options, each with pros and cons. Find out as much as possible, and decide what's right for you. Your boyfriend may beg you to keep the baby. Your girlfriend may advise you to have the baby, then give it up for adoption. Your parents may urge you to get an abortion. Easy for all of them to say. What do *you* want to do?

Think about yourself first—before boyfriend or baby, friends or family.

I'm going to tell you about your choices. You're the one who has to make the decision and live with it.

Keeping the Baby

Before you decide you want to have and keep the baby, think about what you're getting into. Having a baby is not like having a doll or baby-sitting for two hours, then leaving with money jingling in your pocket. A baby is a huge responsibility. I hope to have a family someday, but at twenty-seven, I'm still not ready for that responsibility. Are you sure you are?

Over a half-million teens each year decide to have and keep their babies. Some end up feeling trapped, resentful, and cheated of their childhood. Child abuse and neglect of babies born to teens is more common than among older mothers. Would you find it frustrating to wear maternity clothes while slim friends wear sexy dresses? To be stuck inside changing diapers, while buddies are out partying? To drop out or have to attend a school for pregnant women or go on welfare while friends are graduating from high school and getting jobs? Maybe you want to finish being a kid before having a kid. Maybe you aren't ready to be tied down. You probably will be able to offer a baby more in the future. Being a mother with no money, no husband, and no degree is hard. Grim but true: Suicide is seven times more common among girls who are mothers than among girls who are not.

Be realistic. Can you afford a baby? Are you mature enough to handle having a baby now? Healthy enough for labor and motherhood? Willing to give the baby all the attention it demands? Will you get married or raise the child alone? Picture your situation a year from now; five years from now. Will the baby's father or your parents be able to help you during all this?

Some teens decide to have and keep their baby and it is a wise, happy choice. The baby's father is proud and supportive and can earn a living for the couple and the toddler. Or the teen girl's parents care for mother and baby and the teen is able to continue her education and career plans. Obviously if you are an older teen and you and your boyfriend are already engaged, your chances of feeling good about keeping the baby are better than if you are fifteen and the baby's father doesn't want a thing to do with you. But many couples who marry because Baby's on the way end up miserable. Don't forget that 90 percent of teen marriages end in divorce—and that's counting teens who aren't parents.

If you do decide to have the baby, see a doctor now and start getting prenatal care and taking prenatal classes. If you think you might have a sexually transmissible disease, go to a doctor for tests and possible treatment or your baby could be born blind, deaf, or otherwise defective. To make sure your baby is born as healthy as possible, eat nutritiously (cut out junk food!) and don't drink, smoke, or do drugs while pregnant. Drinking is linked to birth defects; smoking to small, weak babies and premature births. The incidence of premature and underweight infants and infant mortality is higher among teen mothers than mothers in their twenties.

If you decide to have your baby—if your baby is a wanted baby— do all you can to start its life right.

Getting an Abortion

Many teens with unwanted pregnancies end up having an abortion. It's not an easy decision, and afterward, some feel guilty and sad and wistful. But many also feel a deep sense of relief, especially if the pregnancy was the result of rape or incest or loveless sex or if the girl knew in advance (perhaps through amniocentesis or a pelvic sonogram) that the baby would be abnormal or unhealthy.

A first-trimester abortion (one that is performed during the first 12 weeks of pregnancy) is safer, cheaper, and simpler than a second-trimester abortion. In most cases, you cannot have an abortion during the last three months of pregnancy. (So make up your mind. Don't let time make the what-to-do-if-you're-pregnant decision for you.) Having one abortion by a competent gynecologist won't damage your reproductive organs, but having several abortions, particularly late abortions, may make it hard for you to carry a future pregnancy to term. The longer you wait, the more complicated and expensive the abortion.

In 1973, the Supreme Court legalized abortion in all fifty states. Decades ago, some girls who could not turn to doctors tried their own abortions. They shoved coat hangers up themselves or drank horrid solutions or threw themselves down stairways. Many died. If you jump out a second-story window in hopes of ending your pregnancy, you could end your life. Or you could end up pregnant and crippled.

Miscarriage is not uncommon. Your pregnancy may end itself. But don't count on it. And don't try to make it happen.

Early abortions can be performed quickly for around $150 to $300 in clinics. Doctors use the suction method: Your cervix is dilated, and a cannula tube is inserted and attached to a suctioning device that removes the fetus and placental tissues. (Picture a very gentle mini-vacuum cleaner.) The whole procedure takes two to seven minutes, usually involves local anesthesia, and is often followed by a few hours of recovery in the clinic, and sometimes a few days of taking it easy at home.

What if you are more than three months pregnant? Abortions performed in weeks twelve, thirteen, fourteen, and up to eighteen often take ten to twenty minutes (not counting recovery time), may involve general anesthesia, and cost around $300 to $400. In the D-and-C method (dilation and curettage), the doctor dilates the cervix (with a dilator or laminaria, a matchlike stick of dried seaweed that absorbs liquid and expands gently), and uses a curette (picture a skinny, long-handled spoon) to remove the fetus and excess uterine lining. The D-and-E method (dilation and evacuation) is a suction procedure using a bigger cannula than that used in first-trimester abortions.

Two techniques for sixteenth- to twenty-fourth-week abortions are the saline and prostaglandin methods. In the first, the doctor withdraws some amniotic fluid from the uterus and replaces it with a salty liquid. In the second, he or she injects a prostaglandin solution into the amniotic sac or administers it via a vaginal or rectal suppository. Both techniques induce uterine contractions, and the fetus is expelled some hours later through the vagina. A local anesthetic is used, and an overnight hospital stay is usually required. Cost? Around $300 to $700. Psychological cost? These methods can be somewhat traumatic, since the girl is essentially going through labor.

Some doctors use other methods. Ask. Some states require parental consent or the approval of a judge. For more information, call toll-free:

National Abortion Federation (1-800-772-9100)
Abortion Advice and Referral (1-800-438-3550)

or contact:

Planned Parenthood Federation of America, Inc.
810 Seventh Avenue

New York, N.Y. 10019
(212) 541-7800

or

Family Service Association of America
44 East 23rd Street
New York, N.Y. 10010
(212) 674-6100

Giving Up Your Baby

Maybe you're too far along in your pregnancy to have a safe abortion. Or maybe abortion is against your principles. So you're going through with your pregnancy. You're seeing a doctor and taking good care of yourself because you want to deliver a healthy baby.

But you've decided not to keep it. Twenty thousand teens each year choose the adoption option. They realize they are too young or too alone to be the kind of mother they'd like to be.

If you are considering adoption, some may ask, "How can you give away your baby?" but you have to ask yourself, "How can I keep it?" Some may think you should pay for your "mistake," but the emotional and financial cost of delivery and adoption are certainly price enough. Others may think you're coldhearted. I think it is bighearted to offer your baby to a couple that desperately wants a child, has been waiting for one, and is ready and able to give yours the future it deserves. There are more couples who want to adopt than available babies to be adopted.

Contact a licensed adoption agency that belongs to the Child Welfare League. (Look up Adoption Agency in the phone book or ask your doctor or prenatal care counselors for referrals.) Find out as much as you can before you sign any papers. In many cases, when your child is eighteen, he or she can try to contact you (or you can contact him or her) through the agency. Some such reunions are heartwarming; others are disillusioning. If you never want to get in touch with your baby, you don't have to. In many cases, the mother may hold her newborn infant and say a final good-bye. Some mothers write a letter to their baby and give it to the agency to give to the child years later.

Another alternative is to leave your baby temporarily in a foster home that you visit regularly while you decide whether to keep it or give it up. Drawback? If you choose to give up your child after all, the waiting period can make separation harder. And it is best for the child to have one stable home as soon as possible.

All these choices are hard. Once you have made your decision, commit yourself to it and try to feel good about it. I wish you luck now and I beg you to use birth control in the future. Be careful, not careless. Remember: Three-fifths of all teen pregnancies are repeat pregnancies.

If you think I'm coming down hard on you, let me add that plenty of older and married women also get pregnant without intending to.

Here's hoping you can make the most of your life before you start someone else's.

DO-IT-YOURSELF ORGASMS

I have nothing against masturbation, but I hate the word. It sounds so serious. So clinical. About as sexy as the word *genitalia.* Plus *masturbation* conjures some of the leftover hogwash that people used to preach: how boys who play with themselves go blind and girls who touch themselves go crazy.

More teen boys than teen girls masturbate regularly, but the girl who has discovered that stimulating her clitoris or clitoral area can bring pleasure and relieve tension is far from rare. I'm writing this not so you'll jump into bed with yourself once you get to the last paragraph. I write so that if you sometimes engage in what has been wrongly labeled self-abuse, you'll know there is nothing shameful or even unusual about it. So put away the guilt.

Some "sexperts" even argue in favor of self-stimulation and say it is a healthy way for a young woman to get acquainted with her body. She can show her body how to climax, feel confident about her ability to have an orgasm, and later, when making love with a guy, be more apt to come or better able to show him how to help her come. That beats feeling frustrated or worrying that you're frigid or thinking you're the only one who has never felt the rhythmic throbbing and doesn't know what the fuss is about. Masturbation also makes more sense than having sex when you're in lust but not love.

Some girls worry that they are "spoiling themselves"—they fear they'll never come "the regular way" with a guy once their body has grown used to manual stimulation. Yet only a minority of women regularly reach orgasm during intercourse without additional stimulation of the clitoris. Some macho lovers may feel that if the friction going on between his penis and your vagina isn't enough to make you come, it's your fault. More mature and understanding men may be eager to help you climax by touching your sensitive clitoris before, during, or after intercourse.

Some girls find their own private orgasms may be more intense than orgasms with a lover. No crime in that. Sex with a caring partner is still more gratifying than sex by yourself. So unless you feel you are becoming dependent on or obsessed by masturbation, there is no cause for concern. Besides, solo sex can't make you pregnant or give you a disease.

I don't mean to be making a sales pitch for masturbation. But if you've already discovered that you can give yourself an orgasm alone—you don't have to apologize. Because it's not so terrible to love thyself.

ARE YOU GAY?

Probably not. You may sometimes wonder if you're gay, but while most women may feel they love their women friends, most want to make love with men.

Of course being lesbian is not sick or perverted. Life may be hard for gays sometimes, because some cruel, insecure people make fun of women and men whose sexual choices differ from their own.

Don't assume you are homosexual if you once had a lesbian encounter. Or if you are a teenage tomboy. Or if you had a crush on a woman. Or if you are a vehement feminist. Or if you had an erotic dream about a female friend. We are surrounded by magazines and movies brimming with supersexy women; it'd be nearly impossible not to notice their appeal, but that doesn't mean we're gay or bisexual.

No one knows for sure why some people are homosexual. It may not be a choice but a given, an orientation determined by genetic, hormonal, and/or environmental factors.

Why label yourself or announce that you are gay unless you are really sure and have excellent reasons for making your private life public? If you are gay or think you may be and are having trouble with your feelings about it, talk to a counselor or call a hot line or the Gay Switchboard (215-592-8419, evenings). Some estimate that one out of ten American men and women are gay, so the lesbian woman is hardly alone.

SEXUALLY TRANSMITTED DISEASES

You used to worry about cooties. Now you worry about herpes.

I don't want to give you the impression that sex is scary and will leave you either pregnant or diseased. Sex is wonderful. But it's most wonderful when it's worry-free. And it's most worry-free when you're informed, careful, and responsible.

We'll zip through this section as fast as possible. I'm not up for thinking about pus, pain, itches, and sores any more than you are. But what you don't know can hurt you. And it's better to have the facts than to have VD.

VD stands for *venereal disease* and can be very dangerous. Lately the term *STDs* has also been used to mean *sexually transmissible diseases.*

Anybody can get STDs; they are contracted by sexual relations with an infected person. Common? Yes. Over ten million cases of STDs are caught in the United States every year. About seven million American women (ages fifteen to thirty-four) now have STDs. Unfortunately, because the symptoms in women are often internal and hard to detect, many don't even know they are carrying the disease until it has done its damage. You can catch a disease, get cured, and get it again. And you can have more than one type at one time.

STDs are particularly serious in pregnant women, because certain diseases can be passed on to the baby, who may be born blind, retarded, or otherwise abnormal, or who may die soon after birth. With proper medical care, the threat to the newborn can usually be eliminated.

If you have several sex partners (who have several sex partners who have . . .) or if you have a classic telltale symptom (sore, swelling, unusual discharge, or pain or persistent itch in the genital area), see a doctor and ask for a VD test. Do ask because VD tests are not a routine part of ordinary checkups. Don't second-guess your symptoms or postpone an appointment, because although the symptoms may disappear, the disease won't; it may continue causing trouble inside you.

I do not tell you untrue horror stories. Masturbation will not make you blind or crazy or sterile. But STDs can. If they are left untreated, some types can kill you. They do not go away by themselves. If you suspect you have a sexually transmissible disease, call a doctor, a family planning clinic, or the national VD hot line toll free (1-800-227-8922; in California, 1-800-982-5833), or go to your local Health Department clinic. Pronto! Gynecologists are on your side. You might even be able to stroll in without an appointment. Tests may be free, and your parents don't have to be notified.

The person who gave you the disease, however, should be notified— by you or by a public health adviser who will not reveal your name. That way he, too, can receive treatment and stop spreading the disease. (This is one case in which you *should* kiss and tell.)

Modern drugs (praise be to Sir Alexander Fleming, the discoverer of penicillin!) can cure many cases painlessly. Finish any prescription as directed, and be sure your partner is also being treated. Then go for a follow-up checkup. Even for herpes, which doesn't yet have a sure cure, there are medicines that relieve discomfort.

How can you avoid getting STDs? Be sensible and selective about whom you share your body with. Don't fool around with someone who fools around with lots of girls. Look to see or ask the guy if he has a communicable condition. (You're too embarrassed to ask? What are you doing naked with him!?) Or have him use a condom—that reduces the chance of spreading disease. Contraceptive foams and creams also kill some germs. Some experts say it's a good idea to urinate as soon after sex as possible (to flush out any germs) and to wash your hands and genital area with soap and water before and after contact.

Obviously, if you are a virgin or have one steady, faithful, uninfected boyfriend, you don't have VD and need not feel paranoid.

The following are among the major STDs.

Herpes

Q: What's the difference between love and herpes?
A: Herpes lasts forever.

Alas, there's nothing funny about the herpes epidemic. Anywhere from 5 to 20 million Americans have genital herpes, with up to 600,000 new cases annually. Some estimate that 1 out of 35 teenagers have the virus. Herpes is common in the most well brought up, well educated circles. It has made a lot of people frantic and has slowed others down sexually.

Herpes simplex I is mild. It may appear as a mere cold sore or fever blister in the mouth. Herpes simplex II is serious, though not fatal. In women, it may be linked to cervical cancer, and is characterized by recurrent sores around the genital area. Sufferers may experience itching or burning, pain, fever, and an outbreak of genital blisters that dry up and go away in a few weeks but may reappear at unpredictable intervals, often at times of stress and especially during the first year of infection.

You can get genital herpes by having sex with someone who has open herpes sores. Your sores could appear two to fourteen days after exposure. When the herpes victim's symptoms are dormant, his or her condition is much less contagious, but it is still a good idea to reduce the risk of spreading the disease by using a condom and foam or jelly.

Even the not-so-terrible herpes simplex I can become herpes simplex II through oral-genital contact. In plain English, if a woman with blisters in her mouth has oral sex with a man, the next week he could discover blisters on his penis. Guys with herpes simplex I can also inadvertently give their girlfriends herpes simplex II. Similarly, if you touch a mouth or genital herpes lesion and then rub your eyes or tinker with your contact lens without first washing your hands, the virus could move to your eyes (ocular herpes).

If you have genital herpes, keep your genital area clean and dry. Wash with plain soap and water. Consider using a hand-held dryer to dry off. Wear loose-fitting clothes. And forgive yourself.

Many herpes victims feel angry, depressed, guilty, frustrated, and isolated. Imagine sleeping with one person who wasn't considerate or ethical enough to warn you of his active herpes outbreak, then finding you have an incurable disease and feeling like a sexual leper. But there is life after herpes. There are new antiviral drug treatments. And soon there may be a cure or a vaccine.

For more information, contact the Herpes Resource Center, P.O. Box 100, Palo Alto, California, 94306.

Gonorrhea

The "clap" is subtle but serious. Some of the more than one million infected women may notice a puslike vaginal discharge, painful urination, and vaginal soreness, but many notice no conspicuous symptoms at all. Throat and rectal gonorrhea are other variations on the theme. If it is left untreated, gonorrhea can lead to arthritis, heart trouble, inflammation of the reproductive organs, and sometimes sterility. About 100,000 women become sterile each year due to untreated gonorrhea. Pelvic inflammatory disease (PID) is the most common complication of gonorrhea. Symptoms may include abdominal pain, increased menstrual cramps, and lower back pain. PID can result in scar tissue forming inside the fallopian tubes and blocking passage of the egg into the uterus—in other words, sterility. Antibiotics usually work in treating gonorrhea and PID.

Nongonococcal urethritis/cervicitis is a more common disease than gonorrhea that mimics gonorrhea in symptoms and consequences but is treated with different drugs (e.g., tetracycline instead of penicillin).

Syphilis

Syphilis symptoms may include a genital or oral chancre (lesion or sore) followed by a rash anywhere in the body and loss of hair in patches. Then symptoms go away. But the disease, if it is left untreated, continues to do devastating damage to the victim's brain, blood vessels, and heart—damage that may not show up until years, even decades, later. About 100,000 women now have syphilis. And they are in respectable company: Henry VIII, Napoleon, and Beethoven were victims as well.

Vaginitis

Almost all women get some type of vaginitis at least once, and it isn't always contracted from sex. Vaginitis is not very serious but does require treatment with pills, suppositories, and/or creams. Symptoms? Severe vaginal itching or burning and an increase and change in vaginal discharge. You may be more prone to vaginitis if you douche or use deodorant sprays or bubble baths (these can irritate your vulva and kill friendly bacteria). Or if you wear tight pants, or panties or pantyhose with a nylon rather than a cotton crotch (nylon keeps in heat and moisture, allowing organisms to grow). Or if you're taking oral antibiotics and/or birth control pills (they may create vaginal conditions favorable to a yeast or other infection). Or if you have sex with someone who is infected or have sex without enough lubrication. Be sure to wash your vulva with mild soap daily. And always wipe from front to back after a bowel movement.

Cystitis

Almost all women get cystitis at least once. It is a bladder infection, not a venereal disease, but it is associated with sex. If you feel as if you have to pee constantly yet it burns like Hades when you try, and nothing comes out, or your urine is bloody, you may have cystitis. It's been dubbed "the honeymoon disease" because one cause may be a suddenly active, vigorous sex life. See your doctor, but in the meantime, go easy on the sex, soak in a warm tub, and drink plenty (gallons!) of water and liquids, especially cranberry juice with its helpful acidity. Steer clear of alcohol, coffee, or tea, which may irritate your bladder even more.

AIDS

Acquired immune deficiency syndrome (AIDS) is a still incurable and usually fatal disease. Most of its thousands of victims have been homosexual or bisexual men, intravenous drug abusers, and, to a much lesser extent, hemophiliacs and Haitians. Several dozen people have developed AIDS following blood transfusions. Women can get AIDS, too, and their babies can be born with it. AIDS victims' immune systems stop fighting and protecting them against certain infections. Victims may feel profoundly tired, get sick often, lose a lot of weight, develop a cough, and become susceptible to a deadly disease (such as Kaposi's sarcoma or pneumocystis carinii). AIDS may not be a threat in your social/sexual circle, but knowledge doesn't hurt, and everybody may breathe easier when its mysteries are unraveled.

Genital Warts

Genital or venereal warts are caused by a virus. They usually develop one to six months after intercourse with an infected person. Soft pink or red warts may look like tiny cauliflowers and appear in the folds of a woman's labia.

Scabies

A scientist named Bonomo discovered the itch mite in 1687, and scabies continue to plague children, teens, and adults. You can get scabies from having sex, holding hands, or simply sharing a towel with an infected person. Tiny mites mate on the skin, and then the female mite burrows into the skin and lays eggs. They may appear on hands, armpits, breasts, genital, or rectal areas or elsewhere. Scabies can be treated quickly with medicated lotions.

Crabs

Crabs are little parasitic lice that nestle in pubic hair and itch like the devil. They look like moving freckles. They are not a venereal disease but are a sexually transmissible nuisance. Fortunately, over-the-counter shampoos such as Rid or A-200 Pyrinate or prescription shampoos such as Kwell kill 'em off. Make sure you wash and dry all your clothes and linens (on the hot setting) before declaring victory over the little beasties.

Nasty things can happen to everybody, so beware. Let's hope you don't get any STDs. Ever.

RAPE

I am lucky. I have not been raped. But I will share an experience with you that frightened me. Here's what I wrote on February 9 in the diary I kept when I was fourteen:

> . . . Now for the unbelievable thing of the day. I was working on my

math assignment after school in an empty classroom when that stupid janitor walked in. As usual he made remarks about his girl-chasing youth, and he asked whether I played around with the boys, adding, "Sure you do, sure you do" and "You're not afraid of me, are you?" (I hate him so much.) Anyway, once or twice he's touched me around the bra area. That could be unintentional but I doubt it, especially after today. Today I was sitting at the desk wearing a dress. He said, "You must get cold going around in bare legs," then rubbed my leg high above my knee and added, "Oh yes, you're wearing stockings. Are your pantyhose tight?" (What a queer!) I mumbled, "I guess so." Then that guy I hate took his hand away. I yanked down my dress lower and he asked, "Why are you pulling your dress down?" Thinking it was none of his business, I just shrugged. Next he put his hand above my knee again and started working his way up. Suddenly he remarked, surprised, "Oh you have panties on underneath." Not realizing his fingers were up so high, I desperately held down my dress. He said, "What are you worried about?" At this point I was giving him really dirty looks and holding down my dress with all my might!! He said, "What are you afraid of? C'mon, let me have another peek." (I can't stand him. Who does he think he is?) Finally he must have given up and he went back to vacuuming. Now get this. He then said, "I know what you're hiding—your little brown mustache. That's it, isn't it? Do you comb it every night? Sure you do. Well yes or no?" I said no. He added, "Well you put your hand on it." I shot a really mean look at him and went back to my math. He said, "You know I'm doing you a favor letting you in here." I retorted, "Okay. So I won't come here." He said, "You can come. You're not afraid of me." I ignored him and finished my geometry. God!!

I didn't tell a soul back then. Now I wish I had. For all I know, that old man may have harassed—or molested or abused—some younger or more impressionable girl. How could I have been so naive as to think there could have been anything unintentional about his pawing my flat chest? Why did I just sit there? Because he was a grown-up? Because I thought adults were always right? Was I so trusting I didn't realize I didn't have to take that from anybody? So intimidated by and respectful of my elders that I didn't know I could talk back and take off?

That disturbed individual scared me without scarring me. But many women have been less fortunate. The National Center on Child Abuse and Neglect estimates that approximately one out of four American women is sexually abused (not necessarily raped) before age eighteen.

Women are vulnerable. Men don't usually have to think about the possible danger of working alone in an empty classroom or walking unaccompanied at night. Women do. We don't need to be paranoid, but we need to be cautious. And informed.

Did you believe any of the following myths?

Myth #1: Only girls get raped.

Truth: While the majority of rape victims are females between the ages of ten and nineteen, anyone can be raped. Rape is a crime of violence, not passion. Rapists look for easy targets, not sexy figures. Teen girls, old women, even boys get raped.

Myth #2: Most rapists are strangers.

Truth: About 60 percent of reported rapists are "friends," acquaintances, or relatives, and many "date rapes" go unreported. If a guy you're dating forces you to have sex against your will, that's rape. If your neighbor or cousin or friend's brother or the telephone repairman or father of the kids you baby-sit for makes you have sex when you did not freely give consent, that's rape. Most rapists are men between fifteen to twenty-two; many of the offenders are married; many of the crimes were planned.

Myth #3: The victim was asking for it.

Truth: Nobody asks for rape. Rape is sometimes random, but if the victim happens to be wearing a halter top or "provocative" skirt, she is no more to blame than is an elderly nun or a retarded teen girl wearing an overcoat. The rapist is to blame.

Myth #4: Most rapes happen in dark alleys.

Truth: About half of all rapes and assaults happen at home—in the victim's home or at the place where she is baby-sitting or visiting. "Date rapes" or "acquaintance rapes" often occur on the rapist's turf, often on weekend nights.

Myth #5: Most rapes are interracial.

Truth: Most rapes occur between men and women of the same race.

How can you reduce your risk of being attacked? Take a self-defense course or learn judo or karate at school or at the YWCA. I know a 110-pound high school girl who decked a 180-pound mugger. Sure took him by surprise. And for safety's sake:

- If you are in a home or car, make sure the doors and windows are locked.
- If it's nighttime, don't walk alone, especially in rough neighborhoods.
- If you are out alone, walk briskly and with confidence. Don't project fear.

- If you are lost, don't ask a strange man for directions and don't give your home address.
- If you feel suspicious of a man behind you, cross the street or walk in the middle of the street. Don't slow down or go toward bushes, alleyways or dimly lit areas.
- If you've got the willies and see a respectable-looking woman, walk next to her. (A man once saw me enter a movie theater alone, then went in and sat behind me. I spotted another lone woman a few rows back, sidled up, asked if I could join her— and she and I have been friends ever since.)
- If the phone rings, and you're alone, don't let a stranger know. (Why not lift the receiver, shout "I'll get it" to the walls around you, then say hello?)
- If you're alone on a bus, subway, or train, sit near the driver or conductor, and don't prepare to get off until the last moment. No one needs to know ahead of time which stop is yours.
- If a scruffy-looking guy is alone in an elevator, don't get in. If a dubious character gets in and you're alone inside, coolly get off at the next floor.
- If you are carrying more money than usual, carry two billfolds— one with a few bucks in case you are approached, the other for you, safe in an inside pocket.
- If you insist on hitchhiking (not smart), never do it by yourself and never accept a ride with a guy or guys alone. Whenever you're in a car, check the door handle so you'll know how to get out fast.
- If you are nearing your home or car, have your key ready.
- If you and a guy are going to park and kiss, avoid secluded back roads or lovers' lane setups where he or a less trustworthy man could take advantage of you. (My parents encouraged us to park in the driveway. Safe and sensible, though my brother Eric sometimes teased me when he heard the car pull in at 11:30 but didn't hear me walk in until 12:00.)
- If a phone is nearby and you need help, dial 0 or, in many areas, 911 to summon the police.

Since we're imagining the worst (I trust you're not reading this alone at night in a creaky house), let's imagine the worst of the worst. You're jumped by a rapist. What do you do?

Unfortunately, there's no simple answer. It depends on you and the situation. Some advise to be passive, especially if the rapist has a gun or knife. Others say to try to repel him: vomit, drool, pee, tell him you have your period or herpes or AIDS. Many say to be assertive: scream, yell *rape* or *fire* or *help* or *police,* struggle, carry a whistle at all times and blow it like mad. Others say to fight back if you know what you're doing: bite, scratch, knee his shin or groin, gouge his eyes, punch his stomach, bend back his pinky, beat his face with your keys or the heel of your shoe, yank at his testicles when he least expects it. (When you think about it, he may be in a pretty vulnerable position himself.) Some say to go limp: turn into heavy, immobile weight. Others say to use psychology: ask him sympathetically about his life or tell him your father was just killed in a car crash. Shock him; catch him off guard; outsmart him.

I have a friend who was assaulted by a teen when she was a teen. Eleanore was so furious she yelled, "Oh go home and behave yourself!" He left!

What would *you* do if you were approached? Think about it now.

I don't think I'd have the guts or know-how to poke a rapist's eyes out, but if I had my wits about me and thought I stood half a chance—a big *if,* to be sure—I'd scream bloody murder and run like a sprinter.

You knew this was coming. We're about to imagine the worst of the worst of the worst. You've been raped. Now what?

Lie. Promise the rapist you won't tell anybody. Then go straight to the nearest police station or hospital or call one of the nation's seven hundred rape crisis centers—check your phone book. Call even before you bathe, clean up, or change, because authorities usually need physical evidence if you prosecute, and the police may be more sympathetic if you aren't looking fresh as a rose. The majority of rapes go unreported, but if you press charges and land the creep in jail (not always easy), you'll feel good about your revenge and good knowing you probably protected someone else. (Most rapists rape again.) Many rape crisis centers provide a counselor or support team who will accompany you to the hospital or police station and help you begin to deal with your rage, humiliation, guilt, and disgust.

A married friend of mine was raped. She didn't get pregnant, beaten, or STDs, but she was so turned off by men and sex afterward that for a long time she was unable to enjoy making love with her husband. Finally she joined a therapy group that helped her sort out her feelings and retrieve her self-esteem and sense of control. She is now slowly learning to trust again and to blame that one man—not all men and not herself—for her misfortune. She is learning to stop demeaning herself for not having resisted and to start congratulating herself for having survived.

For more information, write to Women Against Rape (WAR), P.O.

Box 02084, Columbus, Ohio, 43202. Their twenty-four-hour crisis telephone number is (614) 221-4447. Or call the National Center for Prevention and Control of Rape at (301) 443-1910.

INCEST

Incest isn't sexy, and if there were a chapter in this book devoted solely to abuse or crisis, I would have included this and the rape section under that heading.

Sexual contact between relatives or family members is taboo and illegal but not as rare as we would like to believe. Since so many cases go unreported, it's tough to guess how common incest is. Some experts estimate that around 2 percent of adult women have been sexually molested by their father or stepfather and that tens of thousands have had sex with a grandfather, brother, stepsibling, uncle, cousin, or other relative. Others cite much higher statistics and numbers. In the *Cosmo Report,* which questioned 106,000 *Cosmopolitan* magazine readers in 1980, 10.7 percent wrote that they had had an incentuous experience. The women surveyed may be neither typical or representative, but that percentage is still too high to ignore.

Alice Walker's prize-winning novel *The Color Purple* gives a heart-rending glimpse of the fear and anguish that usually accompany incest. Incest is alarmingly widespread among so-called all-American families of every color, class, and locale. Offenders may be violent alcoholics or conservative churchgoers. Often the victims are children who don't question their elders and don't realize at first how exploitative and out of the ordinary their situation is. They may mistakenly believe that Father knows best.

"If you don't do as I say," a father or stepfather may threaten, "I'll beat you." "If you don't let me do this now, I'll do something worse next time." "If you tell anybody, I'll kill you." "I'm your father—I should be your first man."

The girl may be afraid to say no. She may be afraid that if she tells her mother, her mother won't believe her. Or will blame her. Or will break up the family, then hate her for it. Or the girl may worry that if she does *not* tell, the experience will happen again—to her or to her little sister.

I've heard accounts from a boy who was sexually approached by his mother and from a girl who was sexually attacked by her grandfather. Those who quip "incest is best" haven't been there.

If you are a victim of incest, you are not alone and you are not at fault. You are the same good person you were before the troubled adult made use of your body. The offender is messed up, not you. But you may want to seek help before your pain, anger, and humiliation can turn to scars that make it hard for you to respect and love other men. Tell a trusted adult who will believe you: a family member, teacher, doctor, group leader, school counselor, minister, or rabbi. Several dozen clinics around the country, like Chicago's Incest Survivors, specialize in helping with incest-related problems. Or call the National Child Abuse Hot Line toll free (1-800-422-4453). Or look in your phone book's Yellow Pages under Mental Health or Social Services or Family Counseling or Community Referral. Your father won't immediately be hauled off to jail, nor will you be thrown into a foster home. In most cases, you and your family can begin to get the therapy you all may need. And you can learn how not to let the difficulties of your past ruin your future, and how not to let someone else's problem become your own.

A final word: The most common form of incest happens between siblings and usually has a less devastating effect on future mental health. Lots of us have played some form of "doctor" with our brothers when we were little children. If you played a more advanced or older version with your brother, and now you don't think about or worry about it, okay. But if past "play" still upsets you or gets in the way of new relationships, talk to a counselor and start feeling better.

5
FAMILY

CAN'T LIVE WITH 'EM, CAN'T LIVE WITHOUT 'EM

So much for sex. If your mom and dad hadn't had it, you wouldn't be here. But they had more than sex. They had a family.

Some say the ideal family provides roots and wings. The catch? Most families aren't ideal.

Novelist Leo Tolstoy wrote, "Happy families are all alike; every unhappy family is unhappy in its own way." The reasons behind some families' unhappiness are, indeed, diverse and complex. You may have problems with parents or parents with problems. Or you may get along fine with your parent or parents but wish you could say the same about your siblings or stepparents.

If yours is an open, affectionate, supportive family, you are lucky. I bet you like yourself and I hope you are appreciative. If your family always bickers, yells, ignores, or hurts each other, these pages can give you clues about how to end destructive patterns. It's worth working toward more communication and caring, possibly even through counseling. You can't just break up with your family as you can with a boyfriend, so strive to improve things on the home front. Love takes work.

This chapter is for every daughter who is growing up, up, and away.

PROBLEMS WITH PARENTS

Why aren't you all getting along as well as you used to? That's a hard one. If it's not the case in your family, terrific. If it is, fluff up a pillow, sit back, and let's try to figure out what went wrong.

Surprise. Nothing went wrong. It's absolutely normal for parents and teenagers to go through some rough times. Why? Because when you were a child, you probably obeyed your parents without question, and now you question everything. You may have thought they were infallible, and now you know they make mistakes.

Consider your parents' point of view. Not so long ago, you idolized them and depended on their approval ("Mom, Dad, watch this, watch this, watch this!"). Now you eat and sleep at home but would just as soon be with your friends. You reached for your mother's hand when crossing the street, and now, when she occasionally reaches for yours—right in public—you could just die. You may give Tuffy and Tiger more affection than Mom and Dad. Yet your parents, like you, need to feel needed and loved. They want to get along with you as much as you want to get along with them. And they have to put up with you as much as you have to put up with them.

You think it's easy for your mother? She's noticing a wrinkle here, a gray hair there—and you wake up more attractive every day. She may feel her life is becoming routine, whereas yours is (or is about to be) brimming with kisses and compliments, new people and places. Of course she's proud and happy for you, but she may also feel a tinge of envy— and hate herself for it. Even if she works outside the home (as most mothers do), it may be tough for her to see you as a person who won't need much mothering anymore.

And your father? You think it's easy for him to see his darling daughter's eyes light up with every mention of Tom, Rick, or Larry? He remembers his wild teenage times and may hate to think of his princess getting tangled up with guys. Plus, he probably thinks you're as pretty as the woman he proposed to, and that may be hard for him to handle. If he's going through his own mid-life crisis ("Have I accomplished what I set out to do? Is there more to life than this?"), he may be too preoccupied to sympathize or help with your adolescent identity crisis ("Who am I? What do I want to become?").

So everybody's got a different perspective, and you're all butting horns. You may quarrel because your parents are too protective, permissive, indifferent, nosy, demanding, critical of your friends, or embarrassing. Or maybe they're mired in problems of their own.

One of every five teens live with a single parent, usually the mother. Although I refer to *parents* in the plural, the following suggestions apply to single parents, too.

If Your Parents Are Overprotective . . .

They probably mean well. They probably want to know where you're going and with whom and when you'll be back ("Not later than 10:30!") because they love you and worry about you. Even so, it's hard if you have the strictest parents and earliest curfew around. How do you get your parents to stop treating you like a baby? Not, I repeat, not, by throwing a conniption fit, stomp, stomp, stomping to your room, slamming the door, and blasting your music. If you want them to start treating you like an adult, act like an adult. If you want more privileges, take on more responsibilities. To get your folks off your back, you may have to show that you can manage on your own—whether by getting up in the morning or getting a job or doing your chores—without needing to be nagged.

What if you'd like a later curfew? Don't whine, "Everybody else gets to stay out until midnight!" Instead, wait for a relaxed moment and ask your parents if you could have a trial compromise curfew this weekend. Try to sound rational, not emotional, as you ask if they'll let you stay out until 11:15. Say you want to learn to become gradually more independent so you'll be able to handle college and living away. Then make an effort to be more responsible. You might volunteer to do another chore around the house—vacuuming the living room? mopping the kitchen floor?—in exchange for more freedom.

(If you're thinking, "Another chore! Whose side are you on anyway?" let me point out that a carefree childhood can be misleading. The "lucky" girls who don't have to pitch in at home often freak out when they're on their own or married because they hadn't realized how many tasks need doing. I agree, however, that it is unfair if your parents distribute chores in a sexist way. You *can* mow the lawn and your brother *can* wash dishes.)

If your parents don't agree to the later curfew, tell them they're almost asking you to be disobedient or resentful. Or simply ask again next week, perhaps upping the check-in time by only fifteen minutes.

If they agree to give the 11:15 curfew a try, *get home on time.* If you walk in at 11:25, you've blown it. If you won't make it in until 11:20, phone ahead. If you arrive at 11:05, you may have won their trust and earned a new improved curfew.

As far as parents' wanting to know where you're going, forgive me again, but I think that's fairly reasonable. No, they shouldn't give you the third degree and, no, you don't have to fill them in on every detail. But parents tell each other where they're off to and until when. It shows they care and it's important in an emergency. From my diary when I was thirteen: *"Mom, Dad, and Mark got home after 1:00 A.M. and didn't call—worrying me and Eric to death."* See? If they're going to be late, they should phone, too.

How come you don't want to tell them where you're going, anyway? Because they'd disapprove? If you are doing drugs at your boyfriend's while his parents are away, maybe you can see why your parents worry.

One more thought: Sometimes life is easier when you have cut-and-dried rules. Back when nice girls wouldn't think of doing drugs or having premarital sex, they didn't really have to deal with those pressures. The answer was no, and that was that. Now, since many young women can make up their own minds about such matters, it can be a struggle to decide what to do. My point? That it sometimes helps to know what's off limits and what isn't. It's a relief to have rules—not unfair, inconsistent rules, but not no rules.

If Your Parents Are Too Permissive . . .

Maybe you feel your parents would let you do anything, and that they don't, as Rhett told Scarlett, give a damn. Frankly, they probably do.

Your parents may believe that since you'll have to learn to be self-sufficient eventually, better now, under their roof, than later by yourself. Or maybe they worry that if they say "No TV before dinner" or "No dates on weeknights," you won't like them as much. As with overprotective parents, it may be that they are raising you the best way they know how and with your well-being in mind.

My parents were fairly permissive. They made me absolutely promise I'd never ride a motorcycle, but otherwise I had a lot of leeway. Mom and Dad's easygoing attitude made me feel trusted, not neglected.

How about *you?* If your parents' lack of rules makes you uncomfortable and you'd like more reassurance that they care, tell them. Shock them with: "Believe it or not, I wish I had a curfew" or "Give me some guidelines."

Many teens nowadays wish their parents would provide more rules. If your parents just won't, or can't, give yourself rules. You will make your bed every day. You will start your homework before dinner. You will be tucked in by eleven. Eventually you live by your own rules, so it doesn't hurt to start disciplining yourself early.

If Your Parents Seem Indifferent . . .

What if your parents not only haven't set rules but never ask about your life, friends, schoolwork? They're so busy with their jobs and friends, they don't seem to have time for you. What if communication is zilch?

That hurts. Of course they may be patting themselves on the back for not being nosy, nagging, interfering parents. If so, you need to let them know you'd like to have more talks. They may be flattered, but unsure as to how to bridge the gap. Sometimes a man who has spent his whole adult life getting ahead in business may not know how to be a sensitive father. You may not be able to convert him and may have to accept him as is, flaws and all. Or reject him. Or in a few years, closeness may be easier.

It *is* worth trying to get through to a stony parent. Are you trying? If your dad asks, "Where have you been?" and you say, "No place," that's not setting the groundwork for friendship. Rather than being upset that your parents aren't attentive right when you come home from school or the minute they walk in from work, plan a time for a visit. Say to one or both, "How about if we make popcorn or play cards and talk tonight after we all get our work done?" Or, "Let's take a walk after dinner." Or, "I'll treat at Burger King for lunch this Saturday." Or, "Whoever keeps me company while I make cookies gets the first one warm from the oven—and a plateful to take to the office tomorrow." Sound too idealistic? Try informality. If one parent is running an errand, go along. If both are relaxing in front of the television, join them for a while. Or leave a note on their bed: "I don't say it often, but I love you."

Try to draw your parents out. Try: "How was work today?" When your parent grunts, "Fine," say, "No, tell me about it. I hardly even know what you do." If your folks are in a good mood at dinner, ask about how they met, about their first date, first kiss, honeymoon.

Don't forget the little ways to show you care. Compliment the person who made dinner. Praise your dad for trying to quit smoking or your mom for trying to lose weight. Empty the dishwasher if you know your mom hates to. Ask your dad if his cold is going away. My father used to stock the refrigerator with mushrooms (I adore mushrooms) when he knew I was coming home for vacation. It was a small detail, but it made me feel loved. By the way, if you do something loving, then afterward wait for applause, toasts, and thank-you notes, it doesn't count as much.

No getting around it, some parents really don't or won't or can't care. You can bend over backward to please or displease them, and it doesn't make a dent. Maybe you can forgive them someday for being emotional rocks. In the meantime, work to please yourself and reach out to other peers, adults, and family members for role models and for the love you deserve.

If Your Parents Give You No Privacy . . .

According to a recent survey, about one-third of American teenagers feel their parents invade their privacy. If your parents ransack your drawers, rummage through your purse, enter your room without knocking (or without waiting for you to say "come in"), read your mail and diaries, listen in on your phone calls, throw out your old clothes or magazines, or borrow your belongings without consulting you first, you can legitimately be mad.

Have you given them reason to be suspicious? If parents find out that their daughter smokes or drinks or has sex, they may—again, for Daughter's own good—try to keep track of what she's up to.

Try to get your parents to trust you more by being more open about your whereabouts. Satisfy their curiosity by telling them a little about your friends, activities, and schoolwork.

They are wrong if they think they have a right to know everything you do, but you are wrong if you think your life is none of their business.

In person or in a note, gently ask them to try to respect your privacy and your need to keep some things to yourself. Don't shout "Leave me alone!" Explain that you aren't doing anything bad and that you love and need them but that you have your own separate life.

If they won't stop snooping, you could consider hiding or locking up your personal things, or leaving them in a school locker. What a shame. But take heart. Pretty soon you *will* be on your own.

If Your Parents Expect Too Much . . .

Some parents' expectations are so high that nothing you do is enough.

When I was sixteen, I wrote in my diary about a time when I fell short of my father's expectations. My verbal PSAT score was fine, but not as fine as he had hoped. *"Dad said, 'Read the paper, Carol, and you'll do better next year. Eric's score went way up; Mark's did, too. Don't be disappointed.' Dammit—I wasn't disappointed!"*

Because I was a good student, my parents got used to good report cards. At first, I wanted Mom and Dad to go nuts with pride every quarter, yet they seemed to take my grades for granted. Finally I told them how I felt. They said they were proud even when they didn't show it. More important, I began working to please myself, not them.

If your parents expect the world, they may mean well. They may even want you to accomplish what they meant to but didn't. If they encourage you (as my parents usually did), they are being helpful. But if their plans for you are too lofty, they may be setting everybody up for disappointment.

You may have to sit them down and explain that you *are* trying hard in school. Or that mastering the flute is their dream, not yours—you'd rather concentrate on photography. Or that it's not reasonable for them to expect you to do all the cooking and cleaning and still lead your own life.

Some parents may never be satisfied. Try to accept this as their shortcoming and recognize your strengths even if they don't. This isn't easy, but you can do it.

Other parents may have difficulty giving praise because they're feeling jealous or inferior. If this is the case, you could subtly remind your parents how grateful you are for their help and encouragement along the way.

Still others are convinced their kid is God no matter how much the kid screws up. That way they get to award themselves the Best Parent Prize every year. Positive reinforcement is the key to good parenting, but not when Mom and Dad go overboard. If you start believing you're picture-perfect, you'll be in for it later when you have to face up to your failings.

Finally, some parents—the kind I hope you have—have high hopes for you and encourage you, without undue pressure, to reach for the sky, yet want for you what you want for yourself and will love you unconditionally.

(P.S.: That's a lot to ask. And sweetie, you can't expect your parents to be SuperMom and SuperDad any more than they can rightfully expect you to be SuperDaughter.)

If Your Parents Don't Like
Your Friends or Boyfriend . . .

In fifth grade, one of my friends said, "I hate you!" to her mother, and her mother told her to stop playing with me. Me! Mild-mannered level-headed polite little me! She had decided I was a bad influence on her innocent child. I'm biased, of course, but I think she was mistaken. Sometimes parents' judgments are wrong.

But sometimes they are right. Come to think of it, I was an unpredictable ten-year-old. That very week I'd pilfered five colored thumbtacks from the police department headquarters during a Girl Scout trip!

Anyway, just as you don't like all your parents' friends, they won't like all yours. But do introduce everybody so they can give each other a chance. And make sure you aren't picking friends to please or spite your parents.

If they like some of your friends but dislike one in particular or don't like your boyfriend, obviously you aren't going to dump that person heartlessly. But ask yourself—and them—why they disapprove. Maybe your father would have trouble watching Daddy's little girl waltz off with *any* young man. Maybe your mother is jealous of your closeness with girls your age. If so, their opinions of your friends may not be valid. Why not meet your buddies outside, at school, and at their homes more often than at yours?

Perhaps your parents have reason to believe that Greg is dishonest, is taking advantage of you, or drives too fast; or that Paula has a bad reputation, is ill-mannered, or deals drugs. Have you been swearing more than usual or acting surly or listless or sullen? Have your grades dropped? It's possible your parents put down your friend (I know you're tired of hearing this, but picture yourself in their position) for your own good.

My parents never warmed up to my brothers' friend Zeke. One evening we three kids gave a big summer party, and Mom and Dad were nice enough to stay upstairs and out of the way. Dad did, however, peer out their bedroom window from time to time to check on things. That's when he saw Zeke, slightly wasted, tossing lighted matches into the forsythia. Dad came down yelling, and I couldn't blame him.

Your parents may be particularly touchy about your boyfriend because they may be afraid you're going to get pregnant or run off and marry him. Tell them you're responsible and having fun, not making life commitments. If they haven't met your boyfriend, have them meet informally. They may decide he's not such a bad guy.

Some parents are going to like your friends so much that they may not know when to leave. If your parents always try to be too buddy-buddy with your buddies, handle the situation with care, because they may be feeling a little middle-aged or lonely. Meet your friends elsewhere. Or have a short visit with your parents at your home, then explain that you are all going to your room to talk. You're entitled.

If Your Parents Embarrass You . . .

I have a friend who is embarrassed by her parents because her parents are poor. They also happen to be one of the warmest, most giving, most down-to-earth couples I know.

Other friends get embarrassed because their parents are rich. You compliment the grand piano in the hall or the painting on the wall, and the friend starts apologizing.

Try to appreciate whatever it is your parents offer and stop cringing just because your foreign-born mother makes occasional grammar mistakes or your individualist father shops in shorts and knee-highs and always smokes a fat cigar.

If you are embarrassed because your parents have drinking problems or bad reputations, the problem is stickier, but remember that you are your own separate person. If someone mocks you, you can admit, "My mother's behavior bothers me, too, but it also bothers me when people judge me because of her." Or you can tell a teacher, "I feel terrible that my father called to complain about my grade. I'm really sorry."

Can you speak directly to your parents about how they humiliate you in front of their friends or yours? Maybe. You can't say, "Mom, get rid of your accent." But you can say, "Mom, I know you meant well telling Tish to stand up straighter, but I don't think it's your place to comment on her posture." You can say, "Dad, please don't compliment me in front of friends. It was sweet of you, but I felt ridiculous when you wolf-whistled in front of Lloyd." Or tell your parents, "Please stop asking me to play the horn for company. I feel like a complete idiot when I have to perform." If your parents love to tease, you can't change them, but you can warn your friends they may be in for some ribbing.

Decide for yourself if a showdown is worth it. My father sometimes had me speak a few lines of French when we had dinner guests. I usually obliged because although I got a little embarrassed by it, he got a big kick out of it.

I also had to develop a sense of humor about Dad's quips on my budding figure. From my diary, age fifteen: *"I was going to the dance and Mom said to Dad, 'Doesn't Carol look nice?' Dad put in his usual, 'Yes, but what are those bumps on her chest?' "* Thank heavens he kept such cracks in the family!

In most cases, the soundest advice is to be open, caring, and honest, and to try to talk as adult to adult, not child to parent. Tackle problems as they arise. You and your parents are separate individuals. Agreement isn't always possible. But harmony is worth working toward.

PARENTS WITH PROBLEMS

When you're a kid, you don't think of your parents as having any problems. Now you know better.

Family strife may come from parental problems that have almost nothing to do with you. If your parents fight or get divorced, it is probably because of problems between them: changing values, loss of trust or respect, money troubles, infidelity. Or your family may be in turmoil because of alcoholism, illness, or unemployment. You may get caught in the middle and you may ache because of their problems, but their problems are not your fault. And just as your parents aren't failures if you're not happy, you aren't a failure if they aren't happy.

If Your Parents Fight a Lot . . .

My parents had a happy marriage, complete with occasional arguments. When I was fourteen, I wrote in my diary, *"It hurts and upsets me when Dad uses a harsh manner with Mom because I know twenty years ago they were newlyweds."* Yet now I realize it's impossible to feel and show intense love every minute after years with someone. And in a way, arguing shows caring.

When you go out with a guy, you're trying to have fun for a limited time. When you're married, you're trying to have fun and take care of each other and make a living and pay taxes and keep a tidy home and get food on the table and maybe raise a family for an unlimited time. It's a bigger challenge. Your parents may be very much in love yet sometimes feel the need to let off steam. A little airing of tension is healthy and productive. It may not be pleasant or even fair, but it is tolerable and normal.

And if they quarrel constantly? It's hard on you, but it's not because of you (or your siblings). Childless couples squabble, too. Even if your parents do blame you or use you as a scapegoat (I hope they don't), how well they get along is up to them, not you. Their happiness is their responsibility, just as yours is yours. If you worry that they'll split up as soon as you leave the nest, you need to realize that you can't live at home forever to serve as buffer zone or keeper of the peace.

What can you do if they're always blowing up at each other? Not much. Accept their troubles as their troubles and try not to take sides or become the confidante of either one. Go on living your life, because you can't make their problems dissolve.

You *can* attempt to make things easier on them. Try to be less demanding during their rocky times. Clean up after yourself around the house, be extra kind, offer to fix dinner for your younger siblings so your parents can go out alone. If things are getting out of control, you could (easier said than done) suggest they talk to a marriage counselor, adding, "I love you both and I hope you can work out your differences." This may help. Or may not.

Keep things in perspective. You and your siblings probably fight even though you love each other. Some well-matched parents fight a lot. Some fight for a few months, then go back to being their quiet, resilient selves. And—I hate to say it—some hold hands all the time, then end up in divorce court. Just because your parents raise their voices is no reason for you to jump to conclusions. Even if your parents are separated, they may get back together, though it's best not to count on it.

If Your Parents Get Divorced . . .

Ouch. This is official. Since one of two marriages ends in divorce, it's also common, and you're not alone. But it's painful. And it may force you to grow up before you're ready. Your parents may start leaning on you. You may be alone more than you like. Money may become scarcer, responsibilities more plentiful. You may move. Or have to deal with stepparents. Or be separated from a sibling. You may wish things were back to normal.

They aren't. And even if you'd been a total angel-pie every second your parents were together, it's almost guaranteed they'd still be apart now. So if you're feeling guilty, stop it. If you're hoping they'll get back together, try to stop that, too. Get yourself to remember, if only for a few minutes, some of their worst fights.

Accepting hard times is part of maturing. It rains on everybody's life once in a while, and then the sun comes out again. In the meantime, your umbrella is to try to get on with your world—friends, school, work, sports. You need a lot right now. Don't cry alone. Talk about how you feel to your parents. Or talk to a teacher, relative, school counselor, therapist, or friend (maybe one whose parents are divorced).

If one parent starts telling you things you don't want to hear, be understanding (your parent is hurting) but gently say, "Mom, I don't want to hear about how stingy Dad is or how rotten your sex life was," or "Dad, please don't tell me about Mom's affair; I can't do anything about it and it just upsets me—I'm sorry." It's not fair for you to have to play parent to your parent. (On the other hand, if your parents act falsely brave, tell them it's okay to share their sadness with you.)

It's tricky if one parent tries to use you to find out what the other is up to. You might say you are having a hard enough time adjusting and you don't want to be a go-between. Say, "Ask *him* if he's dating, not me." It's also awkward if your parents try to win you over with gifts. Don't let your loyalties be bought. And don't let one parent make you bad-mouth or stop seeing the other.

It might be a good idea to try to be part of any discussions about custody and visitation rights. Keep at least a spare toothbrush at the house where you may spend weekends or vacations. Better yet, make one bedroom drawer and one bathroom shelf officially yours.

Some kids are relieved when their parents divorce. The war is over, and the parents may end up more content, alone or remarried. Some kids have more independence than ever and some enjoy a new closeness to both parents. One friend told me she thinks of her family not as a broken home but as two happy homes.

Other kids are devastated. They'd accepted their parents' marriage as a given, and now their family is one more statistic. Is your parents' marriage over? Coming to terms with that sad truth gets easier with time and distraction. But you can't deal with it until you believe it. Be patient with yourself. Allow yourself time to feel angry and depressed.

It takes a long while to get from one part of your life to another. Remember that the end of one chapter marks the start of the next. Take your time grieving for the way your family was, then turn the page. Things won't be the same, but they may come out better than you expected. And by simply surviving this terrible time, you'll probably emerge a stronger, deeper, more compassionate person. (If, instead, you let yourself become glum, cynical, or an object of pity, you aren't doing yourself any favors.)

Although your parents don't love each other the same way anymore, they probably each love you as much as—or more than—ever. If one of your parents does suddenly drop out of the picture, it's going to hurt like hell. Parents are irreplaceable. But new people always come into your life, too, and two out of three divorced or widowed people remarry. You'll be loved because you are lovable.

If Your Parents Drink Too Much . . .

The *Drinks, Drugs, Etc.* chapter talks about alcohol. But if your parents (not you) have the problem, they (not you) are going to have to recognize it and deal with it. If your parents have one or two drinks after work every day, that doesn't point to alcohol dependency. But if that one drink changes their character, or if they can't control the drinking or become mean, supermoody, sloppy drunk, or just plain pass out, then your parents may be alcoholics and you are indeed in a difficult situation. You may feel disgusted, ashamed, angry, resentful, disappointed. Keep in mind that alcoholism is a disease—partly acquired, partly inherited. And you can't get your parents to change until they admit that they have a problem and are ready to work on it. I know one boy who poured out his mother's entire liquor supply, but the mother replenished it that week.

What can you do? Stay out of the way when your parents are drunk, and don't provoke them. Look up Alateen in your Yellow Pages (under Alcoholism Information and Treatment Centers) and talk to other teens whose parents are alcoholics. Many of the approximately 13 million problem drinkers in America are parents with children who, like you, are caught in a love/hate bind. Al-Anon is for entire families of alcoholics. You could also talk to an adult you trust, a counselor, a member of the clergy. And you could suggest (results not guaranteed) that your parents attend an Alcoholics Anonymous meeting. Be encouraging, not critical. If your parents have come to grips with the problem, they may be ready to get help. But if you keep making excuses for them, covering their tracks, or letting them be abusive, they are getting away with being irresponsible and may not feel motivated to change. (You may want to escape the whole scene at times, but don't do it by drinking.)

If Your Parent Is Ill . . .

Losing a parent is the number-one teen fear, according to the Norman-Harris survey reported in *The Private Life of the American Teenager*. But for the moment, let's not assume ill means dying, okay? Many of my friends' parents have survived heart attacks and cancer and complicated operations. In each case, the scare brought the family closer.

If your parent is ill, it's hard on everybody. How you did in the track meet doesn't seem to matter to anyone anymore—maybe not even to you. Your whole family is frightened, near tears, and tiptoeing around. Hospital bills may be using up the family money. You may have to take on more responsibilities than you can handle.

Talk about your worries with each other and show your love to the ailing parent with words, hugs, cards. You all need each other a lot right now. Be thoughtful and helpful. If the strains are too much, talk to a relative, a friend, or an adult outside the family.

If Your Parent Loses
His or Her Job . . .

Be supportive. Your parent's self-esteem may be suffering, and your understanding, love, and respect will be appreciated. The parent may be cranky or withdrawn or may sleep or drink more than usual. Cut back your own spending and try to make extra cash baby-sitting or at other work. Maybe you could even treat for some groceries. Even if your admiration is more genuine when your parent is on top of things, your parent needs your love now. Take advantage of the parent's extra time by doing things together: walking, cooking, going to the zoo, playing games. Every family crisis provides an opportunity for new family closeness.

If Your Parents Both Work . . .

Ha! Just checking to see if you were paying attention! If your parents both work, that's not—or doesn't have to be—a problem. Coming home to quiet may be a jolt if Mom or Dad had always been a house spouse and you'd gotten used to milk, snacks, and conversation after school. You may miss that time of closeness, but there are advantages of having two working parents, besides the obvious economic ones. Since both my parents worked, I learned independence early and didn't struggle with the career-versus-marriage question because I knew that women, like men, can have kids *and* careers. Some sacrifices have to be made, but both parents can be breadwinners and breadbakers.

If your working parents like their jobs, that can be a plus, too. If they lead stimulating lives of their own, they might be less likely to invade your privacy; be overprotective or abusive; or become dependent on alcohol, drugs, food, soap operas, or you.

If Your Parents Are Abusive . . .

If you frequently get hit or threatened, it probably doesn't help to know that millions of other teens are also beaten, neglected, or abused by their parents, or to know that parents who punish their children like this are sick and in the wrong. If you are a victim of abuse, you need help. Your parent needs help. Your siblings need protection. You should report your parent.

It's one thing if your parent lost control once and slapped you harder than he or she meant to. That's not praiseworthy, but it may, if followed by apologies and explanations, be forgivable. But if your parent uses you as a punching bag, *you* could grow up with physical and emotional scars even though your *parent* is the one at fault.

If you've been brutally smacked around more than once, consider calling the National Child Abuse Hot Line, toll free at (800) 422-4453. Or call the police (juvenile department) or talk to a doctor, relative, teacher, minister, rabbi, or school counselor. In your phone book, look up your state or city government and check under Social Services. Or check the Yellow Pages under Mental Health. Or just call your operator and ask for one of these numbers. You deserve to be treated better.

Emotional abuse may not leave you visibly black and blue, but it's horrible to be picked on all the time. If the nicest thing your parents ever say to you is "Get lost" or "Our lives were easier before you came along," it becomes difficult for you to believe in yourself. Your family needs counseling, and if they won't go with you, you should go alone. Making the initial call is hard. Talking to the therapist or social worker is not so hard—it's a relief and a release.

If you cannot stay in your home, there are places to go, besides your friends' or neighbors' homes. Don't rush into marriage or you may find yourself in another trap. And don't run away without knowing where you're running to. Too many runaways end up desperate and poor and deceived; many become prostitutes or pushers or porno "movie stars." That doesn't have to happen! There are halfway houses and shelters and federal service agencies for battered teens and wives. If you are under eighteen, you have a legal right to shelter, protection, education, and support. The Legal Aid Society, Civil Liberties Union, and Child Welfare Bureau can help you.

The national toll-free numbers for runaways are (800) MISS-YOU, (800) 231-6946, and (800) 621-4000. Switchboards can serve as go-betweens for parents and teens and can tell you about running away. Over one million teenagers run away from home each year—that's too many!

In most cases, if you have terrible problems with parents or parents with terrible problems or a bit of both, you'd be wise to get some family counseling before things worsen. There's no longer any stigma attached to getting outside help. It's a lot smarter than staying in a no-win situation. So keep reading!

YOU'RE CRAZY IF YOU NEED COUNSELING AND DON'T SEEK IT

Therapy is not only for the weak or the wacko. It's for the person who is smart enough to realize she could be happier and strong enough to realize a trained professional could help her find that happiness.

Let me be clear. You don't trot off to the doctor's each time your tummy hurts, and I'm not saying you should run to get your head shrunk (or expanded) each time you're upset.

From my diary when I was sixteen:

Life is like a rerun. There's no one to talk to and I don't want to be alone. I'm sick of pressure, even peer pressure. I'm sick of being told to pick up Eric here and there. I'm sick of Fran and I haven't even seen her yet. I'm sick of my driving teacher flirting with Danielle. I'm sick of my bosses at the pharmacy thinking I'm high-strung. I'm sick of my messy room—I never clean it. I'm sick of getting no sleep—it's 1:11 A.M. now. I'm sick of not improving at piano—I hardly practice . . .

That's not jolly, but it's okay. It's the kind of mood that feels awful, yet mostly disappears by morning. Part of being a teen—and a person— is getting into life's ups and downs, smiles and frowns. (Now you know why I'm not a poet.)

But some problems, ruts, and moods are too big to handle alone. If you're anorexic or alcoholic or suicidal, you probably can't recover without outside support. If you've been abused, talking to a therapist may speed the healing. If your parents divorced or your sister died, an objective listener can help you cope with your sorrow. If the idea of kissing petrifies you, a counselor can help you be more comfortable with your sexuality. If you've been shoplifting or binge buying, a counselor can help you control your urges. If you've been generally down, a therapist can help you buoy yourself back up. Sometimes you feel trapped when you're not. A psychiatrist can also find out if your depression is due to a chemical imbalance and, if so, can prescribe not talking but medication and possibly a diet.

It may be that your whole family could benefit from therapy. For instance, if your home life is unbearable—not warm, but freezing or boiling. Or if your father is the heavy, your mother never even disciplines the dog, and it's screwing you up. Or if it's next to impossible to adjust to your stepparent or half-brothers. Or if your home is full of misdirected anger: You all yell at each other when you're actually mad at friends, teachers, bosses. You could put up with family friction and assume—accurately, perhaps—that you'll all get along in a few years. But why deny yourselves the possibility of getting along now?

Not that counseling guarantees instant family or personal happiness. You have to work toward that. But counseling is a step in the right direction. And if you're carrying around a lot of excess emotional baggage, sooner or later, you'll want to unpack.

How do you find a good therapist? Your school guidance counselor may be able to help you or refer you to competent counselors or counseling agencies. You won't be found out or "exposed." The referral can be confidential, and your sessions can be your secret.

If you belong to a church or synagogue, counseling may be available free. Ask.

Your family doctor may be able to recommend a psychologist, a psychiatrist, or a licensed social worker. Private sessions could cost up to $75 an hour, part of which may be covered by insurance.

In your telephone directory under Youth or Mental Health or Social Services or Family Services, you may find therapists and agencies that don't charge for counseling or that charge a sliding-scale pay-according-to-what-you-have fee that can run anywhere from zero to $40 an hour. The United Way can also help you find someone who can guide you to understanding and liking yourself better.

Short-term therapy may be all you need. Going for counseling doesn't have to mean years on the couch.

You may decide you don't feel comfortable with a particular counselor. Fine. Find someone else. Or try group therapy. Or perhaps an anonymous phone call to a hot line can provide comfort, insights, and reassurance.

The point is, if you need help, it's out there. If you've lost your appetite or can't sleep or work because of troubles, don't come apart at the seams. If some people envy your popularity or money or brains, but you can't see past the 8,600 logical reasons you have for feeling miserable, seek help. It's no disgrace. What is unfair to yourself and your loved ones is to be chronically depressed for months on end, with or without good reason, yet to do nothing about it except cry and complain.

Teen Suicide

Grim statistics: Suicides among 15- to 24-year-olds have tripled in the last twenty years. Many more girls than boys try to kill themselves, but boys seem to go about it more decisively and succeed four times more often.

In the 15- to 24-year-old age group, suicide is the number-two cause of death, trailing traffic accidents—many of which may be suicides. More than 6,500 teens commit suicide each year. (The actual numbers may be much higher because so many suicides are reported as accidental deaths.)

Experts estimate that 400,000 teenagers attempt suicide annually, often as a cry for help, hoping to be found and rescued. Sometimes suicides follow a ripple effect: A teen will commit suicide in an affluent suburb and suddenly several other local teens will do the same. Many experts believe suicide is more common among adolescents than among any other age group.

Listen, kiddo, there are always reasons to feel despondent, just as there are always reasons to feel happy. You may have considered suicide briefly at some moment. You may have thought, "That'll show 'em," then realized it would show you, too. If you have ever contemplated suicide, please please please see a counselor or make a call to a suicide hot line—if you like, from the privacy of a phone booth. Get help.

Do you have a friend or sibling who is talking about suicide? Who is more than a little accident-prone? Who isn't eating or sleeping? Who is suddenly giving away valued possessions or withdrawing from favorite activities? Don't brush it off. You owe it to him or her and to your own peace of mind to alert a responsible adult. If a friend mentions that he has considered suicide, take him seriously.

More than three hundred suicide prevention centers exist across the country. Hot lines vary from state to state, but if you look up Crisis or Suicide in your phone book, you'll probably find a number to call.

I'm not going to tell you, "It's your party and you can die if you want to." Because I don't think you want to end your life. I think you want to change your life. And there's a big difference.

BROTHERS AND SISTERS

I have a friend whose big brother swore that if she cupped her hands around a bumble bee and held them together, the bee would become tame. She spent months hunting bumblebees, finally caught one, clamped her hands, and—well, you can guess what happened. (Hint: She wasn't pleased.)

Brothers and sisters. When I was growing up, I had no sisters, but brother, did I have brothers! Just two older ones, actually. Mark and Eric. Yet it felt like a houseful.

We three sometimes got along, sometimes squabbled, and sometimes played tricks on each other. It's all in my diary.

I was about to go to bed when I found out Eric had set my alarm for 2:00

A.M.! . . . Mark and I tried hard to convince Eric he was balding. . . . Eric told me my faults for about half an hour including that he'd rather have been an only child. . . . Eric was mad at me so he slammed the car door shut. But its window shattered and that made him even madder because he'll have to pay. . . . I drove to Jen's but Eric bicycled over and quietly drove the car away. When I was ready to drive home, I thought the car was stolen and I got hysterical. . . . Judy, Eric, and I visited Mark at Brown University. The visit was fun except that besides giving Mark and his roommate Charlie a dozen cupcakes, we were a pain. For example, Mark had a huge test and we gave him no time to study. We twisted Charlie's pipe cleaners into little animals. We insulted their sloppy room. We made them find extra beds. We put a peeled banana in Mark's bed and he thought it was something else. I parked illegally and the car got towed and Mark had to pay to retrieve it, etc. etc.

Somehow we've all forgiven each other, and we're very compatible now (well, not aalllwaaays but most of the time).

Becoming lifelong friends with your siblings isn't easy. But a sibling is a sibling forever. And your bond may be all the deeper for the mischief you shared. The expression "Blood is thicker than water" is a sort of gross way to put it, yet it's true you can count on family even when friends let you down. Besides, who else knows you and your parents inside out and remembers the day your kitten got stuck in the filing cabinet and how Grandmom always brought hermit cookies when she visited?

I know, I know. I'm making it sound ever so rosy, but some of you are stuck between a snobby bossy know-it-all big sister and a bratty kid brother who gets away with murder. Or you've got a 100 percent perfect, can-do-no-wrong sis, and only you know that behind the charming facade, she's a number-one jerk. Siblings are for keeps? That may be the last thing you want to be reminded of.

Hold it right there. For openers, are you even half as nice to your siblings as you are to friends and strangers? If not, that's one reason they aren't always nice back. It's wonderful that family members feel comfortable together. You can take your shoes and makeup off. But if you're so familiar that you don't bother being kind, civil, or interested in each other's doings, then no wonder communication breaks down.

Example. If your brother says, "Nice haircut," and you got your hair cut *last* week, you could say with a sneer, "You're real observant," or you could say, "Thanks."

It's hard to get along with someone who hogs not only bathroom and television, but parents' attention as well. Here are some tips on handling siblings' feelings and making your own feelings known.

- *If you're jealous of your brother*, tell him. You may find he envies or admires qualities in you, or that deep down he's sometimes insecure, too.
- *If you think your parents favor your sister*, don't hope they'll pick up on your gloom—express it. If your parents are lavishing time on your sister because she's got mono or is getting married, be patient. Their attention doesn't mean they love her more. It may mean they think she needs them more right now. (Direct from my diary: *"I feel like crying. Dinner was awful and the conversation was Eric's college choices again. What originality!"*)
- *If they label you two The Smart One and The Pretty One*, either of you could tell them Smart is beginning to feel ugly and Pretty is starting to feel dumb.
- *If your parents favor you*, you could bask in the glory, but be generous. Say things to them like, "Isn't Lynn a marvelous actress?" or "Can you believe how good Lisa is in science?" When your parents play favorites (their mistake), you and your siblings may become competitive and jealous (your loss).
- *If your brother acts like he knows everything*, tell him you're glad he's there when you need help, but you wish he wouldn't volunteer advice when you don't ask for it. Tell him you want to make up your own mind, not conform to or rebel against his ideas. He may be in a let-me-prove-how-mature-I-am phase. Things get easier once you're both secure and independent.
- *If you always idolized your sister and then find out she's a regular human being*, that's called growing up. It's okay.
- *If your sister is Ms Amazing*, stop competing and focus on what's amazing about you. Think of your family as a team: The "better" each member, the "better" the team.
- *If you and your sibling are rivals in school or athletics*, figure out what area *you* like best and work on excelling in different subjects or sports (unless you both absolutely love the same fields). Learning to cooperate and compromise with siblings is often how you first learn to deal with strangers.
- *If your kid brother always wants to tag along*, spend a little time with him, but explain that you want to go out alone with your friends. If you occasionally offer him your undivided attention and let him say hello to your friends, he may be more willing to respect your time out.
- *If your sister steals your boyfriends*, tell her she's hurting you. And that you're glad she approves of your taste, but even if she "wins" Kirk, she's losing more than she's gaining. She may be sacrificing sisterly love for a fleeting romance.

- *If you want to get to know a brother better,* start a conversation and listen. Instead of doing chores separately, do them together and talk. Go for a bike ride and ask his advice or tell him what you like best about him. Knock on his door and confide in him: You have a crush on Bob, or Mom has been on your case and it's driving you nuts. Ask what worries him most. Stop making fun of each other.
- *If you like your brother's friend and think feelings might be mutual,* maybe, just maybe, he can arrange a casual double date to the bowling alley. (Eric did it for me!)
- *If you and your sister share a room,* try to set a few rules about neatness and privacy and try not to let petty things get to you. Tell each other (calmly) what you like and dislike about the arrangement. And get a curtain or room divider if the going is tough.
- *If your sister goes to camp or college,* call and write; it may strengthen your bond.
- *If your sister is a nerd,* don't tease her about what a nerd she is or she'll become nerdier and hate you, too. Praise her for what she does well and boost her confidence.
- *If your brother is getting married and you're worried you won't be as close to him,* expect to feel a little jealous and left out at first (I did when Eric married Cynthia), but give your brother credit for knowing a great person when he finds one. You may gain a sister, not lose a brother.
- *If your brother discourages you from taking on challenges,* prove him wrong by excelling.
- *If your sister's recent eating or drinking habits worry you,* say, "It may be none of my business, but I care and it concerns me that you're getting so thin (or drunk). Is something bothering you?" Don't expect her to thank you and reform immediately, but continue to show love, and she will appreciate it. If you're very worried, you could tip your parents off. (I don't mean tattling about your sister's sneaking one beer. I mean getting help if you think she's losing control of her life.)

That's enough *ifs* for now, don't you think? It's hard to generalize, because each family, sibling, and situation is different. It depends on many things, like how old you are and your relationship and family size and age gap and birth order.

Birth order. Have you heard the popular birth order theories? Some experts believe where you fit in your family may determine where you fit in the world. They contend:

- The firstborn, since he or she deals with adults right off and teaches younger siblings, is often bright and verbal and achievement oriented, but may be stubborn or a worrier.
- The middle child, since he or she is a practiced diplomat and referee (who, alas, may occasionally feel overlooked by Mom and Dad) is likable and socially adept.
- The youngest child, since she may get heaps of attention, might grow up confident, secure, sociable—and a little spoiled.

Of course, your individuality is far more important than family position. Besides, if you're the only daughter in a family of five (like my friend Judy, a middle child), you're going to get more attention than an average middle child. And if you were born long after your siblings (like my sister-in-law Sally), you may sometimes feel like an only child.

What does it feel like to be an only child? It depends. My sister-in-law Cynthia says it felt just fine. "When I went to other people's houses, I thought, 'Nice place to visit, but I wouldn't want to live here—too chaotic!' " The pros of being an only child are that you may get undivided attention and feel very loved, you never have to share a room or get punched out by a bully of a brother, and you learn early to be independent and, perhaps, imaginative and a good reader. The cons are that you may get more parental attention and solitude than you'd like, you won't get the inside scoop on what makes boys tick, and you may feel less comfortable in a group of kids. If you are an only child, work on making tight friendships. And if your parents will let you, think about getting a pet. A pet can be an important family member. (I've had the same sweet Siamese for fourteen years!)

My husband's mother is a twin. She experienced the advantages of always having a playmate and best friend and the disadvantages of rarely getting Mom and Dad all to herself. Famous twins Dear Abby and Ann Landers were compatible and competitive. If you're a twin, you two might consider attending different schools. The connection you share will probably never fade, but it's crucial to develop separate identities.

If you are adopted, you may not know your natural parents or have any natural siblings, but you probably know that families who share their home and love are as close as families who share genes. I hope you feel special knowing how much your parents wanted you.

STEPPARENTS AND STEPSIBLINGS:
STEP BY STEP

Just about everything I said about parents and siblings goes for stepparents and stepsiblings, too, but getting used to new family members is a whole 'nother sack of potatoes.

One in six American children is a stepchild. According to *Newsweek,* only 38 percent of America's young people live with both natural parents. By 1990, there will be more stepparent families in the United States than traditional or single-parent families. If you're suddenly a stepchild, perhaps you can make friends with someone who has gone through the adjustments you now face. Some teens accept a parent's death or divorce and welcome new family members. *You* may wish your stepparent or stepparents would make a grand exit, or that a good fairy would appear and whisk you away. (It worked for Cinderella.)

If you were happier before the stepmother, stepfather, or live-in lover came along, keep these thoughts in mind.

- You may bristle at your stepparent because you miss your natural parent. You may even feel like a traitor for chumming up to the "replacement." But play fair. Treating the newcomer like a substitute teacher or blaming the stepparent for family upheaval makes life harder for everybody. Befriending the stepparent doesn't diminish your love for your absent parent.
- You may chafe because you feel left out. A lot of parental attention that went to you now goes to someone else. Ask your parent to go for a walk or shopping or jogging or museum visiting or to do *something* alone with you. Make a date of it. Make a weekly date of it. Then don't bitch about The Invader; talk about positive things.
- Try to be happy for your happy parent. Just as you need friends your own age, your parent—though he or she probably adores you to pieces—may have felt lonely at times and wished for adult company. If you are happy for your parent and sad for yourself, it's okay to say so.
- Be relieved: With someone else to care for Mom or Dad, you won't feel depended on. You will feel freer to go out with pals or go away to college.
- Think of the stepparent as a plus, not a minus. Arrange time alone together. Don't expect prefab love. Let rapport or friendship develop. Who knows? If your stepparent has natural kids elsewhere, he or she may feel the same odd sense of betrayal and

disloyalty you do about investing in a new relationship while missing a former one. Ask yourself if you'd still think she was a shrew, or he was a thug, if she or he had been introduced as a friend's parent.

- Try not to let your feelings toward your stepparent depend on whether he or she is generous or permissive. If you're expected to follow a whole new set of rules, try to obey, or have a family talk about compromises and tradeoffs.
- Allow time for transition. Instant harmony won't happen. It may take a year or two to settle in as a family, more if you see each other only on weekends or vacations.
- Don't forget that your stepparent is making adjustments, too. Consider this: Your stepparent fell for your parent yet married a package deal. Fine. No reason for any guilt. But it's not all stars-and-stripes from that end, either. If you want to get closer, one way to begin is, "I've been sort of stubborn, but I'm ready for us to get along." Stilted? Maybe. Effective? Probably. Or try, "It must be weird having an instant family." (If the stepparent grunts and grumbles, "It ain't what I bargained for," then my sympathy is with you.)
- If you've really tried and just can't get along—sigh—learning to deal with the stepparent will teach you tolerance and social skills. Watching the stepparent's interactions with your family will give you insights on how other families operate. If the situation is beastly, you might be able to move in with your other natural parent or with a relative or friend.
- Stepsiblings add more confusions, rivalries, dimensions, love, and good times to the pot. You're not obliged to adore your stepsiblings, but it's worth working toward (1) truce, (2) friendship, and (3) family feeling. *The Brady Bunch* aside, some stepsiblings get along better than natural siblings. If you're the newcomer and you think the daughter feels threatened, say, "We both know you're your mother's one and only, but I appreciate her trying to make me feel at home." If you're the one who will receive new siblings, call or write before the marriage and say "Welcome to the family." Realize that your parent, too, may be going out of the way to show the newcomer goodwill.

Take it one step at a time. Share your feelings. As John Lennon sang, "Give peace a chance."

RELATIVES IN THE PARLOR
AND SKELETONS IN THE CLOSET

It's easy to take relatives for granted. It's easy to think of your parents' folks as old fogies and not as the ones who cradled your mom, taught your dad to drive, baked birthday cakes, walked down the aisle on their wedding day, and watched with excitement as your mother, pregnant with you, got bigger and bigger.

Your relatives shared memories before you were born, and they've been through crises and quarrels like the ones you're going through now. Sure it's important to dress up, be polite, and show them respect, but why not really get to know them? You probably won't like all of them, and not all of them will find time for you, but you may find you adore many of your relatives and vice versa.

If you have a complete set of doting grandparents, you are very lucky. Let them know you love them. If one of your parents' parents died before your birth, ask about him or her. Your parent may welcome the chance to tell you stories.

Get to know your older relatives while you have the chance. Get them to tell you their stories firsthand. What was their childhood like? What were their hardest and happiest times? What were *their* parents like? What are they most proud of? How did they meet? What was your dad like in grade school? What was your mother like in high school?

You may treasure the advice older relatives give you. When I was sixteen, I wrote in my diary, *"Granddad told me to 'spar with the boys' but not to fall in love, but Grandmom said I'd be in and out of love many times before marriage."* (Grandmom was right.) If you have a tape recorder, you may want to tape relatives' stories.

Or have them write stories down. The best present I ever gave my father was a journal of blank pages in which I asked lots of questions. Some of the questions were light, such as "What are your favorite forms of exercise?" (Dad wrote, "Jogging to refrigerator, fetching the mail, signing checks.") Others were more serious, such as "What was it like meeting Mom?" (Dad wrote, ". . . From about the third date, we were bonded for good.") Now that I don't have my father, I can't tell you how glad I am to have some of his thoughts written in his own hand.

Years ago, when families didn't scatter so much, grandparents often lived with the family. In some places, they still do. When I stayed on a French farm, grandparents Mémé and Pépé lived with us, as did great-uncle TonTon. It caused some tensions, sure, but mostly it was nice for the teens to learn from the elders' wisdom and skills, and for the elders to enjoy the teens' energy and enthusiasm.

Don't be embarrassed by your relatives. You are you, and they are they, and besides, nearly everybody's family has at least one eccentric but sweet uncle who saves paper bags and wears wide, garish ties and socks that slip down because the elastic has worn out.

Do you have any problem relatives? If you look deep inside almost any family—including all relatives and in-laws—and open the closet door, skeletons will come toppling out. Never mind the adulterous half-brother or the bisexual aunt. I'm talking about real lulus. In my extended family, a cousin shot her husband and then herself, only she died and he lived and . . . well, I don't mean to one-up you on family sagas but to let you know that if your step-grandfather drinks and your second cousin is in jail, *you* need not feel ashamed.

If you feel you got gypped in the Relative Department—you hardly have any or the ones you have are indifferent or uninteresting—take heart. I bet certain teachers, parents of friends, and friends of parents will become like loving relatives to you.

WHEN LOVED ONES DIE

When someone you love dies, it feels like the worst thing in the world. I wish I could tell you that you get over the loss in a hurry, but you don't. I will say that after you have mourned, you may end up stronger (if you've survived this, you can survive anything), you may have a better perspective on your setbacks (you won't pout and say "This was the lousiest day of my life" after merely flunking a test), you may become more sensitive (since you've "been there," you can empathize with other people's sorrows), and the rest of your family may grow closer than ever.

Of course, you'd probably prefer to be less strong, less wise, less sensitive, and less close to your family than to have to deal with death. Yet Death doesn't ask. And if you're lucky enough to be long-lived, you probably will have to deal with the death of loved ones somewhere down the line.

About 5 percent of Americans under age eighteen have lost a parent, in most cases, a father. Thinking about death may help us appreciate our finite lives and may remind us to show our love to those who make our lives richer.

My father died in his sleep when he was sixty-eight, about two years ago. I still cry about it once in a while and I still sometimes say "my parents" when I mean "my mother." But I have finally gotten to the point where I can smile when I remember Scrabble games and driving lessons and cooking side by side. Or when I remember that among his things was a leather eyeglass case I'd made for him in Shop when I was in sixth grade. Or when I recall that whenever he left after visiting me at college, I waited the hour and a quarter it took for him to drive home, then phoned, and he always picked up the receiver and said without hesitation, "Yes, Snippo, I got back safely."

It took a long time, but I can finally feel thankful that I had such a caring father rather than feeling heartsick that I had him for only twenty-five years. I can feel thankful that the bond we shared is sealed and safe. And that you lose your father only once.

But it still hurts. Remember that journal I told you I gave him? One of my questions was a fill-in-the-blank. I wrote, "I'd think it was pretty neat if Carol _____ ." Dad answered, "published a book." Well, here's the book, but I can't give Dad an autographed copy.

Mourning is the pits. Dad was my biggest fan, and when he died, I felt stranded. My mother and brothers and I comforted each other, but we were all in pretty bad shape. Suddenly a huge hole was in our lives, and we kept falling in because we didn't know how to step around it. I also felt guilty about sobbing to Mom; she had just lost her husband, yet I was asking her for solace.

Seven weeks after Dad's death, I was still a mess: unable to work, unable to play. Dad's life was over and mine was at a standstill. A friend suggested I "talk to someone," meaning that I see a therapist. The words stung, because I'd always "had my head screwed on right"—as Dad had often put it. But I knew my friend was right.

What I didn't know was whom to call. (I didn't have one of these handy-dandy books around.) Baffled, I started leafing through the phone book under P for psychology, T for therapy, and at last, M for mental health.

I was shaking as I dialed the first number. The receptionist said someone could return my call after the weekend. The weekend? I couldn't wait that long. I dialed another number, got no reply. I dialed a third number.

"My father died and . . ." my voice cracked, ". . . I'm having a hard time dealing with it." The woman on the other end said, "Do you want to come in and talk about it?" Did I ever!

I got on my bicycle, rode to the Evanston Hospital Crisis Intervention Center, met Mickey Jordan, and blubbered to her for a solid hour. I showed her Dad's picture, described the funeral, told her about the other people in my world. During the next few months, we met seven more times. The sessions with Mickey cost less than $20 each and were invaluable. She helped me accept what I couldn't change and untie some knots that were in the way of my getting on with my life. She helped me figure out how to step around the abyss of my father's death. She helped me regain my lost confidence and realize that although my father is dead, he will always be alive inside me.

If someone you love dies, you may not need or want to seek professional counseling. You may find enough strength in your family, your friends, your religion, your memories, yourself. You may be able to stick to your routines and get through one day at a time. Try to pamper yourself. And don't go by any *should*s: "You should have been nicer"; "you should feel better by now"; "you should cry more"; "you shouldn't be enjoying a dumb television show." It may take months or several years for you to absorb the shock and believe that the loved one is gone forever. There may not be a turning point in your recovery, but there will be a turning time. Almost everybody who has grieved is left with some sense of guilt, some feeling of being robbed, and some unanswered questions. But eventually, you will accept that your life goes on and you will risk loving other people.

What can you do or say if your friend has lost a brother, sister, parent, friend, or relative? Do *not* avoid the friend because you don't know how to act. Your friend needs you now. Say you are sorry. And be there to listen. You don't have to bring up the subject, but don't change it if your friend brings it up. If your friend's mother dies, she can't talk *to* her mother, so she may want to talk *about* her. Listen.

If her mother had been sick for years, it's not your place to say, "Her death was a blessing in disguise" or "Cheer up" or "Be brave" or "You never really got along with her anyway" or "Don't question God's wisdom" or "Maybe your father will remarry someone nice." I also never liked it when people said, "I know how you feel" because I always felt "You do not." But those people meant well, and the grieving need to be tolerant, too.

Just listen to your friend and agree that it must hurt an awful lot. Listen even if she wants to share a detail that seems horrible (how skinny her mother looked in the hospital, what it was like throwing away her pantyhose). Even if your friend acts crabby or neurotic, she probably appreciates your being attentive. Grant her a short-term "fool's license," because she may be spacey for a while. If your friend loses a family member, she may be sadder months after the fact, when the loss really hits her. And she may never be her very same old self again.

When I was in junior high, my mother learned of the death of a friend and cried and carried on for hours. I tiptoed about and stayed out of her way. Later Mom said she wished I'd gone into her room and given her a hug. Now I wouldn't need to be told.

Do you want to write a note to someone faraway who has been through a loss? (I appreciated every single letter I received.) Your card doesn't have to be long. In fact, instead of expressing your sympathy, then going on to say how you've been doing, it's nicer to write a focused card, then follow up later with chattier letters. Often the bereaved are deluged with letters when they are still feeling numb, and then nobody writes when the pain settles in.

If you chickened out of acknowledging someone's loss months ago, do it now. Some of my friends worried about writing a belated sympathy card because they were afraid they'd "remind" me of Dad's death. Believe me, one mourns without reminders. And even when friends' cards made me cry, the tears were welcome and healing.

What do you write? "I was so sorry to hear about your mother's death. I know how much you loved her and how much she loved you. My thoughts are with you." Something like that, but in your own words. It doesn't have to be even that long. If you like, say something wonderful about the person or include a telling anecdote. "I'll always remember how your father took me to the Emergency Room when I cut my chin and my parents were at work. I was so scared, and your dad just kept making jokes and asking me about my teachers and boyfriends. He was a wonderful, funny, generous man."

Whether someone you love dies or someone you know suffers a loss, remember that brighter days are ahead. Time doesn't heal but it helps.

6
EDUCATION

GETTING THROUGH HIGH SCHOOL, GETTING INTO COLLEGE

Just the other year you were in kindergarten and Mrs. Quintano had the whole class pledging allegiance and singing "Good morning to you, Good morning to you; We're all in our places with bright happy faces. . . ." You looked up to the fifth-graders and pretended you had lots of homework because it made you feel grown up.

Now you have lots of homework. Does it make you feel grown-up? No. It makes you feel sick. You have a teacher you dislike and another who plays favorites. You're pressured by college and career decisions. You even have anxiety dreams: You're sitting naked in the stands during homecoming game composing essay answers to SAT math questions.

In the recent Norman-Harris survey of more than 160,000 teens, school was reported as the number-one problem.

This chapter shows how to make the most of your school, even if it's a jail, zoo, or pressure-cooker. It includes tips on improving your study habits, ways to deal with teachers, and alternatives to spending four years in the same high school. For the college bound, it explains how to zero in on the best choices for you and how to write a winning application.

IS SCHOOL UNBEATABLE OR UNBEARABLE?

Adults tend to romanticize their long-lost school years. Many forget how they dreaded that first school day after summer vacation. How they struggled to intercept that first mailed-home report card. How they prayed for snow days. How they couldn't care less about what happens to the half-life of a radioisotope that combines to form a compound.

School is no picnic. I remember that. And if I ever forget, I can always look back at my ninth-grade diary and reread entries such as *"Classes warp creativity!"* or *"Someday I'll be a politician so I can express my views on education: It stinks!"*

In all fairness, school has lots of pluses, many of which I did appreciate at the time. It was great having lunch every day with Judy or Jen or my boyfriend. I loved the English discussions about Salinger, Steinbeck, and Fitzgerald. I miss the two or three inspiring teachers who truly cared about my intellectual growth. And I miss the variety of high school: the way I changed teachers every hour and courses every year. Sometimes I even miss the on-top-of-things feeling I'd get when I got to the QED of a geometry problem or figured out an obscure line of poetry.

Do you realize one-third of the world's people are illiterate? Aren't you grateful to be among the other two-thirds?

Believe it or not, learning *is* often more fun than earning. In many ways, school *is* a picnic—a picnic complete with ants.

WHY SHOULD YOU LEARN ALL
THAT IRRELEVANT STUFF ANYWAY?

While you're in school, it's hard to judge what's relevant. When I took Psych 11a in college, I thought of it as just another class. It turned out to be one of the most useful courses I ever took, for my writing and for my social life. When I took Folklore, I thought it was great fun. It proved fairly worthless in the long run. A friend of mine joined stage crew in high school. Did she become an actress? No. She got interested in stage lighting design, then light in general, and now she's the most zealous (and well paid) young physicist I know.

School exposes you to so much: Shakespeare's plays, Einstein's calculations, Picasso's paintings. Sooner or later, while you're writing a program in Computer, conducting a fruit-fly experiment in Biology, racing around the track, singing in the chorus, putting a pot in the kiln, or reading about political campaigns, you'll feel filled with energy and enthusiasm. You'll begin to figure out what you like to do, what you're best at, what fields of study to pursue or what career to start aiming for. That's an exciting discovery. You'll also learn what you're not good at and not interested in, which is essential in planning your future, too.

Whether you're in junior high or high school, dabble with electives, sports, and extracurrics. Balance your schedule without overloading it. The more you learn, the more things you'll enjoy and the more choices you'll have. If you can't type or aren't computer literate, you're limiting your marketable skills. If you don't like reading or theater or sculpture, you have fewer ways to enjoy yourself than someone who does. Do you know the basics of auto mechanics? You're one up on the person who panics whenever his or her car sputters.

You'll never regret having that education edge. School teaches you to think, to analyze, to solve problems, and to work with discipline. Not all your teachers are brilliant and amiable, but not all your future employers will be, either. Not every assignment is scintillating and important, but in the Real World, there are dirty dishes to wash and boring bills to pay no matter how exhilarating your profession is. Besides, the best ticket out of a boring school is to do well there.

Your education, in and out of school, is for you—so you'll be able to lead your life instead of being led by it.

CRAM COURSE IN STUDY HABITS

Students who always ask "Whadja get, whadja get?" and teachers who give tests back in order with 98s on top and 38s on the bottom aren't on my Christmas list. I think working solely for a grade rather than working to learn is a shame. But grades matter. Especially if you are college bound. Besides, if you're making As and Bs, you're probably learning a lot and feeling good about yourself. And since you're in school anyway, you might as well do your best.

A few natural-born brains make the honor roll without even cracking a book. Me? I got good grades by working my buns off. Some subjects came more easily to me than others, but I'm not a fast reader and I couldn't coast along in anything. At times, I couldn't believe how much homework I'd have per class per day—some high school courses are harder than college ones—but I slogged through and it paid off. I'm glad I learned as much as I did in high school and I'm glad I got into the college I wanted.

There are many ways you can learn more and improve your grade point average.

1   *Aim high.* Shoot for 100 and you might get a 90. Shoot to pass and you might flunk. Spend a few minutes before each class looking over your homework or reviewing the assigned chapter. If you tune in, take notes, and move up a row, your classes will go by faster. Don't fall behind. And don't watch the clock and doodle, then, when called upon, have to ask, "What page are we on?" Try to excel in at least one subject. Acing one may inspire you to try harder in others. The cliché is true: The more you put into school, the more you get out of it. So don't get by—get ahead.

2 *Make lists.* Assignment pads are lifesavers. Write down which pages you have to read for History and which problems you have to do for Geometry. Sometimes I'll even write down things like "jog" or "send Granddad birthday card." It's not that I'd necessarily forget otherwise, but writing down plans frees my mind to think of other things. It also adds to my sense of accomplishment later when I cross off what I got done. (Am I making myself sound like a hopeless nerd in high school? I wasn't. I swear. Ask Judy.)

3 *Study actively for tests. Passive* studying means flipping through your notes and leafing through books. *Active* studying means taking notes on your notes, reading them aloud, reciting information to yourself, making an outline. If you own the book, highlight important lines and paragraphs with a yellow marker. Give yourself practice vocabulary quizzes or hard math problems to figure out. Have someone drill you on your foreign verb conjugations.

Think up mnemonic (memory-boosting) devices. When I was studying for Mr. Wildman's essay test on the Renaissance, I concocted the word *pranchimy* to remind me to write about perspective, religion, anatomy, nature, classics, humanities, intellectualism, materialism, and youth. My essay was full of specifics.

Listen when your teacher explains what the test will cover, so you'll know precisely what to study. I used to study for tests the night before, then look over the material again right before class. The risk of counting purely on last-minute cramming is that something may come between you and your books. The guy you like may choose that day to sit next to you in study hall. Or your teacher may chat with you before class or have you hand out the tests when you were depending on those two minutes to commit a poem or formula to memory.

Before you begin an exam, look it over. Carefully. Find out how long it is. Read the essay questions. Pace yourself, leaving time to proofread or check your answers. If you have a lot of time for a short math quiz, you might even take it twice, then compare your results. Approach tests like sporting events—psych yourself for victory.

4 *Write and rewrite papers.* Second drafts are better than first drafts. Don't hand in a half-baked composition you scribbled off an hour before class. Don't think on paper, rambling on as you figure out what you want to say. Think first. Then write. Then do something else. Then return to your paper and revise it.

Be lively: Steer clear of stilted words such as *thus* and *thereby* and bland, overused words such as *nice* and *interesting.* Be clear and succinct: Don't write *significant increase* when you mean *more,* or *at this point in time* when you mean *now.* Be precise: Don't say *very very worried* when you mean *frantic.* Eliminate unnecessary and repeated words. Read your paper aloud—does it sound okay? Check for spelling mistakes. (I dare you to find *drownded, alright* or *alot* in your dictionary.) Watch your grammar—*between he and I* is wrong. Learn to type—not hunt and peck—and type your papers. At college and on the job, papers and reports must be typed, so get in practice now.

The academic art of paper writing doesn't have to seem as hard as the Oriental art of paper folding. If you want to develop better writing skills, read *The Elements of Style* by William Strunk, Jr., and E. B. White. Or read William Zinsser's *On Writing Well.*

Can't get your paper started? Pretend it's an essay question on a one-hour exam. Or pretend you're writing a letter to a friend. ("Dear Jen, Students who always ask, 'Whadja get? . . .'.")

5   *Cheat and plagiarize.* (Only kidding, gang.) The problem with cheating is that you're only _____ _____ (fill in the blanks). As your grades go up, your self-respect goes down. Yes, you may get an A, but you know you didn't really get it.

I plead guilty. I occasionally planted myself near some know-it-all in the back so I could check my multiple-choice answers against hers. Then one day I stopped. It just didn't seem worth it anymore. I wanted to depend on myself.

If you cheat in French in September, you'll regret it all year because you won't have learned the basics. How can you master the *passé composé* if you don't even have the present tense of *avoir* down? Same principle in math. Besides, you'd feel like an idiot if you and Andy were the only ones to write 23,964 when the answer was 12.

Not that cheating is uncommon. A recent statistic revealed that over half the high school students questioned admitted to having cheated at some point. Many colleges try to solve the problem by using the honor system: No one proctors exams because administrators trust you; few end up cheating because few want to betray that trust.

Remember that cheating and plagiarism are illegal. If you're caught, some teachers will give you an automatic zero and some schools will suspend or expel you. The plagiarists who steal from Cliff Notes or turn in papers written by former students are often caught. I knew a guy at college who was kicked out for a year for having plagiarized a paper. He'd copied it straight from an obscure tome—written by a friend of his professor's!

6   *Love your library.* Even if your desk at home is big and well lit, there are always distractions, from telephone to television. Some people can concentrate anywhere. Not me. I like studying where it's quiet, where reference books are accessible, and desks are large enough to spread out on. Ask your librarian how to use the *Reader's Guide to Periodical Literature,* so you can find articles in back issues of magazines, and how to use the computer or card catalog, so you can locate books. (Bonus: Libraries even offer exotic cookbooks and manuals to help improve your chess game.)

In high school, I often stayed after school and holed up in a classroom or the library to make a dent in my homework. That way I had fewer books to lug home and more free time at night.

Figure out where you are most comfortable studying.

7   *Study when you're most alert.* I remember spending about an hour a page reading—or trying to read—*The Scarlet Letter* one night at about two A.M. Idiotic, because despite the passing minutes, none of it sunk in. If you don't work efficiently late at night, go to bed and get up early. If it takes you forever to click on in the morning, don't expect to study well before school. Being well prepared is crucial, but so is being well rested. Give yourself study breaks, and switch subjects if you're getting drowsy. It may help to hit the books for an hour, take a fifteen-minute walk or phone break, then study for another limited amount of time. Or it may help to devise a study routine and stick to it.

You can even do some studying and reviewing at the bus stop or in study halls or whenever you get to class before the teacher. I used to study in the library the first ten minutes of lunch period—all I missed were long lines.

8   *Don't procrastinate.* To tell you the truth, I was going to write this section last night. But I went to a movie. And you know what? I didn't totally enjoy the movie, because I knew I should have been working.

Since you've got to do your homework anyway, you might as well get it over with. Figure out your priorities, and don't wait for enough free time to complete everything in one sitting. Instead, break your work into manageable pieces, get motivated, and crank it out bit by bit. You could even set your kitchen timer for thirty minutes and make a deal with yourself that you won't get up from your desk until the timer rings. Once you get started, it isn't so bad. I promise. The way to get into the work mood is to start working. Sometimes getting to your desk is tougher than the assignment. Just begin. Often I'll write the lead paragraph before I go out. That way when I return, my essay is started and is easier to go back to.

Work has a bad name, but hard work usually makes you feel great, especially when it's behind you. Why not reward yourself by planning something fun to do afterward? For instance, since I know I'm going to dinner with my friend Rochelle in two hours, I'm finding it easy to work right now.

Do you do your term projects in a last-minute panic? Or pull all-nighters? Try to start papers early and do them step by step, before you become overwhelmed. It may help to schedule your work: By week one, you'll have completed the research; by week two, you'll have finished the rough draft; by week three, you'll have the project polished.

Have you ever brought homework along on a vacation? I bet you either didn't do it and felt guilty or did it and felt resentful. Next time try to finish it beforehand.

9   *Get help if you need it.* Most teachers are happy to explain a lesson after school and answer questions during class. You can also get help from your friends, siblings, and parents. Are you way behind in math? Don't succumb to math anxiety that could trip you up in years to come. Of course you are *able* to learn math—you're just not entirely willing, or as quick at it as some people. Arrange for a tutor, then work on understanding the concepts, not just getting the correct answer. The one-on-one approach works wonders. Tell your teacher you're getting outside help. He or she will probably be pleased and eager to recognize your improvement. I used to tutor languages for thirteen to eighteen dollars an hour; fees vary. Your school may be able to recommend someone, perhaps even an upperclassman who will volunteer his tutoring services. Some cities even have homework hot lines staffed by people who will help you grapple with student questions. Don't wait until two weeks before finals—start catching up now, before you're in a ditch too deep to climb out of.

10   *Improve your attitude.* Don't believe for a minute that you're a terrible student. Maybe you *were* a terrible student, but as of now, you are a good student. You weren't dumb; you were a professional under-achiever. Expect more from yourself. Remember: Bookworms often laugh last.

And don't swallow any lines about girls not being good at math or about guys preferring dumb girls (a few insecure dumb guys may, but you'd rather date secure bright guys, right?). No law says you can't be both smart and popular.

On the other hand, if you're a perfectionist, try to loosen up a little. Your world won't cave in if you get an A— or even a B or C (it might even be good for you!). And if you do nothing but study, you run the risk of burning out.

Straight-A students should also be careful not to flaunt their grades or wail, "I flunked that test" when they missed only two questions. And many still need to learn to accept criticism. Most overachievers have mastered the art of studying, but too many haven't learned the equally important art of relaxation.

TEACHERS: THE GOOD, THE BAD, AND THE UGLY

Teachers, like students, come in all types. Some are merciless bores who constantly compare you to your brilliant older sister; they're often the ones with tenure. Others are caring individuals who get so excited they tremble as they explain Newton's laws; they're the ones you may never forget.

My history teacher belonged to the first group. He'd stare at the wall as he droned on and on. He'd show us a movie about the Incas on Monday, then Friday he'd announce he had a movie about the Incas to show us. We'd watch it again. And again. And again. He knew he was absentminded, but that just made matters worse. "I didn't give you this test yet, did I?" he'd ask as he passed out exams. "Yes you did! We took it yesterday!" we'd lie in unison. Most of us depended on his class to get our math homework done.

Are you having trouble with any of your teachers? Do you have a teacher who calls you "numbskull"? Ask yourself whether you are being singled out. Maybe the teacher calls everyone numbskull, and does so affectionately. Or maybe he or she is hard on you because you've been loud or disrespectful in class or because you've been caught cheating or passing notes. Or maybe you're called on often because you can be counted on to know the answer.

If you feel you are being treated unfairly, try to make the best of it or speak to your teacher. If you favor confrontation, do it in private, and try to keep your emotions in check. Don't ask, "Why do you always pick on me?" Say, for instance, "I'm trying really hard, but I feel as though you still think of me as the class clown I was last year. I've grown since then."

Most teachers will respect you for coming to talk with them and will make an effort to judge your work or actions in a new light. So speak up if you think you don't deserve ten points off just because you spelled the last word in *A Separate Peace* as "Piece." I've even spilled tears in front of a few teachers, and although it's embarrassing, I survived.

What if your teacher is unreasonable or terrifying? What if Mr. Castel requires you to regurgitate his words verbatim on exams and docks points when you defend ideas of your own? Tell yourself his small-mindedness is his problem, not yours. Don't let him undermine your self-confidence. You might also consider discussing the matter with your parents or guidance counselor. After all, if, as the headlines put it, Johnny Can't Read because teachers can't teach, you should be outraged—you're getting cheated.

Some students are bothered not because they're being taken apart all the time, but because they're teachers' pets. While most teachers try to hide their feelings and treat everybody equally, others are open with favoritism. If a teacher takes to you, why not feel flattered and enjoy that attention? The teacher's supportiveness may motivate you to learn even more and may boost your self-confidence. (But don't let it go to your head or cause undue pressure to make an A+ every time.)

The situation can be a problem if the teacher dotes aloud and a lot about you, and if other students, feeling left out, tease you or call you a brown-nose. Look, if you sincerely like Mr. Wollenberg because he is sensitive and inspiring, that's wonderful. But if you are apple polishing because you hope he'll give you a higher grade, or if you're befriending teachers while estranging peers, who can blame your classmates for resenting you?

I came across this item in one of my old diaries: *"You know who I despise the guts of? Myra! She's pathetic. She's a brain and every teacher's pet, but I don't feel any envy—just disgust."* Now I can admit that I must indeed have felt envy, but if Myra had been as friendly to students as she was to teachers, who knows?—she and I might have become buddies.

What about crushes? I had crushes on several male teachers from fifth grade on, and I looked up to a few female teachers, too. It's healthy to have role models besides your parents, and it's okay to have crushes—so long as you don't make it obvious. A crush on a teacher, like one on a singer or an actor, is a fairly safe way to feel romantic. It can even put some zing into an otherwise dry class period.

In ninth grade, I had a certified crush on my bio teacher. I could handle it fine—until I confessed to my mother, who, on Parent's Night, asked Mr. Pavlica if he was married. Can you imagine? When he kidded me about it the next day, I nearly died. Fortunately I soon got interested in going out with biology students instead of dreaming about the instructor.

A harmless crush can become harmful if a teacher tries to exploit it by becoming sexually involved with a student. Don't confess your crush to your teacher (it puts him in a bind). Most teachers welcome your admiration and have no intention of letting your friendship get out of hand. But in every truckload of melons, a few turn up rotten. And although sex with a minor is statutory rape, a few teachers do jeopardize job and dignity to take advantage of young women. (You, my dear, are jail bait.) If you are ever a victim of sexual harassment—for example, if a teacher says he'll up your grade or write you a shining recommendation in exchange for a sexual favor—report the incident to a family member, school counselor, principal, or headmaster.

A final word about teachers. A boring teacher can take the fun out of a course on modern movies. A great teacher can make any subject fascinating. In grad school, I took a course on the Spanish Subjunctive at 8:30 A.M., and would you believe Jesús Fernández made it super exciting? (On the other hand, don't start hating computers just because you hate the computer teacher.)

In high school, you may not have much chance to pick your teachers, but if you do, grab the opportunity. If your school's French teachers are considered terrible but the Spanish teachers are terrific, and you're up in the air about which to take anyway, opt for Spanish. If you can choose one elective and everybody loves Mr. Stout, take his course—even if you don't know archaeology from a hole in the ground.

Go for the classes taught by the best teachers. You won't be sorry.

ALTERNATIVES: DROPPING OUT, STUDYING ABROAD, GOING TO PRIVATE SCHOOL, DOING A SUMMER PROGRAM, GOING TO COLLEGE EARLY OR LATE

Restless? Sick of school? Need a change? Some students, like some batteries, have to be recharged once in a while. What can you do to liven up your education?

Plenty. Travel, switch schools, plan an out-of-the-ordinary summer, take a course at a local college, shake up your high school routine.

Although the dropout rate is rising nationwide, dropping out isn't a hot alternative because you're closing yourself off. It may seem fabulous: You'd be making big bucks clerking or packing boxes. But what happens later if you want to try more interesting work, meet new people, face new challenges, or make more money? Since most jobs require a high school diploma, you could be left in the cold. Plus, not having that diploma eats at your self-esteem.

Sure you could go back to school later, but it'd be a lot harder. You'd have to attend night classes with people of different ages, and you might have trouble summoning the discipline to study after so many years away from the books.

Some restless students drop out to become folksingers, actresses, models, or athletes. Fine, but what if their dreams don't pan out? It makes sense to have a degree to fall back on. There are better ideas than dropping out for the student who needs a change.

I was restless my junior year of high school. I'd been a student in the same public school since seventh grade, and I felt I'd already had all the best teachers and taken all the best courses. My brother Mark was in college, and my brother Eric and my boyfriend were both about to go to college. I was worried that all I had to look forward to was Senior Slump.

Then my mother found an enticing ad in the back of *The New York Times Magazine* for School Year Abroad (Phillips Academy, Andover, Massachusetts 01810), a small program that enables dozens of high school students to study in Rennes, France, or Barcelona, Spain, during their junior or senior year of high school. I applied, was accepted, and spent my senior year living with a French family!

It was expensive, but four of the credits I earned counted at college, so I made up the money. It was hard, but taking courses from native French teachers and Exeter and Andover professors made my transition to college easier. Mostly, it was wonderful.

If you'd like to travel during the summer or school year, I highly (highly!) recommend you do so. Teens can travel more readily than adults because they have more time, can arrange to live with families, and can make dollars stretch further. Seeing a country from the inside is a great way to grow. You soak up another culture firsthand. Your history studies come alive. Away from family and old friends, you become more independent. And because you're exposed to another nation's values, you rethink and gain a better understanding of your own background.

Ask your guidance counselor about travel possibilities. Your local Rotary Club probably offers study-abroad fellowships. Or dial these toll-free numbers. Call the American Field Service at (800) AFS-INFO. Or Youth for Understanding at (800) TEEN-AGE. Or the American Institute for Foreign Study at (800) 243-4567. Or the Experiment in International Living (EIL) at (800) 451-4465. (I spent an EIL summer with an enchanting farming family in the south of France, where I survived with no hot water, no indoor toilet, no English. Survived? I loved it! I helped vaccinate sheep, hunt for snails, bail hay, feed rabbits. . . .)

If your grades have been mediocre and you don't think you'd be accepted by these programs, or if you want to create your own itinerary, consider summer travel. Maybe an exciting summer is what you need rather than a huge shift in your academic path. Do you know anyone who knows anyone who knows a foreign family? Perhaps you can arrange to live abroad and be a mother's helper for them. Afterward, if you'd like to return for a school year with credit, let the Eiffel Tower or Vatican City be your incentive to improve your grades. The world's the limit!

Now that I'm twenty-seven, married, and have professional commitments, it would be nearly impossible for *me* to finagle a summer abroad, much less a year. But *you* can do it.

Would a few weeks of summertime rock climbing or cycling appeal to you? Call Outward Bound at (800) 243-8520. They offer strenuous programs worldwide, and also offer financial aid.

What if you can't face another year in the same school but you're not up for anything as drastic as dropping out or going overseas? Consider transferring to a private school. The drawback? It's expensive, but financial aid may be available.

Don't think that if you were in private school, your chances of getting into a good college necessarily go up. Your chances of getting a solid education and developing intellectually may increase, and that's terrific, but private school competition to get into "name" colleges is fierce. Instead of being the outstanding student at your public school and the only one to apply to Princeton, you could find you'd be just one more student, one more applicant.

If you do choose to apply to a private school, visit it first and be sure it offers what you feel your public school lacks. Are you willing to wear a uniform, take harder courses, and face stiffer competition, as may be the case?

Is it possible that instead of making the costly switch, you could improve your situation at high school? Join the student council and fight for changes. Ease out of a clique that has grown boring. Sign up for new electives, sports, extracurrics. (How about voice lessons, folk dancing, Dungeons and Dragons, yearbook layout, service clubs?) Do you want to discuss computers or improve your Spanish? Start a once-a-week science or language table at lunch, and let everybody know where and when it meets.

What if it's senior year, your parents are moving, and you don't want to start at a new school? See if you can arrange to stay behind with relatives or a best friend.

What if you're a formidable musician or painter, and you're ready to focus, even at the risk of narrowing your options? Consider applying to a music or art secondary school. I know an actor who left public school after ninth grade to enroll in a performing arts school. He still earned a high school diploma, but he was able to devote a lot of time to his talent and he met people with similar aspirations.

Interested in, say, carpentry or fabric? Try an apprenticeship with a cabinet maker or textile manufacturer. Vocational schools and junior colleges are also worth investigating, as are vocational-educational programs offered in some schools, like TOP, a Training Opportunities Program in New York City. Ask your guidance counselor or librarian for information.

If you want to skip senior year, your grades have been high, and you are self-reliant and adaptable, look into the possibility of starting college early. Ask your guidance counselor or write to colleges for specifics.

You're wondering how hard college will be, or you're ready for one really rigorous course? Take a class or two in a local university after school. Or enroll in a summer program at a prep school such as Dana Hall or a college such as Rhode Island School of Design, Brown, Bennington,

Penn, Syracuse, Northwestern, Harvard, or the University of Tampa. There are hundreds of programs worth looking into.

If you don't feel ready for college yet, apply for deferred or delayed college admission, get your high school degree, and take time off. Some students benefit a lot from a year in the Real World. Many land a routine job, earn money, realize they don't want to wipe tables forever, and begin to appreciate and value education. Others work for free or for pay in a stimulating job that helps define their career interests. Or spend another year at a private school to become better prepared academically for college. Or travel and become better prepared emotionally.

Your parents may scowl, but if you're buckling under the pressure and don't want to go from high school to college without a break, you don't have to. Explore your alternatives. Think about your short-term and long-term goals. Learn as much as you can. You're not running a race in which a diploma is the finish line.

COLLEGE: CHOOSING AND GETTING CHOSEN

Mark Twain, who didn't graduate from grade school, said, "I never let my schooling interfere with my education." I agree that loads of learning occurs outside the classroom. And I take my hat off to all the accomplished people who never had the benefit of four years of college, from Henry Ford, Thomas Edison, and Eleanor Roosevelt to Abe Lincoln and my father.

Nevertheless, nowadays, unless you're positive the academic environment is not for you, I think continuing your formal education is a privilege well worth taking advantage of. Because less than 20 percent of Americans now twenty-five years old or over have earned a college diploma, that piece of paper still makes a big difference when you're job hunting. It won't guarantee you a lucrative job right away, but it will provide professional flexibility and make it easier to find work. Besides, careers aside, college is a valuable time to grow. You have your whole life to be a homemaker and wage earner, but only a short time to devote yourself entirely to improving your mind. And it can be unbelievably fun to meet dozens—hundreds—of young men and women interested in what interests you, be it film, marine biology, psychology, German, medicine, or graphic design.

If you are college bound, here's what to do.

1 *Think ahead.* That doesn't mean devote your four high school years to preparing for the next four years. But being suddenly impressive in twelfth grade may not impress the school of your choice. Be aware of

what most college admission committees look at: grades, board scores, extracurrics, recommendations, and, in many cases, your essays on their application and your interview with them. They scrutinize junior year transcripts and also study freshman, sophomore, and senior year records, including the second senior semester in borderline cases.

• Enroll in serious, not watered-down, courses, and work hard. The best colleges like to see three years of math, four of English, and at least two or three years of history, science, and foreign language. They look at how many years you devote to each subject, not just how many subjects you study.

• Consider taking the two-hour Preliminary Scholastic Aptitude Tests (PSATs) in October of your junior year, and the three-hour SATs the following spring. The national average score for the math SAT is about 425, while the verbal average is about 468. (My whiz-kid brother Mark got the top score, 800, on his math SAT; the lowest possible score is 200.) About two-thirds of the students who take the test again, often the following December, improve their score, but one-third does worse. You can't cancel your SAT score once it's recorded, though you can cancel it immediately after taking the exam. (Did you hear about the fiasco of 1984, in which the completed SATs of 195 seniors at Sheepshead Bay (N.Y.) High School were accidentally put through a paper shredder at the Newark Post Office? Talk about nightmares!)

It's wise to take several achievement tests right after you complete the corresponding courses, for example, in English, calculus, or advanced biology. And some high schools encourage students to take the American College Test (ACT).

Signing up for an expensive program to prime you for standardized tests is not essential, but do study the workbooks that provide sample tests. For instance, it helps to know what to expect on the SATs: analogies, antonyms, sentence completions, reading comprehension, and math problem-solving. Workbooks also advise you to pace yourself, make educated but not wild guesses, and mark the answer grid carefully. Among the latest good workbooks are *10 SAT's: Scholastic Aptitude Tests of the College Board* and *The College Board Achievement Tests: 14 Tests in 13 Subjects.*

• Get involved. While I don't think you should do anything simply because it will look good on your application, this *is* the time to pursue interests and expand horizons. In the long run, if the only reason you joined band, went away to a college summer school, served as class treasurer, or volunteered at a center for the homeless was to impress the deans of admissions, that still beats having spent your afternoons or summers sitting on your rump. Do something interesting, whether it's getting a job, running a VD hot line, going to computer or music camp, or taking a night course at a nearby college. Do it for yourself: for your here-and-now and your future.

- Start figuring out which teachers you get along best with. A teacher with whom you have a good rapport now will be willing to work overtime later to write you a sparkling recommendation.

2   *Explore your financial options.* Yes, college is expensive. *Not* counting room, board, or books (which may add up to an annual $2500), the average tuition per year in a four-year private college is about $4600. The average tuition per year in a four-year public college is about $1100. Some schools cost an annual ten grand, while other state-run institutions charge only five or six hundred dollars each year.

Ask your guidance counselor and librarian about information on long-term low-interest student loans, merit- and need-based scholarships, grants, fellowships, college work-study programs, and part-time jobs. Or call the Student Information Center at (301) 984-4070 weekdays to find out about federal financial aid for postsecondary education. Or write to Student Guide, Public Documents Distribution Center, Dept. 84, Pueblo, Colorado, 81009, for a free booklet called *The Student Guide: Five Federal Financial Aid Programs.* American taxpayers are funding about $10 billion of student grants and loans. If you deserve some of that loot, let the government know. And let the school you're applying to know. At best, you may end up attending college nearly scot-free.

Most colleges don't let whether you're requesting aid affect their admissions decisions. Do you think everyone in the Ivies is rich? Think again. Nearly 60 percent of all Ivy League undergrads receive some financial aid.

It's easiest to receive aid if you apply early (before March 15) and demonstrate need (your family income doesn't exceed $30,000 and you have siblings in college, for instance). Some uncommon aid sources exist that offer scholarships to good singers or glassblowers or students who have sold shoes at Thom McAn's. Sometimes a particular college has money in store for qualified members of a particular religion or descendants of a particular family. Or a club, corporation, or civic group may have dollars to offer. The National Merit Corporation awards money to students who ace their PSATs.

I saved one semester's tuition by converting my advanced placement (AP) scores into college credit. AP courses may exempt you from college course requirements as well as save you thousands of dollars and enable you to get your diploma in less than four years.

3   *Find the colleges that most appeal to you.* You have about three thousand in the United States to choose from. Do you want to go near or far? South or north? Do you prefer an urban or a country setting? Do you

want your school to be big or small? Two-year or four-year? Private or public? Coed or single-sex? Should it have a strong department of English or Physics? Fraternities and sororities? Religious emphasis? If you attend a small all-girls' prep school now, do you really want to go to a small all-women's college?

What matters to you? Don't go by where your friends and boyfriends are applying. College is your opportunity to strike out on your own. Friendships and true love can endure separation, but if you follow their lead and wind up in a school that doesn't suit you, you could end up resenting your boyfriend (or your ex-boyfriend!).

Visit your high school guidance office or library and peruse the college guidebooks. Or buy one. (*Comparative Guide to American Colleges, The Insider's Guide to the Colleges, Barron's Profiles of American Colleges, Peterson's Travel Guide to Colleges,* and *The College Handbook* are among many helpful choices.) They describe the campus atmosphere, tell how many freshmen returned for sophomore year (95%? 50%?), report the student-to-faculty and male-to-female ratios, and give the percentage of minority students and financial aid recipients. Guidebooks also list the average SAT scores, class size, cost, most popular majors, and statistics on how many people apply and how many are accepted each year, as well as providing information about deadlines and where to write for an application and catalog. (Schools love to send out booklets showing attractive students playing Frisbee, lively professors leading intimate discussions, and ivy-wrapped buildings shining in the sun.)

It takes several hours and can cost as much as $35 to apply to each college, so decide carefully where to apply. Did you know that Cornell offers a One-Course-At-A-Time program? That Tufts has language houses? That the University of Indiana is a haven for musicians? That Emory received a $100 million donation not long ago? That you can major in fashion design at Parsons School of Design? That McGill is a good school in Canada and is cheaper than most American colleges? That the first year at MIT is pass/fail? That Middlebury has its own ski area and a program that lets you spend junior year in Moscow? That Yale has an official Shopping Around Period in which you sample classes for over a week before deciding which to take? Did you know that William Smith has only 800 students, while Ohio State has over 40,000? Learn as much about your next home as possible.

And don't overlook local community colleges. For some, two years at an inexpensive college can provide the perfect springboard to a good job or a more demanding and expensive university.

4   *Go college shopping.* You've narrowed your choices. But how can you decide between Stanford and Cal Tech? Kenyon and Georgetown? Agnes Scott and Drake? Keep reading, and try to meet alumni. If possible,

take a trip to the campus. Go alone or with family or friends. Jot down notes or take photos so you don't get your memories of the schools all muddled.

Strolling among the dorms and buildings for the first time is both edifying and exhilarating. Are the students friendly? Is the campus pretty? Is the food palatable? Do you like the libraries? Do you feel as though you could fit in? Ask the students what they like and dislike about the school. (Sure they're content, but are they lukewarm or raving?) If you can, sleep over one night to get the best possible picture of Swarthmore or Pomona. Even if you don't have a friend at the college you're visiting, its admissions program may be able to match you with a student host.

5   *Have an interview.* Interviews are optional, but if you present yourself well, they're a good opportunity for you to learn more about the school and for the school to learn more about you. If you are checking out a college, call to set up an interview beforehand. If you aren't, consider arranging one with an admissions officer visiting your school or a local alum who serves as a college representative. Tell your well-meaning parents to let you go to your interview alone.

Don't let your impressions of the interview affect your impressions of the school too much. When I visited Harvard, it was a rainy day and my interviewer was snooty. So I didn't apply. Dumb. When I visited Yale, it was a sunny day and my interviewer was charming. I ended up going to Yale and loving it, but the point is I shouldn't have let one day's weather or one man's personality color my judgment. (Harvard is a fine place too.)

How do you prepare for the typical twenty- or thirty-minute interview? Dress neatly and fairly formally, read up on the university, arrive early, and be your most poised, mature self. Think up questions ahead of time. If you want to be a doctor, don't ask how many graduates got accepted by med schools, because the answer is in the school catalog. Ask instead how long the laboratories are open and if it would be possible to see them. If you want to know if most graduates liked their alma mater, ask what percentage of alumni contributed to the college that year.

Be prepared to answer the interviewer's questions, too. He or she may ask why you want to attend Scripps or Bryn Mawr or Carleton. (Be enthusiastic!) Other probable questions: Where else are you applying? What out-of-school activity do you find most rewarding? What are your shortcomings? What can you in particular offer the school? If the interviewers ask if you've done volunteer work, and you haven't but you intend to, don't just say no. Say something like, "After studying, practicing with the swim team, working at the deli, practicing flute, and seeing friends, I don't have much free time, but I am hoping to volunteer at a children's hospital ward next year." (That'll spin their bow ties!) The interview is also your chance to explain why your grades recently plummeted (you moved, you were sick, your parents separated) and to ask (unless you're as chicken as I was), "Would you encourage me to apply?"

Toot your horn, but quietly. The woman who interviewed me at Wellesley complimented me afterward on my humility. Believe me, I got *everything* in that I wanted her to know, but subtly, and I'd told her what I learned from being defeated in Student Council. Don't be too modest, but don't be a nonstop boaster.

After your interview, write a thank-you note. It can't hurt—unless it's sloppy or misspelled.

6 *Zero in on a few schools and apply.* It's smart to apply to three to six schools, including a long shot (you may not get in, but it's worth the try) and a safety or fallback or backup school (the others may pass you up, but you're a shoo-in here). Don't forget that schools base their decisions not just on your strengths as a scholar, leader, athlete, humanitarian, and individual, but also on things like who else is applying from your school. If a dozen of your friends are applying to Colgate (or Berkeley or University of Virginia), your chances of acceptance may go down. If all the kids from your school who have gone to a particular college ended up transferring or dropping out, the college will screen you carefully. If you're applying to a state school in another state, your chances are slimmer than the natives'.

• If you're absolutely sure about which school you hope to attend, you may be able to apply Early Decision. Programs vary from college to college, but generally, by applying early to your favorite school, you'll find out early whether you've been accepted or deferred. But play fair. No changing your mind after that early application is in.

• Most students send for seven or eight applications the summer before and fall of their senior year, and then decide which to fill out. Keep records and copies of what you send where. (An accordion file may help.) The first application may seem overwhelming, but you'll find that they are all somewhat similar and don't take forever to complete. The forms may include questions about your parents' jobs and alma maters, but that information alone won't get you in or keep you out. There will be space to write about any honors or prizes you have received, and you can even send in published articles, photographs, slides of your artwork, or a tape of your flute playing. (Do so only if you're sure you're super talented.) Other questions will ask if you need financial aid and what your career goals are.

It's okay to say your prospective major is "Undecided." It may be a plus to lean toward Middle Eastern Studies or Russian Literature instead of being one more English or Business major. But don't lie! If you say you want to be a Geology major and you have hardly taken any science courses, you'll look silly. And if you start out as a Computer Science major just because you think that's the way to get rich quick, you may regret limiting yourself. I have a friend who dropped out of a good school because she realized midstream that she really didn't like numbers all that much. So far, she hasn't found the energy or money to start over in a liberal arts major, but she feels that would have been a better investment of her school years.

- Recommendations? Find teachers (preferably of different subjects) who like you and know you well, and ask if they would write you a supportive letter. Ask at least one month before the deadline; then, two weeks later, politely ask if the person has sent it in. The forms they'll fill out will have questions about your academic performance as well as personality, ability to work with others, and the like. You could refresh the teachers' memories by jotting down projects you did in their courses as well as some of your other activities. Encourage them to keep a copy of the letter in case you need another one, and waive your right to see it. Thank them afterward!

What if your aunt's ex-roommate's second husband's brother is the town mayor and might be persuaded to write a letter on your behalf? Don't bother. Letters should come from teachers, employers, ministers— people who really know you.

- Take time writing and revising your essays. The colleges may ask about the turning points and major influences in your life. About your favorite books and magazines (don't say *Tiger Beat*). About the extracurric you found most valuable. Many colleges ask just one or two questions, while others ask a bunch. (I decided not to apply to Dartmouth because the application included five questions, then instructed the student to come up with a good sixth one and answer it.) Colleges often ask an open-ended, tell-us-more-about-you question. Your answer should be thoughtful, personal, honest, and clear. You should sound intelligent, not cocky. When I finished, I had my parents check my essays, and you may want a family member or teacher to look over yours. It's a good idea to make a photocopy of the original application, type your essay on that copy, and make any last-minute changes in content or format (margins, spacing) before filling out the original.

Here is part of one essay and a complete second essay that helped me get into college. I include them not because they are model answers but because they may help you come up with ideas.

Essay 1: Tell us about yourself.
It is hard to analyze one's own character, particularly when it is still developing. I'm told I'm competitive—I'd say hardworking. But I had to be. As the baby of the family, I had to catch up with two older brothers, and

the competition was pretty rough. Mark had a poem published in Jack & Jill *when he was four; Eric knew the E.R.A.s of all the Yankees.... Then, I discovered French, and in eighth grade I received the "excellence in French" award.*

I'm told I'm thrifty—my brothers would say a miser. I do like to see money and time amount to something. But I'm not a miser because I parted with my entire life's savings two summers ago and bought a trip to France. . . .

Essay 2: Comment on an experience that helped you to discover or define a value that you hold.

Things are valued most after they are lost. While one is camping, one realizes the luxury of running water. During a blackout, one believes he will never again take electricity for granted. After one finds employment, one values leisure.

Life is different. It cannot be temporarily lost in order to be better appreciated. I learned to value life through someone else's death. When I was nine years old, I made friends with a nature counselor at a local day camp. I always rode on his shoulders and we told each other jokes and stories. I guess I was half in love with "Uncle Norm."

That autumn he joined the Marines. I wrote him and he wrote me from Virginia, Guatemala Bay, and finally Vietnam. Uncle Norm had been a teacher and had studied at the Sorbonne. His letters were always so imaginative. He prefaced one letter with "I haven't written you in such a long time, I know you must be mad at me. If you are, just throw this letter on the floor and stomp all over it before you read it." He wrote about spiders he met while hiding in holes, the stars, and once the "pweeng" of bullets and the "thhhump" of bombs.

I was surprised and worried when one carefree letter ended with "The war isn't going just real well; things could be worse, though."

Things did become worse, and that was the last letter I ever received from my friend. He was shot and killed by Vietcong mortar fire in South Vietnam.

I valued his kindness, intelligence, and curiosity about the world. His death made me value human life even more.

7   *Keep things in perspective.* Unless you applied Early Decision, Early Action, or Rolling Admissions, you may have to wait until April 15 to find out which colleges will open their doors to you. Don't spend those months biting off your toenails with worry. Don't get too wound up in the trauma and drama. Don't have a Duke-or-die attitude. For sanity's sake, talk about something else. (Aren't you eager for me to start talking about something else?)

When the letters arrive, keep your chin up. If you get a rejection, it may not be because you're not qualified. It may be bad luck: Thirty other cheerleading valedictorians who are deejays on the side were vying for the same spot. And it's not the end of the world if Rice or Vanderbilt turns you down. Other schools will snap you up. Even though the college you attend does make a difference, you can surround yourself with friendly, thinking people and get a great education anywhere. (That's why it's alarming to read about parents tripping all over each other to get little Muffy into the "right" nursery school so she'll end up in the "right" college.)

Mid-April can put a strain on friendships. Be caring through thick or thin—whether you or your friends receive thick or thin envelopes. Notice whom you're talking to when you express your delight. You'd hate it if someone gushed about Barnard if Barnard just turned you down.

For now, feel psyched, not scared. I bet you'll wind up at a school you adore. So when the good news comes, celebrate!

7
MONEY

Money isn't everything, but it ain't bad for starters. And if records, clothes, makeup, movies, college, gasoline, phone calls, and travel appeal to you, then the more dollars, the merrier.

The problem? Some people become hung up on money, always counting pennies and always envious of those with bigger bank accounts. Others forget that how you earn is more important than how much you earn and get trapped in high-paying jobs they can't stand. Even teens can get messed up by money if they start panicking simply because they haven't picked out a lucrative profession.

That's why I'm torn about this chapter. Since money is the ticket to fun and freedom but "love of money is the root of all evil," I'm in a quandary. On the one hand, I want you to know how to make and save money, become a better baby-sitter, find odd jobs, write a résumé, ace an interview, use connections, get employed, and ultimately find a career not by chance but by choice. On the other hand, I want you to mellow out. In junior high and high school, you can enjoy a fleeting luxury: You don't have to get hyper about bills and taxes. Look ahead, but relax, too. You probably can be whatever you want to be, and you have years to decide what that is.

BE A BETTER (AND BETTER-PAID) BABY-SITTER

I baby-sat around the clock. I baby-sat for one family in the afternoon and another in the evening. I baby-sat my way to Europe, and in Madrid, I worked as a mother's helper. I baby-sat until I got baby-sitter burn-out.

During my primo baby-sitting years, ages twelve to sixteen, I usually loved it. It was fun trying to answer children's questions. Four-year-old Adam, the first boy ever to take any interest in my flat figure, asked, "Do you have big boobies?" And John said, "We learned there is water in the air. Why isn't everything wet?" I liked letting Gary finish the sentences when I read *Goodnight Moon.* I even got a kick out of the Ice Cream Crisis. Leah wanted a taste of her cousin Tim's cone. "Give her a bite," said I. He did—he bit her arm.

Do you like children? Are you patient? Responsible? Honest? Tireless? Diplomatic? Baby-sitting may be for you. Of course, baby-sitting is a misnomer. It's really baby-watching, baby-chasing, baby-feeding, baby-bathing, baby-changing, baby-reading, baby-bedding. Here are more pointers:

- When you say yes to a job, make sure the parent knows how late you can stay and how much you charge. Write down the time and date of the job, the parents' name, address, and phone number, and whether they'll provide transportation. (If you don't know them or know of them, be cautious. Ask your parents for advice.)
- Don't ever cancel at the last minute. In a pinch, call the parent as soon as possible and offer to find a sub—your best friend or one of the parents' regulars.
- Before you leave, let your parents know where you'll be and when you think you'll be back.
- Before the children's parents leave, get the number where they'll be as well as numbers of the police, doctor, neighbors. Ask for any special instructions about bedtime rules, pets, phone messages, what to do if the doorbell rings, or how to work the alarm system (if they have one).
- Don't have friends over unless the parents said you could.
- Lock all doors.
- To prevent mishaps, be sensible. Pick up toys on the stairs. Don't answer the phone, or take it off the hook, while you bathe the children. Don't give medicine to a sick child without permission.
- Play with the children, but be firm, too. If bedtime is at 9:00, don't let them have pillow fights and let's-pretend-the-bed-is-a-trampoline parties until all hours. Say "This is the last story" or "Quiet down" in a tone that shows you mean it. Even ignoring a brief tantrum may be more effective than screaming "GO TO SLEEP" at the top of your lungs. (The little darlings may be testing you to find your breaking point, so don't be a "sitting" duck.)

- Don't snoop or abuse phone or fridge privileges. (I especially wouldn't recommend sipping straight from the juice carton when wearing lipstick.)
- In case of emergency, call the police—try 911 or 0 if the number isn't handy. In case of fire, grab the kids and run, then call the fire department and children's parents from a neighbor's.
- Try to stay awake until the parents return. A quiet house can be your opportunity to make money while doing homework.

Want more jobs? Spread the word. Tell your parents, friends, and the families you sit for. Post a notice on the bulletin board at your grocer's, club, church, or synagogue. Or place an ad in your school or local paper.

Are you being paid fairly? Find out the going rate from your friends. Two dollars an hour? More? Less? When you take care of three rowdy children, you deserve more than when you stay with a sleeping toddler. Let the parents know ahead whether you charge extra for cooking, cleaning dishes, additional children, or postmidnight sitting. Most parents will ask you back if their kids like you and you have common sense—even if you do charge an extra twenty-five cents an hour.

Don't get gypped! I once helped out at a five-year-old's birthday party. I brought Scott a small gift and did my best to entertain his twelve wild buddies. Afterward, the mother wrote me a check (I hated checks) for the exact amount of time at my minimum hourly rate—no tip! I barely broke even, and boy, was I bummed. I should have asked beforehand if she'd pay me more than usual. Or I should have expressed my disappointment then and there. Instead, here I am, a dozen years later, still peeved.

Baby-sitting can lead to mother's helper or day-care jobs. When my friend Jen and I were sixteen, we ran an informal summer day-care center for eight four-year-olds every weekday morning at different parents' houses. The children brought their own lunch, and Jen and I came up with arts, crafts, games, even a few field trips. We had fun and earned much more than we would have if we'd been baby-sitting on our own.

I know some girls now who run and advertise a baby-sitting network. Parents call Naomi to find an available sitter. Naomi keeps track of the schedules of ten or so girls and lines up jobs for them constantly. Her reward? She gets $1.50 for every job she places.

If you *don't* want to sit on a particular night, don't. Say, "Thanks, Mrs. Brennan, I have plans. I'd love to another time." And if *you* have baby-sitter burn-out? Say, "Sorry, I'm not sitting anymore, but thanks for calling." Me, I used to say, "Aahhm, I'm not sure," then bellow, "Mom, can I baby-sit tonight?" while violently shaking my head no and waiting for her to get me off the hook. What a wimp! You can do better.

BEYOND BABY-SITTING
(BUT BEFORE THE BIG TIME)

It's hard for adults to find work; it's even harder to land a job if you're not yet sixteen.

If you are fourteen or fifteen, you can get a free work permit (through school) and Social Security number (through your local Social Security office). You are eligible for some jobs at small businesses or restaurants. In most cases, you may not work legally during school hours or after 7:00 P.M. or in "hazardous" places, such as in a boiler room or meat freezer, or where there are explosives, alcohol, gambling, or dangerous machinery.

However, you may bag groceries, shelve merchandise, pump gas, be a cashier (if the bill came to $1.78 and someone handed you $2.03, you wouldn't panic, would you?), deliver newspapers, bus tables, help in a nursing home, be a companion to an elderly person, set up store displays, work on a farm, be a model or an actress or a junior camp counselor, help clean pet stores or hotel rooms—and the list goes on. Listen for leads and keep your eyes open for help-wanted notices in stores and newspapers.

At any age, you can make money doing odd jobs in your neighborhood. When my brother Eric and I were little kids, we used to go door-to-door shining shoes and selling homemade potholders. We always came home with candy money.

Are you good in the garden? A whiz at baking? Can you make dirty dishes disappear? Are you fast with a rake? Handy with repairs? A marvel at polishing silver? A pro with paint? How do you fare at washing cars? Washing dogs? Walking dogs? Running errands? Speed typing? Hemming and sewing? Dyeing Easter eggs or wrapping holiday gifts? Can you give guitar lessons? Tutor children in English or math? Run a weekend art, sports, or exercise class for kids? Would your penmanship look pretty on invitations? Can you take care of a house while the owners are on vacation—feed the cat, water plants, bring in mail, turn lights on and off—without getting spooked? Are you a snappy photographer?

Yes? Then if you want work, don't just stand there. Hustle your bustle and get your rear in gear! Let your neighbors know how lucky they are. On a piece of paper, write your name, address, phone number, and special talents. Make photocopies and leave them at neighbors' doors. Better yet, dress neatly, knock, hand out your flyer, and explain that for a fee, you're a Jill-of-all-trades.

A "try me" attitude is helpful, but don't insist and don't wander into houses where you don't know anybody who knows the residents.

Every week last winter, a boy rang my doorbell and asked if he could clear our icy walk for three dollars. Partly to encourage him and partly to have an unslippery path, I always said, "You're on." If he didn't show up, shovel in hand, I wouldn't advertise for a shoveler. But because he takes that initiative, he makes three dollars in ten minutes at many houses on our street.

Come up with creative tactics. If you want to start selling your cookies, why not enclose them in envelopes (one per) with your name, phone number, and rates, then distribute them? Add, "Place your order this weekend and get the first half-dozen free." You could also offer to work for free for a limited time period (half an hour for an odd job, up to a week for a summer job) so a reluctant employer can see how useful you are.

Once you're on the job, work hard without constant supervision. Don't be like one of the well-meaning teen housecleaners my working mother once hired who, every ten minutes, interrupted Mom to ask, "Now what?" Instead, you and your employer should thoroughly go over the chores (ironing, dusting, cleaning the refrigerator) when you arrive.

It's most ideal if you can snag a few regular, once-a-week jobs. It's most fun if you and a friend can work together, although you share profits.

When I was fourteen, I told my diary, *"I wish I could get a real job and make lots of $ working for a few weeks. That'd be great."* Finding a "real job" when you're young is not easy. But if you narrow down what you'd like to do and go after it with gusto, you *can* make "lots of $." I'm rooting for you.

ALL IN THE FAMILY

Families differ and allowances differ. Many parents give their kids a few dollars each week and expect them to do a few chores each week. You may be able to make a little extra if you do a little extra.

If your parents work, and you're a good cook, maybe you can have dinner ready on certain days. If they give a party, maybe you can clean up. If you drive, maybe you can run their errands. Would they consider paying you to sibling-sit? To paint dingy closets? To do the family laundry? Would they let you arrange a garage sale? You do most of the work and get most of the profit.

If you think you're getting an insufficient allowance, you can ask for more. (Satisfaction not guaranteed). Keep a list of where your money goes, and be reasonable and willing to compromise. Your family probably isn't charging you for room and board, so it's not fair to expect megabucks every time you're helpful. Plus, their spending money may not be astronomical. After all, they may be trying to put some aside for your education and future.

Many teens work for their parents outside the home. Does your mother the caterer need a hand on weekends? Offer both of yours. Does your father the shoe store owner need help on busy days? You may be a shoo-in for the job.

Working for your parents has its payoffs. You don't have to go through the job hunt runaround. You may be able to call in sick once in a while to study for a final or go to a game. The transportation problem to and from work is simplified. You may find you have more on-the-job responsibility than a stranger would trust you with. And understanding what your mother or father does all day may bring you closer.

Drawbacks? Plenty. Parent-daughter scolding often hurts more than employer-employee criticism. And other employees might resent you or cater to you rather than simply accepting you. My friend Laura said she felt caught in the middle when she worked for her father. "The people I worked with felt comfortable with me and sometimes they'd bad-mouth the boss—but the boss was my dad!"

Many disillusioned adult sons and daughters complain that because their parents needed them, they got stuck in the family business and never developed their own skills or tested their own dreams. If you work for your parents, let them know when you feel put-upon. But also let them know if you're happy and grateful for the job.

FIGURING OUT YOUR FUTURE

Once you're sixteen, you can get more jobs and more money. But before you run off to apply to be a waitress or fast-food counter person, take a minute—no, many minutes—to grapple with the old "What do you want to be when you grow up?"

You don't have to have an instant answer, but now is the time to ask yourself questions, whether you are college bound or not. Do you have short-term and long-term goals? What are your interests and strengths? Some of you may think, "I'm good at lots of things." Some of you may mistakenly believe, "I'm not good at anything." And others may be good in one subject but tilt toward another. (Case in point: My math SAT score was 140 points higher than my verbal, but since I loathed numbers and loved words, I stuck with words.)

You have years to decide to be a teacher, advertising executive, lawyer, zoologist, real estate agent, computer progammer, flight attendant, pilot, social worker, health care coordinator, interior decorator, robot engineer, or whatever, but think ahead. Think of The Big Picture.

Deciding what sort of job you want is a job in itself. But it's settling to find a direction. Besides, if you know what you're aiming for (I didn't), you may be able to get a part-time or summer job in your chosen field (I didn't). Don't let your parents or anyone else choose a profession for you. And don't worry that your decisions are being set in stone.

Do you want a career? It's okay if you don't, but I hope you do. A career can offer money and fulfillment and friends. And it gives a woman options: She can be single and self-sufficient; she can support herself and her children if her-husband-the-good-provider dies or gets fired or files for divorce; or she can leave him if he becomes abusive or unfaithful or if she feels she'd be happier without him. Let's hope this is never your story, but divorce is commonplace, and one out of four divorced or separated women is now on welfare. Furthermore, women live an average of eight years longer than men. It's risky not to know how to take care of yourself.

According to a recent *New York Times* poll, even if they could afford to stay home, over half of American working women would rather work. I'd keep writing even if I won a million-dollar sweepstakes. Well-chosen work can be enjoyable. That's why rich filmmakers, business executives, and Nobel Prize laureats don't quit and go golfing. If you're lucky, you can decide later to be a full-time mother and homemaker, but in the meantime, keep your possibilities open. Don't shortchange yourself.

Today you may want just a job. But later you may seek a career. "Just a job" forever could be boring. It's sad to think that many people spend over forty hours a week selling their time for money and impatiently watching the minute hand creep (or the digit cards flip) until quitting time. The Thank-God-It's-Friday crowd isn't enjoying Monday, Tuesday, Wednesday, and Thursday enough.

What kind of career matches your talents and interests? What are you naturally good at? Would you like the security of a nine-to-five job with salary and colleagues, or do you have the discipline and desire to be self-employed? What are your dreams? When you're older, how would you like to look back on your life?

I'm not asking all this to worry you. When I was in high school, I wasn't sure what I wanted to be. I thought I might become a writer or psychologist or teacher or chef or. . . . And I confess, one line in my diary reveals: *"I probably will get married, etc., rather than have a neat career."* As though it were either/or!

Take out a piece of paper (this is not a pop quiz, I promise) and write down your best and/or favorite school subjects. Next add the extracurrics that mean the most to you. If you're not the star of the track team or the lead of the musical, but you love running and acting, write that down. What do you do in your free time? Read? Make jewelry? Play tennis? How would you describe yourself? Open? Creative? Methodical? What are you secretly proud of? The way your room looks? Your eye for fashion? How you can smooth out arguments? What achievements do you feel good about, and which skills did they involve? What are some of your values? Friendship? Knowledge? Power? Helping others? Jot this all down.

You're on your way to writing a résumé (more on that coming up). For now, use this personal profile, and look for patterns and clues about what sort of job to head for. Persuasive sorts might enjoy sales jobs. At a sporting-goods store? Stereo outlet? Clothes shop? Quiet organizers might prefer clerical work. At a travel agency? Radio station? Government office? If you're good with numbers, you may eventually end up on Wall Street or in the field of science, engineering, or computers.

Does your list say art, going to museums, sketching portraits, making clay figures? Do yourself a favor: Forget fast food and look for artsy employment. Aim to be the arts-and-crafts instructor at a camp, or ask if help is needed at galleries, graphic design businesses, nearby paint shops, or museums. Maybe a local artist or craftsman would welcome an apprentice.

Does your list say English, school newspaper, reading, writing letters, keeping a journal? If you're motivated, don't settle for a cashier job as I did; get a head start on a literary career. Work in a library or bookstore. See if a local newspaper needs a "stringer" to report school happenings. (Jody, a spunky 14-year-old I know, called a paper and offered to write sports features. The editors okayed the idea and pay $20 a column.) Could you be an intern, copy girl, or go-fer at a local magazine, running errands while meeting editors and seeing the business from within? Or try to sell your own writing to a teen magazine. Study the magazine carefully before you send out your typed masterpiece, or it may boomerang back. And if it does? Remember that it is better to have written and been rejected than never to have written at all.

Maybe your most stunning quality is your appearance. Many teens wish they could be models, but only a few can. So don't kid yourself. If you're petite and adorable, you're petite and adorable and probably not model material. But if you're healthy, slender, tall (we're talking 5'7" minimum), photogenic, out-and-out beautiful, and you have straight teeth and a perfect complexion (most of us would be quite content with two of the above, thank you), consider checking out a modeling agency. Bring along recent pictures.

Your school guidance counselor can provide more job opportunities as well as internship information, and many communities have federally funded youth employment placement centers and services. The library is a gold mine, too. A librarian can lead you to helpful reference books, such as the government's *Occupational Outlook Handbook,* or *Writer's Digest's Internships,* or *Summer Employment Directory of the U.S.,* which is updated annually and includes available jobs at camps, campuses, ranches, holiday resorts, amusement parks, and restaurants. Adults don't get to try out different careers each summer, but you can. So experiment!

If you can afford to forgo a salary, don't overlook nonpaying work. Volunteer at a hospital, YWCA, Boys' Club, children's clinic, veterans' center, or Red Cross agency. Your pay is the good feeling that you are helping others unselfishly. Plus you may become deeper, more confident, more mature. When you've spent the afternoon in a hospital with a life-loving boy who was seriously burned when his house caught fire, you tend to stop feeling annoyed that your best friend gets a clothes allowance and you don't.

Still determined to waitress? Stretch yourself by doing it in a new environment. Ask your aunt or grandparents if you could live with them one summer.

And don't forget that the odd jobs that were available to you when you were younger are still around—at higher wages. Do you have your license and access to a car? Add "grocery shopping" and "chauffeur service to the airport" to your flyer.

Don't wait until summer to apply for a summer job. The early bird gets the work.

WRITING A RÉSUMÉ

"He or she who gets hired is not necessarily the one who can do that job best, but the one who knows the most about how to get hired." Richard Bolles wrote that in *What Color Is Your Parachute?*

If you want a job, you've got to market your skills. That means you have to let the bosses out there know why they'd be lucky to have you. And that means you may have to write a résumé.

A résumé is like your scribbled list of strengths and interests but is organized, on one page, typed, and includes your experience, education, and any pertinent special courses you've taken (like accounting, shorthand, computer programming). From your résumé, an employer should be able in a glance to get an idea about who you are and what you've done.

When you write your résumé, sell yourself. If your grades are lousy, don't mention them. If you got a varsity letter in gymnastics, say so. If you speak Japanese because your father is from Tokyo, write that down. You may have skills that you take for granted but that could knock an employer's socks off. Remember: Everybody started with no experience.

There are various résumé formats; some include job objective and references. Whatever you choose, be neat, concise, and positive. Then update your résumé often to include any new activities, jobs, or awards.

You may want to come up with more than one résumé if you are applying for different kinds of jobs. For instance, if you want to work in a summer repertory theater, you should make a big deal of your singing and dancing parts in school plays, your two years of voice lessons, and your ushering at a local theater. If you're simultaneously applying for a clerical position in an office and a job to assist a veterinarian, highlight other skills and interests.

Maybe you think all you've done in the last few years is pass your courses and pig out on Twinkies. Think harder. There's bound to be something you can include in a résumé. No? You're sure? Then do yourself the favor of signing up for some extracurrics. Not just to add zest to your résumé but to add zest to your life!

Have a parent, teacher, or counselor check your résumé, because it should be perfect before you make copies.

Send it with a neatly typed cover letter to various individuals. Then cross your fingers and hope the employer invites you in for an interview. If weeks pass and you don't hear from your prospective employer, you could call him or her.

Here is a sample cover letter and résumé that a girl seeking a position as a camp swim instructor might write.

(P.S.: If you're getting a funny feeling in the pit of your stomach and thinking, "But I'm still a kid," maybe *you* don't need to know all this yet. This book is your personal encyclopedia, remember? It's so you know where to find out about résumé writing—or breakups, or sex, or college applications, or alcohol—when you *do* want to know.)

10 Maple Way
Armonk, NY 10504
March 10, 1985

Mrs. Lisel Jeffrey
Camp Clearwater
19 Asbury Avenue
Wilderness, VT 01010

Dear Mrs. Jeffrey,

I would love to be a swim instructor at your camp this summer. I have my lifesaving certificate, have worked as a lifeguard, and am an active member of my school and club swim team. I adore children and baby-sit often.

Enclosed you'll find my résumé. Thank you for considering me for the position. I look forward to hearing from you.

All the best,

Sue Denim

Sue Denim

Sue Denim
10 Maple Way
Armonk, N.Y. 10504
(914) 121-2121

Education

Byram Hills High School, Armonk, N.Y.
expect to graduate June 1986

Experience

Summer, 1985   Lifeguard at Windmill Club
Summer, 1984   Baby-sat every morning for children of
                Mrs. Little, Upland Lane, Armonk, New York

Awards

Most Valuable Team Member, Windmill Swim Team 1984
Third place, Westchester County 50-meter breaststroke

Skills

Lifesaving certification, white water canoeing, diving, typing,
two years of Spanish, driving

Activities

Byram Hills Swim Team Co-captain
Candystriper at Mount Kisco Hospital
Outdoors Club, secretary

Age

16, born June 28, 1969

ACING THE INTERVIEW

Whether you are having a job or a college interview, you want to come off as mature, intelligent, enthusiastic, polite, and hardworking. The tips given in the *Education* chapter apply at the workplace as well. In a nutshell:

- Read up on the company and prepare questions.
- Anticipate the interviewer's questions and prepare answers.
- Dress neatly and conservatively.
- Plan to arrive alone and early—count on a traffic snarl en route.
- Introduce yourself and shake hands firmly; maintain eye contact; smile; sit up straight; use complete sentences.
- Don't gesticulate wildly, scratch, chew gum, smoke, ramble on and on, or talk about what a jerk your last boss was.
- As succinctly and positively as possible, state what you hope to offer the company, not what you hope to learn or gain from it.
- Don't be bashful about discussing hours and wages. (Can you handle working more than 15 hours in a school week? Are you available weeknights? Is minimum wage—currently $3.35—okay with you?)
- Shake hands again and follow up with a thank-you note.

Last week a friend had an interview at a bank. Together we staged a practice interview. He had terrific answers for "Why should I hire you?" "What do you expect to be doing in ten years?" and "Tell me about yourself." But when I asked "What are your weaknesses?" he blew it. He said, "I'm not good with numbers." A bank doesn't want to hear that! (Later he realized he shouldn't have been applying for a bank job anyway. That was his *father*'s aspiration, not his.)

If an interviewer asks about *your* weaknesses, don't volunteer that you're a procrastinator or are hopelessly disorganized. A better answer would be, "I'm a perfectionist," or "Sometimes I get so involved with a project I don't know when to quit." Don't lie, but put your best foot forward. Talk your way into the job!

Last but not least: the thank-you note. It can make or break you. Write to everyone who has been of service. Try to notice the assistant's name, too, then mention how much you appreciated Terri's help. The thank-you note can also be your chance to say anything important that you forgot to mention in person.

Hey, and don't be discouraged if you don't get the first, second, or even tenth job. Your interviewing skills improve with practice. And you need only one boss to say "You're hired!"

CONNECTIONS IS NOT A DIRTY WORD

When my sister-in-law planned to apply to my alma mater, I planned to write her a glowing recommendation. Sally is helping me edit this book, and I couldn't wait to tell Yale what an all-around smart person she is.

But then she did something dumb. She asked me not to gush on her behalf. She nobly worried about the applicants who didn't have Yalie sisters-in-law, and besides, she wanted to Get In On Her Own. Sally ended up at a tiptop school, but the point is, it's not so terrible to let people help you get ahead.

Students are notorious for resisting connections and even resenting those who use them. But don't forget that the ones who have the connections have often earned them. After all, no one is going to go out on a limb to praise a nincompoop. I wouldn't have offered to recommend Sally if she hadn't won my respect. And I wanted to write the letter not only for her sake but for Yale's. A connection is a two-way favor.

Not that my letter alone would have done the trick. Connections merely help you get a foot in the door. You still have to squeeze the rest of your body in by yourself.

Are they worth making? Absolutely. Weaving and pulling strings isn't cheating; it's a skill; it's being professional.

It won't kill you to be nice to the head honcho your parents know (who could someday offer you a job), just as you should be nice to all your parents' friends. If you don't have any family connections, make your own. Meet people who know people. Work hard and develop confidence in your abilities. Find someone you admire and let him or her know it. Get over the idea that biggies are unapproachable.

When she was still in college, my friend Henny Wright landed a position at the White House. How? One morning during her freshman year, Jimmy Carter (then a little-known candidate) was a guest in Henny's political science class. She was impressed by him and decided to skip her classes and follow Carter around campus. After his final speech, Henny didn't beeline home for popcorn in the dorm. She stuck around and talked to Carter. And he offered her a job! She accepted without hesitation. Years later, when Henny eventually applied to Yale Law School, she had impressive and much-deserved letters of recommendation.

It pays to have gumption. I had never interviewed anybody, and then I interviewed Joanne Woodward. She was performing at the nearby

Kenyon Festival Theater in Ohio, and I told myself, "You have nothing to lose, you have nothing to lose. . . ." as I circled my phone like a pilot above an airport. Finally I dialed and, after preliminaries, asked, "May I interview you?" "Yes," she said. Just like that.

My husband Rob got a job with Broadway director Hal Prince when he was fresh out of theater grad school. How? On day one, Rob saw and loved Prince's *Madame Butterfly* in Chicago. On day two, he spotted Prince at Northwestern University and congratulated him. On day three, Rob sent Prince a letter and résumé. Upshot: even Big Time Successes respond to genuine admiration and may remember that sometime someone somewhere gave them a break. During the New York interview that followed, when Prince asked, "What can I do for you?" Rob answered, "Hire me." Prince did. Just like that.

If the stars of your chosen profession are not on the horizon, contacts can be made from afar. And small connections can lead to bigger ones. Teachers may become principals; assistant editors may become editors-in-chief; actors may become directors; paralegals may become law partners; and so on.

There is such a thing as the Old Boy and Old Girl Network, and you can use it if you want to. Everyone knows somebody who knows somebody who can be of help.

It doesn't hurt to be friendly, not too modest, and willing to boost someone else's ego with a sincere compliment. I consider it cordial, not calculated, to acknowledge a favor with a thank-you note. (I thank people who can help me and people who can't.) I wish the girl I helped last week had felt the same. She wants to be a writer, so she came over and I spent two hours talking with her. Fine. But she should have followed up with a simple thank-you. It's not that I stand on ceremony. It's that if she had seemed more appreciative, she would have made a better impression, and I might have been more eager to pass her name on to editors. (When you're looking for work, your personality counts, too, not just your talent.)

In the future, you won't be the kind who forgets initial votes of confidence, will you? Stay in touch with past mentors. And be sure you lend a hand to people who could use your help.

For now, if you want a job, don't sit back and wait to be discovered. Write a letter to someone you admire. Let your peers and adult friends know you'd like to meet someone in certain career fields or from certain colleges. Don't give up your dreams before giving yourself a chance. As the poet Emily Dickinson put it, "Luck is not chance/It's toil—/Fortune's expensive smile/Is earned."

Success with no strings attached is great. But it's okay to cultivate connections and tug strings without guilt or apology. It beats feeling beaten.

ONCE YOU'RE HIRED, DON'T GET
FIRED—OR SHOULD YOU QUIT?

It's more fun to be given a raise than to be given the ax, so on the job, try to be (take a deep breath): punctual, dependable, cheerful, honest, busy, polite, open-minded, neatly dressed, professional, able to take criticism, willing to do more than the expected, and (phew) not the first to leave at the end of the day.

But what if you decide enough is enough? You can't wash another plate, serve another salad, add another column of figures, or tell another customer how becoming the yukky skirt looks. What if you've worked over a year and still get minimum wage even though you requested a raise (pointing out not that you need it but deserve it)? What if you've learned quite enough about dry cleaning, thank you, and want to explore other fields? What if you've tried but just can't get along with catty Connie or lecherous Larry? What if you're not earning all that much anyway after taxes? (Don't assume you're exempt.) What if your grades are sinking, your friendships are threadbare, and you're always tired and rushed? In short, what if your job is no longer paying off?

Consider quitting. You're allowed. (Even Snoopy considered leaving the comics when he got tired of working for Peanuts!) Be sure to give two weeks' notice and leave without hard feelings. Tell your boss you enjoyed and learned from and appreciated the experience. Your last employer can be a valuable reference on your next résumé.

WHEN TO BE CHEAP, WHEN NOT TO

Many moons ago, my grandfather bounced me up and down on his knee and said, "Always save your money and be cunning as a fox, and you'll always have some money in the old tobacco box."

Money is for spending and enjoying, so you shouldn't save it all. And instead of a tobacco box, you should probably save yours in an interest-earning savings account. But Granddad's message is a good one: It pays to be thrifty. For instance:

- If every dollar counts and you're going to want a box of Raisinets at the movies, buy it at a store, not at the theater. You'll bypass lines and save dimes.
- Buy woolly socks on sale in spring. In general, compare prices, look for sales, and buy items out of season.

- Try not to live by the adage, When the going gets tough, the tough go shopping!
- Look for interesting and affordable clothes and sundries in thrift shops, Salvation Army outlets, and antique stores.
- Read magazines and check out books at the library. (Except, of course, this book, a copy of which belongs in your permanent collection. Only kidding.)
- Trade clothes, magazines, records, and accessories with your friends and out-of-town cousins. (You can also tape each other's records.)
- If your message is short, send postcards instead of letters.
- Make or bake presents instead of buying them.
- When pennies count, order water in restaurants, not soda. Don't order more than you can eat.
- When shopping, always check expiration dates. No point spending today's money on yesterday's yogurt.
- Don't buy a faddish dress right after you cash your paycheck. Ask a clerk to hold it. Go home and see if your wardrobe runneth over. If you still want the dress, then buy it. (It's dry clean only? Add those costs into your budget.)
- Check boys' departments for bargains on T-shirts and other androgynous clothes.
- Don't always go for name brands. Sometimes generic will do.
- When you go shopping, bring a short list and a restrained friend, and leave your checkbook (if you have one) at home.
- No matter how cute, patient, or insistent the salesperson is, never buy too-tight shoes or anything else you don't want.
- Remember that the same restaurant is usually cheaper at lunch than at dinner, and the same movie is often cheaper at noon than at night.
- Don't spend lots of money on your boyfriend. Spend lots of time with him.

The other side of the coin is that you don't want to be a penny-pincher. Sometimes it's not worth it to scrimp. For instance:

- If you and two friends go out for dinner and their meals are a little more expensive than yours, split the bill in three anyway. It can be crass and mood dampening to whip out your calculator after a fun evening. If your meal cost a lot more than theirs, put that extra amount in the pot.
- If you're only parking for ten minutes, put a coin in the meter anyway. Spending the dime avoids risking the fine.

- If you're sending photos or a fat letter, stick on enough postage, even if it means getting the missive weighed. It's worth another stamp for the letter to get there without delay.
- Get your silk blouse dry-cleaned and your leather shoes reheeled. You'll save in the long run.
- If you're making a major purchase that should last many years, like a typewriter, computer, stereo, or car, it may be worth the extra bills to get the best product.
- If you're short on money and the gang is going for burgers, don't sit home. Go and order a drink or side dish.
- Tip. As a teen girl, you can probably get away with not tipping, and, yes, you could even leave a lonely penny in the sundae sauce, but it's decidedly not nice. And if you ever work as a waitress, you'll know that no tips is no fun. (Waitresses are underpaid because bosses expect them to make up the difference in tips.)

   How much should you tip? Waiters and waitresses: at least 15 percent of the total bill. Taxi drivers: 15 percent of the fare. Hairstylists: 15 percent to 20 percent of the bill, unless the person owns the salon (in which case you don't have to tip). Give at least a quarter or two to the person who shampooed your hair. The man at the airport who helps you with luggage: 50 cents to a dollar per bag. The person who checks your coat: at least a quarter. The valet who parks your car (my, you *are* fancy!): 50 cents minimum. The lady in the ladies room: You could scoot by her, but would you want that job? Put a dime or a quarter in her dish. When you are tipping, have a heart—round up. If you are at a club, you may not have to leave any tips. And in some restaurants, if eight or more of you gather for dinner, the tip will already be included in the bill.

Don't be a tightwad or a spendthrift. Money isn't fun if it's all stashed away. But if you binge-spend or never check prices, you may have to put yourself on a budget.

MONEY MISCELLANY

- Over half the women in America work outside the home, most for anywhere from 20 to 40 years.
- Women make up nearly half of the American work force and fill nearly one-third of the management jobs.
- When a man and a woman do the same job, the man almost

always earns more. (Of course we deserve equal pay for equal work, and if we fight for it, we may get it.)

- When a man and a woman do different jobs, the man often earns more because even today, many women settle for jobs that bring in less than $15,000 a year (bank teller, receptionist, secretary) rather than aiming for jobs that require more skills and offer more creativity, independence, and money.

- Check out classified ads. They show what jobs are available and at what salaries.

- Every contest has a winner. But your essay or photograph or beauty won't win the prize if you don't enter.

- The T-shirt that reads, "Anyone who says, 'Money Can't Buy Happiness' . . . Doesn't Know Where to Shop" is funny, but wrong.

- The song that goes, "All I need is the air that I breathe and to love you," is romantic, but wrong.

- Unless your boyfriend has an orchard full of money trees, share expenses when you go out. It's only fair.

- If you have a rich boyfriend, examine your motives. Be sure you'd love him if the stock market crashed. (I went out briefly with a guy who always treated for lobster—lobster!—sandwiches. I thought, "Boy, if we got married, I could travel to Rio, Peking, Cairo, Fiji." Then I thought, "I'd have to go there with him." We broke up.)

- If you have rich parents, try not to become spoiled, feel guilty, or take material comforts for granted. Treat your friends once in a while, but don't try to buy friends. Do volunteer work. And hope that someday you can be generous with your children.

- If your parents don't have wealth to spare, try not to resent friends who are handed money when you have to work for it. You're learning the value of a buck and how to make a living. That gives you an edge. And since you know how much life costs, you're not in for such a shock in the Real World.

- Stop comparing. There will always be people better off and worse off than you.

- When you first live on your own, half your salary may go toward rent and food. (Unless you live in Manhattan, in which case half may cover just rent. Could *that* be why New Yorkers stay slim?)

- Cars eat money. Don't buy one unless you need one.

- People who make fast money dealing drugs often wind up in jail and sometimes wind up dead before their time.

- Don't get robbed. Your purse should not be grabbable in a restaurant, disco, or public bathroom. Don't carry more money than you need. On trips, take traveler's checks.

- Theft is common; try not to get too attached to material objects. Remember the heirloom diamond engagement ring I told you I stopped biting my nails for? Well, I recently took it to a posh jeweler's for a slight repair. When I went to pick it up, I was told it had been a small part of a huge jewelry heist! Yes, I was distraught. But the ring was insured, and at least I still have my nails—and my husband!

- Don't stuff loose money into your purse; put it in your wallet. If you do lose a five-dollar bill, think how happy the person who finds it will be. Then be more careful.

- From my teen diary: *"I wrote down 'Dad owes me $10,' but I can't remember why, so he won't give it to me."* Keep *your* IOUs and UOMes straight and complete with explanations.

- If you save $1 a day, you'll have $365 at the end of the year.

- There's usually just enough money. There's rarely more than enough.

- Don't say, "Mr. Hollings is worth three million dollars." If he's a decent human being, he, like you, is worth more than money.

- "What is a cynic? A man who knows the price of everything and the value of nothing." So wrote Oscar Wilde.

- What is success? Not a mountain of money. According to Ralph Waldo Emerson, "To laugh often and much; to win the respect of intelligent people and the affection of children; to earn the appreciation of honest critics and endure the betrayal of false friends; to appreciate beauty; to find the best in others; to leave the world a bit better whether by a healthy child, a garden patch, or a redeemed social condition; to know even one life has breathed easier because you have lived. This is to have succeeded."

8
DRINK, DRUGS, etc.

AND I PROMISE NOT TO LECTURE

Did you know that girls who smoke and are on the Pill are running a serious health risk? That if you down a Quaalude with a few drinks, you could die?

This chapter is about cigarettes, pot, harder drugs, alcohol, and drunk driving.

You may already know a lot about this stuff. You may think you've heard it all. But I too knew a lot in high school, and I learned tons more researching this chapter. I hadn't realized, for instance, that booze and butts cause many more deaths than heroin. I hadn't even realized that a Planter's Punch has as many calories as a bowl of ice cream.

This chapter on substance use and abuse is not alarmist propaganda, although it does contain some alarming facts. And I admit: I'm hoping you don't smoke and drink and do drugs. At least not regularly. Many of the patterns you set now will be yours for keeps. You owe it to yourself to find out what you are getting into.

TOBACCO: WHEN IT'S GOOD TO BE A QUITTER

Test your smoking savvy.

1. How much money does a pack-a-day smoker spend on cigarettes each year?
   a. Under $100.
   b. About $200.
   c. Over $400.

2. How much tar does a pack-a-day smoker inhale each year?

    a.   A negligible amount.
    b.   About two tablespoons.
    c.   A full cup.

3. How long does it take for cigarettes to do a smoker any harm?
    a.   About three seconds.
    b.   About three weeks.
    c.   About three months.

4. How many adult smokers would like to kick the habit?
    a.   About 25 percent.
    b.   About 50 percent.
    c.   About 85 percent.

5. How much does the average smoker smoke per day?
    a.   Less than ten cigarettes.
    b.   Ten to twenty cigarettes.
    c.   Over twenty cigarettes.

6. How many lung cancer victims die within five years of diagnosis?
    a.   About 30 percent.
    b.   About 60 percent.
    c.   About 90 percent.

7. *True or False:* Smoking affects the smoker's sense of taste or smell.

8. *True or False:* If a pregnant woman smokes, her baby has an increased chance of being born small, weak, or dead.

9. *True or False:* Smokers die younger than nonsmokers.

10. *True or False:* If you smoke without inhaling, you don't up your risk of cancer.

11. *True or False:* Most adult smokers started as teen smokers.

12. *True or False:* It's easy to quit smoking.

And the answers are . . .

1.c. Think about the clothes, records, tickets, and gifts you could buy with $400. If your habit costs over a dollar a day, in less than three years, that's over $1000 going up in smoke!

2.c. Ugh. And tar, made up of thousands of solid chemicals, is carcinogenic (cancer-causing).

3.a. One puff speeds your heartbeat, raises your blood pressure, decreases the body temperature of your hands and feet, and replaces some of the oxygen in your blood with carbon monoxide—right when your accelerated heartbeat requires more oxygen. The smoke you inhale attacks the living tissue it encounters as it travels through your body, from throat and lungs to stomach and bladder.

4.c. Most adults smokers want to quit. Only 29 percent of adult Americans still smoke, down from 42 percent in 1964, according to a Gallup poll. Many got hooked before they knew how harmful tobacco was. Now that they are wising up, fewer are lighting up.

5.c. Less than 15 percent of high school seniors smoke more than half a pack a day, however.

6.c. Frightening. Yet lung cancer, which kills more Americans than any other cancer, is usually preventable. About 90 percent of lung cancer victims are smokers. Up to 90 percent of chronic lung disease is attributable to smoking. Thanks to cigarettes, almost as many women now die of lung cancer as breast cancer.

7. True. Not only does smoking stink, smokers have smoky-smelling clothes and bad breath (who was it who first said kissing a smoker is like licking an ashtray?), but the smoker's sense of smell and taste are impaired. Food tastes yummier and flowers smell prettier to nonsmokers and ex-smokers.

8. True. If you're pregnant, you're smoking for two. Your fetus is not getting as much oxygen as it normally would and is growing more slowly and with more difficulty. It's especially harmful to smoke after the fourth month of pregnancy. Crib death is more common among babies whose mothers smoked during pregnancy.

9. True. An average smoker's life is shortened by about the number of minutes spent puffing away, which usually comes out to six to eight years. At every age, there's a greater percentage of deaths among smokers than nonsmokers. (No, I'm not making this up. It's based on research of the American Cancer Society.) The good news: Once a smoker stops smoking, unless irreversible damage has been done, his or her body works immediately to clean up the mess and replace ravaged cells with healthy ones. Ten years after a heavy smoker quits smoking, he or she has the same chances of living a good long life as a nonsmoker.

10. False. Your chances of getting lung cancer are less than those of someone who inhales, but you've heard of mouth, lip, and tongue cancer, haven't you?

11. True. And 85 percent of them wish they could quit, remember?

12. False. Mark Twain claimed quitting was easy and said he'd "done it one hundred times." Quitting isn't easy. But over 33 million Americans have kicked the habit. Some quit cold turkey; others taper off. If you smoke, cut down on how much you smoke, don't smoke each cigarette to the very end, and inhale less deeply or less often. Filter, low-tar, or low-nicotine brands may be less harmful than regular brands, but each puff still contains such treats as formaldehyde, hydrogen cyanide, ammonia, and lead. The younger you are when you start smoking and the longer you smoke, the tougher it is to quit. But if you make it through your teens without starting, you probably never will take up the habit.

Among adults, per capita cigarette smoking recently dropped to a thirty-four-year low. Yet the percentage of teen girls who smoke is going up, not down. As many as 25 percent of teen girls smoke.

To you, emphysema, chronic bronchitis, and ulcers may not seem ominous. So what if smoking accounts for 30 percent of all cancers and doubles your chance of heart attack? No biggie. Teen smokers may not even know where the pharynx and larynx are, let alone worry about getting cancer there. But even young smokers catch colds and get winded and cough more often than nonsmokers. The ads that show smoking skiers, dancers, and mountain climbers are misleading, because smoking impairs athletic ability.

Smokers on the Pill further increase their chances of strokes, heart attack, blood clots. Cigarettes and oral contraceptives don't mix.

Here's a danger you may not have considered: More than 25 percent of all United States fires are caused by smokers.

If you smoke, stop kidding yourself. Stop killing yourself.

Tips on Quitting

- Throw away your cigarettes, lighters, ashtrays. (Or if you're cutting down in preparation for quitting, lock or wrap them up so that they will be hard to get at. Or buy a cigarette brand you don't like much.)
- Think about the surgeon general's printed warnings right on your cigarette packs. Make yourself read the warning every time you reach for a cigarette or read a cigarette ad.
- Write your own "Why I Want to Quit" list and read it whenever you feel like lighting up.
- If you crave smoking, the American Cancer Society suggests you try to crave quitting.
- If you smoke to relax, try quitting over vacation or after exams.
- Have a friend or family member quit (or break any bad habit) with you, or bet your friend $10 you won't smoke for two weeks. Cheer each other on; don't nag.
- Think: one day at a time. The first two days are the hardest.
- Spend those first days in no-smoking places: libraries, movies, theaters, stores.
- Tell your friends you've quit.
- Tell yourself you are stronger than your habits. Prove it.
- Stock up on sugarless gum, mints, celery sticks, carrots, grapes, popcorn, and other low-cal munchies. You won't gain weight

when you quit unless you start eating more than you used to. Which you won't do, right? Many quitters do gain weight, but one of four quitters loses weight, possibly because he or she feels more energetic and active after quitting.

- Consider chewing nicotine gum. It's not a solution, but it will satisfy your craving without polluting your lungs.
- Take up knitting or have a coin or bead to fool with when your hands want to play.
- Change your routine. If you love an after-lunch cigarette, get right up after lunch instead of lingering.
- If smoking gives you a lift, try taking walks and getting more sleep so you won't feel tired.
- Reward yourself by stashing away your cigarette money, and at the end of a week or two, treat yourself to a new pair of earrings or other little luxury. Think of what you want in terms of the cost in cigarette packs.
- Stay out of smoky bars and request the no-smoking section of planes, restaurants, and trains.
- If you slip up, don't give up. Lots of quitters succeed in unlearning and conquering the habit on the third or fourth try.
- Once you've kicked the habit, get rid of those yellow stains on your teeth and smile!

What If You Don't Smoke?

Congratulations. Unfortunately, your parents, boyfriend, fellow car poolers, and other folks who may blow smoke in your face are doing more than making your hair and clothes reek. They're increasing your chances of an unnecessary illness. Secondhand smoke is hazardous to your health. Pneumonia, bronchitis, and lung troubles are more common among children whose parents smoke than among other kids.

Sidestream smoke is particularly dangerous in closed or poorly ventilated rooms. When nonsmokers sit in a smoke-filled room, the amount of carbon monoxide in their blood doubles.

My parents smoked, so when someone next to me lights up, I've never been one to protest or flap my arms. Once a month or so, I've even said, "May I bum a cigarette?" But ever since I've read the American Lung Association and American Cancer Association brochures and seen their gross photos of diseased lungs, I haven't been at all tempted to smoke. Who knows? Next time a friend says, "Mind if I smoke?" I might even say, "Yes, because I like you."

MARIJUANA—IN MODERATION?

Okay, who out there has tried marijuana? Let's see some hands. I have. That doesn't make me cool and it doesn't make me a druggie. I mention it just so you won't think, "What does she know?" Getting high every once in a while is something I can't fully condemn (without being a hypocrite). But getting high regularly is something I could never encourage (without being a fool).

When you're a teen and are working to achieve independence, why become psychologically dependent on a drug? While you're growing and developing, why risk tampering with your mental and physical health? While you're striving to forge your future, why let a chemical slow you down and dampen your ambition?

Don't forget that pot is illegal, although laws and punishment for possession differ from state to state. And because joints aren't government regulated, you can never be sure of what you're putting into your body. Pot is generally stronger now than it was a few years ago. Sometimes half a toke of potent marijuana (particularly "sinsemilla") can leave you so disoriented, it's scary. Some pot is laced with unpredictable—and dangerous—angel dust (PCP). Some contains the poisonous herbicide paraquat.

Remember all those cigarette findings? Well, there's more tar in marijuana than in tobacco. And pot has been linked with respiratory disease. Pot smoke is inhaled deeply and held inside for a long time—not good news if you're a lung. Joints are smoked right down to the end, where tar is most heavily concentrated. Sure, you can argue that marijuana users smoke much less than cigarette fiends. Yet ignoring the possible connection between "killer weed" and cancer is naive.

Marijuana can make you gain weight, too. Oh, I know pot has no calories. But when you're high and get an attack of the munchies, your willpower goes down the tubes.

Are there other not-so-nifty long-term physical effects? Does THC—tetrahydrocannabinol, the main mind-altering chemical in pot—damage chromosomes or the body's ability to ward off infection? Does heavy pot smoking mess up women's menstrual cycles and fertility or lessen men's sperm count and sperm concentration? Does pot impair intellectual performance? Many researchers say yes. Why expose yourself to such risks? Why be a guinea pig? After all, it took decades for scientists to discover the hazards of tobacco.

Never smoke pot if you're driving or if you're pregnant. Playing with your life is one thing; taking chances with someone else's is another.

The short-term effects you may know about. Someone who is stoned usually has red eyes, a quickened heart rate, a distorted sense of time and space, not-so-hot coordination, and a faulty short-term memory. He or she may become extra withdrawn or talkative or euphoric. Or hungry or sleepy or horny. While the short-term effects last only several hours, THC can remain in the body for weeks, settling especially in the brain, reproductive organs, and fatty tissues.

How would getting stoned affect *you?* It depends on the pot, your mood, and whom you're with. First-time users may feel little effect. Regular users may find that marijuana magnifies moods. You're sad? You may get forlorn or paranoid. You're merry? You may get gales of giggles. Listening to music may seem more fun. The distortion of your perceptions can be a problem, however, if you make an important decision while stoned. For instance, don't imagine the romantic time you're having with a guy is based on love and respect when credit for the TLC may belong to the THC.

If you've ever been the straight one in a room full of wasted acquaintances, you know that the stoned sometimes think they're being mind-bogglingly insightful or so hilarious that it's a crime nobody brought a tape recorder. Yet their deep reasoning is usually off-target, their jokes more silly than witty. They may even seem zombielike.

Because marijuana sometimes provides a temporary sense of well-being, it often lessens an individual's drive and reorganizes priorities. It's easier to get stoned than to tackle your history homework. Heavy pot users may find their days are a daze; entire months may dribble away with little to show for them. Some potheads wind up listless, unproductive, insecure, apathetic, and sapped of energy and motivation. Some smokers may be less mature than their peers because they've been avoiding certain social encounters and academic challenges while their classmates have been learning to deal with responsibility.

How do you resist peer pressure if one of the nation's sixteen million regular pot users offers to "do" a bowl or offers a hit off a bong or a bite of an Alice B. Toklas brownie? Just say "No thanks." Don't go into the *why*s and *wherefore*s, and don't give any unwelcome holier-than-thou I-get-high-on-life sermons.

I don't think pot necessarily leads to harder drugs, but addicts start somewhere. Hash comes from the same *Cannibis sativa* plant that is harvested for marijuana. Because hash has more THC than pot, it is a stronger drug.

Speaking of stronger drugs . . .

HARDER DRUGS: FROM COCAINE TO HEROIN

Most kids who pop pills with friends in the basement of suburban homes don't end up as thieves, prostitutes, or murderers mainlining heroin with unsterile needles. But that doesn't make pill popping any safer.

More teens are deciding it's not worth it to take long-range risks for short-lived pleasure. According to one survey, however, 64 percent of high school seniors had used an illicit drug (in many cases marijuana) at some time. If drugs tempt you, remember:

- Never mix drugs and driving. You could kill someone, including youself.
- Never mix drugs and alcohol. You could die.
- Never mix different drugs. One plus one can equal five.
- Never take drugs if you're pregnant, unless a doctor prescribes them. Your baby could be born addicted or with defects.
- When abused, even over-the-counter drugs can be dangerous.
- Don't use illegal drugs blatantly or in public. You could go to jail without passing go.
- Don't make big decisions (about sex or work or love or . . .) while under the influence. You could use bad judgment and regret it afterward.
- Don't buy drugs on the street. The person pushing downers may be passing out sleeping pills—or poison.

Consider drug dependence. If you become physically dependent on a drug, you'll probably get sick when you try to go without it. You may suffer withdrawal symptoms like nausea, dizziness, chills, or worse. If you become psychologically dependent on a drug, you may feel nervous, bored, and depressed without it.

Consider the law. A college buddy of mine was caught selling LSD to a plainclothes policewoman. He ended up spending a lot of summer vacation in a drug rehabilitation institution and a lot of money on legal fees. And he was fortunate: Instead of throwing him in prison for up to twenty years, the judge put him on probation and assigned him two years' community service work.

Some people are in the money because of drug dealing. Others are in the slammer. Others are dead. Drug dealing carries all the risks of organized crime.

If you're with someone who overdoses on illegal drugs, however, don't sit around worrying about the legal ramifications of getting help. Call an ambulance. Your friend could die while you're weighing your options.

If you haven't dabbled with illegal drugs, don't. If you have, stop, or be extremely careful. For information about particular drugs, one place to write is: Do It Now, P.O. Box 5115, Phoenix, Arizona 85010.

If you have been misusing drugs and want to get your life together again, drug-free, discreet help is available. You can go to a treatment center without getting into legal trouble. Many counselors are ex-drug users. They don't judge; they understand and they help. If you don't know of a nearby center, call Alcoholics Anonymous or Narcotics Anonymous for referrals. Or call **PRIDE**, the National Parents' Resource Institute for Drug Education, (800-241-7946). In the evenings, try the Teen Troubles Hot Line (213-855-HOPE). In New York, you can call the New York State Drug Abuse Information Line (800-522-5353).

Step one to recovery is to eat well, exercise, get enough sleep and rest, and take vitamins to replenish what drugs have depleted. Respect your body. Don't be self-destructive. Your will, not my words, will determine whether you abstain or abuse.

Types of Drugs

I don't recommend these drugs. I recommend you know about them.

- *Narcotics* are painkillers that induce sleep and relaxation. Doctors often use them for patients who've had accidents or surgery. Narcotics come in two types: opiates and synthetics. Opiates are made from the opium poppy; examples are opium, morphine, codeine, methadone, and heroin. Synthetics are made in labs; examples are Demerol, Dilaudid, Perkadan, and Darvon.

Not only are narcotics extremely addictive, but they create tolerance, so addicts need more and more to get high and to keep from getting sick. Someone who injects drugs with an unsterile needle could wind up with hepatitis, abscesses, blood poisoning, fatal heart infections, or AIDS. Someone who needs to support a $1000-a-day heroin habit often resorts to crime. Overdoses can be fatal. And the life expectancy of an addict is much lower than that of a nonaddict.

- *Stimulants* speed up your nervous system and make you less tired and hungry but more restless or agitated.

If you take speed repeatedly, upping your blood pressure and increasing your heartbeat rate, you reduce your resistance and literally wear yourself out. You may sometimes seem paranoid, manic, hyperactive, even depraved. When you come down off speed, or "crash," you may feel irritable, lethargic, and exhausted, and your appetite returns in full force.

Someone who is crashing shouldn't take more speed but should sleep well, eat nutritiously, drink water and juices, and take vitamins. Many speed users, however, ignore their physical limits and do more speed, taxing and overloading their systems. They feel the "rush," and may stay thin and on the go, but they may also die younger. Speed damages the liver and kidneys. Speed really does kill.

A friend confided, "When I was a college sophomore, I studied by pulling all-nighters with the help of speed. Trouble is, the next few days were torture. So I got more and more behind on my work."

Amphetamines, once widely prescribed as diet pills, are now fairly scarce. Amphetamine lookalikes are sold on the street and often contain uncontrolled amounts of the drugs in decongestants, antihistamines, and diet aids, which include a lot of caffeine. Some users have died because their blood pressure shot up too high too fast.

Caffeine? Yes, it's an addictive drug found in coffee, tea, cola drinks, chocolate, and some over-the-counter drugs. There are lots of caffeine fiends around—it's the most widely used and abused stimulant in America. If you down over six or so coffees or even more colas a day, you may be hooked. The drug gives you get-up-and-go, but when it wears off, you may be more tired than before. Controversy is brewing as to the health hazards of caffeine. It's smart to cut back and opt for decaf or other drinks. Why strain your system, irritate your stomach lining, disturb your sleep patterns, and invite gastrointestinal problems? When heavy coffee drinkers first cut down, they may get headaches or feel drowsy, but before long, they rediscover the natural energy within themselves. Over half the nation drinks coffee—down from nearly 75 percent back in 1962. The number of coffee drinkers under age thirty has dropped dramatically.

Some people think they are "chocoholics." I wouldn't walk a mile for a Camel, but I might for a brownie. And if there's an open bag of peanut M & M's in the pantry, watch out. Am I hooked? No, because I don't need chocolate fixes. Even true chocolate addicts should take heart: Frozen Milky Ways are not illegal and won't change your consciousness so that you'd be useless in an emergency or would whisper a passionate "I love you" to some guy you scarcely know. Still, if you overindulge, try to cut back.

Cocaine is a stimulant used by over ten million Americans. Its popularity is on the rise, especially among professionals and preppies. At up to $3000 an ounce (and how do you know it's pure?), cocaine costs far more than gold. Its effects last briefly. Many users experience a tremendous short-lived high, and when the drug wears off, they want to reexperience it. They take repeated doses and become psychologically addicted, even obsessed. Many neglect responsibilities and relationships and become virtual slaves to the seductive drug. In college, I knew of a guy whose values got so distorted that he robbed a friend for cocaine. And I knew a girl who continued going out with a guy long after her feelings had faded because "he was always good for some lines of coke."

Coke strains the system and can cause cardiac and respiratory arrest. It can also cause nausea and insomnia and can damage nasal passages (if snorted) or veins (if injected). Some smoke the glamorized drug in a purified form called freebase, which can increase the chance of overdose and health problems. Cocaine used to be one of the ingredients in Coca-Cola until 1906, when the government stepped in. Any questions? Call the twenty-four-hour coke line at (800) COCAINE. They get about a thousand calls a day.

• *Hallucinogens* are psychedelic drugs that affect mind more than body, altering mood and changing perception. LSD, PCP, psilocybin mushrooms, peyote, mescaline, and MDA are examples.

LSD, dubbed "acid," was popular twenty years ago and is making a comeback now on some campuses. A little LSD goes a long way and can cause a whole kaleidoscopic sound and light show in your mind. A trip may begin around thirty minutes after taking a "hit" and may last for three to twelve hours. It may seem fun, profound, truth revealing, love inspired, colorful. Or it may be hell, particularly if the setting is wrong or the user was depressed or fearful or if the LSD is impure or the dose too high. In a single trip, the user may switch from seeming bliss to terror, insight to insanity, delusions of grandeur to feelings of insignificance. The following day users may feel sluggish, lightheaded, or downright horrible. LSD can cause nausea, but it is not addicting. Long-term side effects are still being studied. If someone you know ever panics because of a frightening trip, try to be warm, calm, and reassuring. Remind the user that the drug effects will wear off. (I for one am playing it safe— "depriving" myself of a possible good trip and not risking a bad trip or bad side effects.)

PCP, dubbed "angel dust," "tic," "tac," and "crystal," among other names, is an animal tranquilizer that is not only a hallucinogen but is also an anesthetic, a stimulant, and a depressant. Overdose is not uncommon, and the user can go into a coma. PCP is intense, strange, and dangerously unpredictable. A trip can last from several hours to several days. The body stores PCP, and regular use creates tolerance—the user needs more to get the same effect. PCP has gotten bad press from many drug users, but profit-minded dealers keep selling it in new forms with new names or mixing it with pot, heroin, LSD, or other drugs.

Continued use of LSD or PCP can impair memory and leave the user fried and strung out. In rare cases, a user may experience a flashback long after taking either drug. Flashbacks are unexpectedly going through part of the trip again and may be triggered by stress, fatigue, or use of other drugs.

Peyote buttons come from certain cacti. The user chews and swallows them, feels nauseated and often vomits, and "gets off" for a six- to ten-hour trip.

True pure mescaline is rarely available, although street dealers often dilute LSD or mix other substances and pass it off as mescaline. Other "kitchen chemists" sprinkle store-bought or even poisonous mushrooms with LSD and try to sell them as psilocybin mushrooms.

• *Inhalants* are chemicals that are sniffed or inhaled. They are cheap, accessible, and extremely dangerous. The high is neither exotic nor mystical. It's like being intoxicated with alcohol, but it takes place quickly and lasts for only five to fifteen minutes. The person who sniffs a volatile solvent like glue, gasoline, cement, paint, paint thinner, nail polish remover, or typing correction fluid may feel drunk for a short while—or may OD and go unconscious. The person who sniffs too much of an aerosol spray, like Pam, hairspray, deodorant, or spray shoe polish, can coat and clog his or her lungs and suffocate. Inhalants are particularly dangerous when mixed with alcohol.

Nitrous oxide or "laughing gas" makes users giddy and dreamy and is sometimes used as an anesthetic. When it is inhaled, the gas replaces the oxygen in the lungs. If users are not careful to breathe in fresh air and oxygen while taking nitrous oxide, they can vomit, become disoriented, and even die. MIT's student newspaper recently published an article about a chemical engineering major, a senior, who died from nitrous overdose. Such accidents are not as uncommon as you might think.

Amyl nitrite ("poppers") and butyl nitrite (sold as room deodorizer or liquid incense) produce short, intense "rushes," often repeatedly. Side effects are headaches, dizziness, nausea, dilated arteries, and lowered blood pressure.

Inhalants may damage the kidneys, liver, nerve endings, or bone marrow and may cause sudden death.

• *Depressants* produce sleep and relieve tension. Also called downers and sedative-hypnotics, they depress the nervous system, reduce the heart rate, and s-l-o-w y-o-u d-o-w-n. Of course, while they calm you or bring on sleep, they aren't changing the problem that was keeping you awake. If you grow used to them, you become less able to relax or sleep without them.

Sleeping pills and barbiturates are psychologically and physically addictive and produce a high level of tolerance. Overdosing can be lethal. Someone who takes a downer may look and act drunk for hours. Mixing alcohol with such drugs is courting death. Addicts should not try to go off these drugs without medical supervision, because withdrawal can be accompanied by complications such as seizure or kidney failure or delirium.

Types of depressants include tranquilizers (such as Librium and Valium, the most popular prescription drug in America) and sedative-hypnotic drugs like sleeping pills or barbiturates (such as Seconal, Tuinal, and Methaqualone, also called Mequin and Quaalude).

Let me stress again that I'm not encouraging you to seek chemical shortcuts to a fleeting, artificial nirvana. I hope I'm providing reasons for you to say no. Drugs are dangerous. These pages offer just bare-bone facts. If you want to know more, go to the library. There's more bad news than good.

THINKING ABOUT DRINKING

What don't you know about alcohol?

1. How long does it take the liver to metabolize and get rid of 12 ounces of beer?
   a. Under twenty minutes.
   b. About forty minutes.
   c. Over sixty minutes.

2. What percent of the population drinks on occasion?
   a. About 33 percent.
   b. About 50 percent.
   c. About 66 percent.

3. What percent of United States homicides and traffic deaths involve alcohol?
   a. About 15 percent.
   b. About 30 percent.
   c. About 50 percent.

4. About how many calories are in a can of beer?

    a.   200.
    b.   150.
    c.   100.

5. If you've drunk too much, what's the best way to sober up?
    a.   Sleep it off.
    b.   Drink black coffee.
    c.   Take a cold shower.

6. If you've drunk too much and wake up with a hangover, what must you do?
    a.   Drink a small dose of alcohol.
    b.   Drink coffee with aspirin.
    c.   Wait it out.

7. *True or False:* How drunk you get depends solely on how much you drink.

8. *True or False:* Alcohol abuse is the number-1 drug problem in the U.S.

9. *True or False:* Smokers who are drinkers increase their chances of getting cancer of the mouth, tongue, or throat.

10. *True or False:* Moderate drinking (one or two drinks a day) poses as many health risks as heavy drinking.

11. *True or False:* It's safe for pregnant women or mothers who are breast-feeding to drink.

12. *True or False:* No matter how much beer you drink, you can't get as drunk as you would if you were drinking the hard stuff.

13. How many synonyms for *drunk* can you come up with?

And the answers are . . .

1.c. It takes the liver over an hour to metabolize one can of beer, one glass of wine, or one shot of vodka. If you drink more than one glass per hour, you're on your way to getting drunk. Age, weight, and sex also affect tolerance. For most girls, a little goes a long way.

2.b. About 50 percent of the population drinks every so often—more if you count just adults. Over 10 million Americans are alcoholics. As many as one in five college students may be a problem drinker. A University of Michigan study of 17,000 high school seniors reported that 93 percent had tried alcohol. One in sixteen teens drinks daily.

3.c. Over half the traffic deaths and murders in America are alcohol related. About one-third of traffic injuries involve alcohol, as do well over two-thirds of all fatal falls, drownings, and fire fatalities.

4.b. Most alcoholic drinks are caloric but not nutritious. Sweet rum drinks (e.g., Planter's Punch) or creamy liqueur drinks (e.g., Sombreros) have many more calories than do wine spritzers or light beer. Plus, if you get buzzed, your willpower to resist the Doritos and dip goes down. Besides, you should never drink on an empty stomach. So although one can of beer may add up to only 150 calories, drinking is fattening. If you drink instead of eating? You'll suffer from malnutrition.

5.a. What do you get when you throw a drunk into an icy shower and administer coffee? A wet, wide-awake drunk. Fresh air isn't sufficiently sobering, either. Time and sleep are.

6.c. There's no surefire hangover helper. If you ever do wake up with the morning-after blehhcks, pour lots of water and fruit juice into your dehydrated body. (It would have been better to do that, between hiccups, before you went to bed.) Alcohol depletes the body's vitamin supply, too, which is another reason for downing juice or munching something healthful, like a banana. To speed your metabolism and help your liver get rid of the poisons you've subjected it to, take a cold shower or brisk walk or jog (unless your head throbs in protest). If you like, take aspirin or a nap. Alcohol disrupts the dreaming REM (rapid eye movement) sleep stage, so if you go to sleep drunk, you wake up less rested.

At the next party, instead of spending an evening getting drunk and blowing the following day recovering, don't drink, or sip just a little. You'll probably have more fun, and as a bonus you get to remember the good time.

By the way, although overindulging in beer can result in a hangover, it's more typical to feel awful after overdoing it on rum, brandy, or bourbon or after mixing different drinks. As a rule, the darker the drink, the higher its hangover potential. Some people get hung over after drinking next to nothing, whereas others drink with seeming impunity.

7. False. How drunk you become depends on how much you drink as well as how much you weigh, how much and how often you're used to drinking, how fast you drink, whether you've eaten, your body chemistry, your mood, where you are, and whether you're psyched to be drunk or sober. If a petite girl who has her period, hasn't eaten, and is not used to drinking chugs a beer at a party in a high-altitude city, it will go to her head much faster than the same drink would affect a large man sipping his daily beer over dinner in Manhattan. *What* you drink makes a difference, too: Straight liquor is absorbed into the bloodstream and makes drinkers drunker faster than liquor diluted with mixers.

8. True. Alcohol is a drug. Parents of alcoholics who sigh and say, "At least she's not into drugs," are deluding themselves.

9. True. Cancer, smoking, and drinking are often related.

10. False. "What is moderate drinking?" is a tricky question. Adults who drink one drink a night and do not become intoxicated are probably not problem drinkers and probably aren't risking heart, liver, or digestive tract problems. Some studies suggest that for *adults*, modest drinking can actually be healthful: A drink or two relieves stress and may decrease the risk of heart attack because it inhibits cholesterol buildup. Other studies suggest that even moderate drinking increases the chances of getting rectal and lung cancer. Mixing drinks with other drugs (legal or illegal) can be out-and-out hazardous, and more than two drinks daily can be physically and psychologically dangerous. To put it plainly: Too much booze pickles the brain.

11. False. Alcohol is the number-1 cause of drug-related birth defects in the United States. When a pregnant woman or nursing mother drinks, her fetus or baby also takes a swig. Women who drink heavily during pregnancy, especially during the first three months, up their odds of having babies who are abnormal, small, or exhibit mental or emotional problems, because the fetus can't metabolize alcohol efficiently. As the notices in many bars and liquor stores say, Drinking Alcoholic Beverages During Pregnancy Can Cause Birth Defects. Some experts say even one drink per week during pregnancy can invite trouble. Others believe once a mother is nursing, it's okay to drink an occasional beer.

12. False. Alcohol is alcohol. Yes, ounce for ounce, whiskey is much more potent than beer, but beer, wine, and whiskey all contain alcohol. Drink a little and you get tipsy. Drink a lot and you pass out.

13. I'm not sure if I'm giving or subtracting points for this one, but if you're smashed, trashed, plastered, plowed, sloshed, looped, crocked, soused, bombed, blotto, blitzed, tight, toasted, tanked, or tractored . . . you drank too much.

Many people don't drink. They don't like the taste, the calories, the blurry feeling. They're taking medication or are pregnant or are in training. They have bad associations with alcohol: a car accident, an abusive father, a negligent mother, a friend who got drunk and was taken advantage of. Or they just don't want to.

That's fine. That's smart.

It can be hard to resist peer pressure, but if you don't want to drink, don't. (Though some may scoff at you for teetotaling, others will admire your strength of character.) There's no point in breaking the law and messing up your body and mind. If you're offered beer at a party, say no thanks. You don't owe anybody any explanations.

If you do choose to drink, be responsible about it. Sip and nibble rather than guzzle on an empty stomach. Know your limit and stick to it. Never mix driving and drinking, and never mix alcohol with other drugs. If you take a cold pill or antihistamine with wine, for instance, you're combining two depressants, which is dangerous. If you're taking an antibiotic and drinking, the antibiotic may be inactivated. If you're combining an illegal barbiturate with booze, you may get so mellow that you never wake up again.

Alcohol is a depressant, not a stimulant. One drink may make you feel peppy and talkative, but that's because alcohol dulls judgment and inhibitions. It also dulls the body. Shakespeare himself elaborated on the paradox in *Macbeth* (II,iii): "Lechery, sir, it provokes and it unprovokes: it provokes the desire, but it takes away the performance."

A lot of alcohol slows your brain, making you slur words and lose coordination. Too much alcohol too fast can even result in coma or death. That's why the party-till-you-puke don't-leave-till-you-heave attitude is so stupid. About a thousand Americans die each year from overdosing on alcohol alone.

Sound scary? It can be. But whereas you get hooked on opiates or tranquilizers in mere weeks, it usually takes longer to become physically addicted to alcohol. Of course, many teens are problem drinkers without being alcoholics. If you regularly drink to get drunk, or throw up after drinking, or end up kissing a guy when you didn't intend to, or make a spectacle of yourself when you are out of it, beware! Strive to control your habit before it starts controlling you.

ALCOHOLISM

For many people, alcohol becomes a poison, a necessity, and a nightmare.

You probably know a few alcoholics. One out of ten people who drink become alcoholic. Less than 5 percent of alcoholics are bowery bum winos or derelicts; most are ordinary working people. About 50 percent have an alcoholic parent. No one is too young to be an alcoholic. Some alcoholics drink regularly; some go on sprees or binges. Most suffer withdrawal symptoms if deprived of the drug.

Alcoholism is a disease. Alcoholics have lost control of their drinking and drink even though the habit wreaks havoc on their health and professional, academic, financial, and/or personal lives. Alcoholism, after heart disease and cancer, is the third great killer in the United States. Is the alcoholic only hurting himself? No. He's often hurting his family and his co-workers, and if he drives drunk, someday he may inadvertently commit murder on the road.

Although alcoholism is a progressive illness, it is treatable. Recovery usually means swearing off liquor for good and forever. The thousands of alcoholics who have been helped through Alcoholics Anonymous swear off booze one day at a time. Families and friends of alcoholics have also found strength and some solutions through Alateen and Al-Anon.

Alcoholics Anonymous (AA) got its start fifty years ago in Ohio. Now groups meet in over 110 countries. At AA meetings, members are committed to staying sober and helping each other stay sober. They share personal stories about their battles with alcohol. The only requirement for AA membership is the desire to stop drinking. Meetings are free; donations are accepted.

AA is not associated with any particular religion, although there is an AA prayer:

> God grant me the serenity to accept
> the things I cannot change,
> courage to change the things I can,
> and wisdom to know the difference.

One more quick quiz. Answer the following questions *yes, no* or *sometimes*.

1. Are your grades sinking because of your drinking?
2. Do you skip class to drink?
3. Do you lie about how much you drink?
4. Do you forget things or have blackouts (memory loss) because of drinking?
5. Do you drink to escape?
6. Do you drink in the morning?
7. Do you need a drink to feel self-confident?
8. Do you get drunk when you hadn't intended to?
9. Do you think about drinking a lot?
10. Do you drink on the sly or hide liquor?
11. Do you drink alone?
12. Do you drink instead of eating?
13. Do you drink a lot in a hurry?
14. Do you drink until you pass out?
15. Do you drink when you're angry or stressed?
16. Do you get into trouble when you drink?
17. Do you look up to friends who drink a lot?
18. Has your drinking affected your reputation and friendships?
19. Has your drinking lowered your ambition?
20. Have you tried to quit or cut down your drinking and failed?

Add up the *yeses* and the *sometimeses*. If you have more than three, take it as a warning. Try a week on the wagon. If you think alcohol is becoming a problem in your life, consider calling Alcoholics Anonymous. No one needs to know that you attended a meeting unless you tell. If there's no listing in your phone book, write to:

General Service Office
Box 459
Grand Central Station
New York, N.Y. 10163

For other alcohol information, write to:

The National Council on Alcoholism
733 Third Avenue
New York, N.Y. 10017

Or for an alcohol or drug problem, call:

Care Unit
(800) 854-0318

If you think it would be hard to stop drinking now, think how much harder it would be to stop later. You can control an addiction, but you can never truly cure it. So don't let yourself get hooked in the first place.

DRUNK DRIVING

If you've ever been in a car in which the driver was drunk, consider yourself lucky to be here. Of the 26,000 people a year who die because of drunk driving, 8,000 to 9,000 are teens. Some were drunk when they fell asleep at the wheel or said hello to a tree. Many were perfectly sober, minding their own business, singing along with Michael Jackson on the car radio, when some inebriated jerk plowed into them. Police officers and coroners don't enjoy telling parents that their kid is dead, but they do it all the time. Highway crashes are the leading cause of death in the sixteen- to-twenty-five-year-old age group, and millions are injured yearly, too. American drunk driving has tripled since 1972 among people under eighteen.

I knew people who died young because they mixed drinking and driving: the brother of a girl I used to baby-sit for, a guy I once worked with, the daughter of a writer friend. What a waste. It's too sad to run into the mother of a classmate at the grocery store and watch her eyes fill with tears as you mumble how sorry you were to hear about the death of her son. It's too sad to hear a middle-aged friend tell you, her voice shaking, that as much as she tries, she can't remember the sound of her daughter's laugh.

Frightening but true: On any given weekend night, many drivers who are sharing the road with you and me are not all there. Alcohol has dulled their reflexes, and if they are distracted for a second, they may crash smack into us.

Teens are just learning to drink and just learning to drive. When they combine the two, many are dangerous to themselves and to others.

Some states have a legal drinking age of twenty-one. Others have a lower legal drinking age. Teen traffic fatalities often occur around the border between such states. A group of teens who are too young to drink in Illinois will drive to Wisconsin and get smashed. Then they'll weave their way home. Most arrive. Some don't.

If a cop catches you driving drunk, you may be asked to touch your nose with your eyes closed, recite the alphabet, walk a straight line heel to toe, stand on one leg, pick up a coin, or perform other tasks that seem laughably simple—if you're sober. You may also take a breathalyzer test to determine if you were driving under the influence. If you are arrested for driving under the influence (DUI), it could cost you hundreds of dollars in legal fees and higher insurance rates. If you're fortunate, it won't cost you car repairs or your life.

The legal limit for intoxication in most states is a blood alcohol level of .10 percent (measured in grams of alcohol per 100 milliliters of blood). Before you even feel drunk, your ability to drive safely goes down. If you've had four or five drinks, you are probably legally intoxicated. If you drive, your chances of getting into an accident quadruple. I hope you don't try to outwit the statistics. (And if you do, I hope I don't happen to be cruising along in the next lane.)

Respect yourself and respect other drivers. If you are drunk at a party, don't drive home. Have a friend drive or call your brother or sister or parents or a cab (always carry enough money to get home on your own). If your date has the car and is drunk, don't risk both your lives. Refuse to let him drive. Do not worry about offending him when he is about to put your life on the line. Take his keys and have someone else do the driving. I know that's hard, but that's what friends are for. Do *not* let a drunk drive.

Some friends have a system: When they go together to a party, one member of the group stays absolutely sober. At the next party, they alternate, and another person keeps away from the booze. Some schools have systems, too. Many have a number you can call if you need transportation home.

Today, this very day, about seventy Americans will die in alcohol-related traffic accidents. It may seem cool to have "road pops," and backseat drinkers may seem more socially acceptable than backseat drivers. But it's not cool to die or maim or kill.

I often drive. I sometimes drink. But I firmly believe: none for the road.

Among the not-for-profit citizen activist groups against drunk driving are:

SADD (Students Against Driving Drunk)
P.O. Box 800
Marlborough, Mass. 01752
(617) 481-3568

MADD (Mothers Against Drunk Driving)
669 Airport Freeway
Suite 330
Hurst, Texas 76053
(817) 268-6233

RID (Remove Intoxicated Drivers)
Box 520
Schenectady, N.Y. 12301
(518) 372-0034

By the way, even sober drivers aren't always safe drivers. A ton of moving metal can be a lethal weapon.

I still remember my boast to a blond junior I had an unrequited crush on. The car I was in won a race to the Bum Steer restaurant. "We got up to ninety miles per hour," said I, oh-so-self-impressed. "That was stupid," he snapped. My bubble burst, but I realized he was right (and wouldn't you know it?—his "caring" and maturity made my crush even stronger).

Reckless driving *is* stupid. Drive carefully. Don't race through the red light on this block just to be first at the red light on the next one. Watch out for the other guy. Stay alert on long and short trips. Two out of three traffic deaths occur within twenty-five miles of the driver's home. And put your seat belt on—traffic cops hardly ever have to unbuckle dead people.

Enough. Let's move on to something more upbeat. How about a chapter of quizzes?

9

A Quintet of
QUIZZES

GETTING TO KNOW YOU

ARE YOU *TOO* NICE?

We all know people who would give us the shirt off their backs, and others who wouldn't give us the time of day. Which are you? After each question, circle the answer that best describes you. Then check the scoring.

1. You just baby-sat from 9:30 A.M. to 2:30 P.M. The children's mother returns, takes out her wallet, and says, "Let's see, I owe you for four hours." You
   a. point out politely that you believe she means five hours.
   b. accept payment for four hours because you hate to contradict her and you want her to ask you back.
   c. tell her you will not be cheated out of money you earned.
   d. say, "Hmm, 9:30 to 10:30, 11:30, 12:30, 1:30, 2:30" in a hesitant voice.

2. You don't like your date that much, but he did take you to a fancy restaurant for dinner. On the way home, he drives down a dark country road, pulls over, and turns to kiss you. You
   a. talk a mile a minute each time he leans toward you.
   b. push him away and demand he drive you home immediately.
   c. kiss him back—you figure you sort of owe it to him.
   d. tell him you enjoyed the evening, but you're not ready to start a romance with him.

3. Your class had an impossible pop quiz in history this morning. The teacher warned you not to tell the afternoon students because they'd take the quiz later and it would be graded on a curve. At noon, a girl with a locker near yours asks, "How was history?" You

    a.   pretend you didn't hear her and compliment her blouse.

    b.   say, "You'll find out," and walk away.

    c.   tell her about the quiz, and when she pleads, whisper the questions, too.

    d.   say, "Not much fun" and change the subject.

4. A guy invites you to the movies and suggests a gory film you're sure you'd hate. You

    a.   say, "Sounds great to me. I've been dying to see it."

    b.   ask, "What else is playing?"

    c.   say, "I will if you really want to."

    d.   say, "No. I can't stand violent movies."

5. You're cramming for tomorrow's French test when a long-winded friend calls. You

    a.   say, "I just can't talk to you now."

    b.   talk to her for nearly an hour.

    c.   say, "Let's talk for five minutes, then I've got to go back to my studying."

    d.   gasp, "My father is calling me—I've got to go!"

6. A classmate who has borrowed lunch money from you before but has never paid you back asks if you'll lend her a few quarters. You

    a.   say no and remind her she still owes you several dollars.

    b.   say, "I don't have any extra money today."

    c.   hand her 75¢.

    d.   say, "Forget it!" and grimace so she knows you can't believe she had the gall to ask.

7. A friend is returning a yellow sweater she borrowed—with a brand new chocolate stain in the front. You

    a.   say, "How dare you try to give my sweater back in this condition!"

    b.   ask her if she tried hand-washing or dry-cleaning the sweater.

    c.   say, "Thank you" and pretend not to notice the stain.

    d.   hold the sweater up in such a way that she knows you see the stain and hope she volunteers an explanation.

8. You and a dozen others are on a committee to plan a class picnic. A meeting was scheduled for tomorrow at 4, but the chairperson suddenly wants to switch it to 3:15. She asks you to phone everyone about the change. You

    a.   say, "I won't be home tonight, so I can't help you."

    b.   start looking up numbers and plan an evening on the phone.

    c.   say, "I'll make a few calls, but let's divide the names."

    d.   declare, "You're the one who's changing things—you make the calls!"

9. Every time you and your buddy Jim get together after school, you end up helping him wash his car or mow the lawn. Today he phones and invites you to keep him company while he builds a bookshelf. You

    a.   say, "No. But if you're ever ready to do something fun outside your house, let me know."

    b.   say, "I'll be right over." After all, he does enjoy being with you.

    c.   say, "Sorry, I'm busy right now."

    d.   say something like, "I'll help you under one condition: Afterward we go for ice cream and a walk."

10. Your elderly aunt has shown you three family scrapbooks, and you're feeling antsy as she opens the fourth. You
    a.   politely ask, "Who is this couple and how do you know them?"
    b.   say, "I'm really tired of scrapbooks."
    c.   suggest you go for a stroll and save the others for later.
    d.   ask, "Aren't your eyes getting tired?"

11. Five girls cut in line in front of you at a concert. You
    a.   step in front of them, shoving each one slightly so they know you're annoyed.
    b.   clear your throat several times loudly and stare at them.
    c.   stand quietly behind them—no point in causing a fuss.
    d.   say, "Excuse me, but the line starts back there."

12. Your crush has finally asked you out, and you've ordered burgers at a crowded restaurant. Suddenly your next door neighbor and her grade school son appear at your table. The mother gives you a cheery hello and asks, "May we join you?" You
    a.   bury your head in the menu until your neighbor, bewildered, walks off.
    b.   say that you look forward to dropping by for a visit later, but that you and your friend have a few things you need to discuss between yourselves.
    c.   say, "We're having a private conversation."
    d.   hear yourself stammer, "Sure, pull up some chairs."

13. A popular girl always asks for your help with math homework during study halls but barely speaks to you outside school. Here she comes, trotting over sweetly, geometry book in hand. You
    a.   say, "Get lost, you hypocrite!"
    b.   help her, but make a point of sighing, drumming your fingers, and checking your watch.
    c.   help her as usual—it's easier than making a scene.
    d.   explain that you'd feel better about helping her in school if she were more friendly out of school.

14. You've already put in plenty of overtime at the store where you clerk. Your quitting time is 5 P.M., but your employer begs you to stay until closing at 9. You're exhausted, you promised your parents you'd be home for dinner, and you have to finish reading a novel for English. You
    a.   say, "I have evening plans, but if you really need me, maybe I can stay."

b.   apologize and refuse to work because you have other commitments.

c.   agree to work without complaint.

d.   complain that she forgets you have a personal life.

15. A guy you don't like at all keeps calling to ask you out. You've made umpteen excuses: baby-sitting, family plans, out-of-town guests, even washing your hair. But he never catches on, and he calls you again. You

   a.   hang up as soon as you recognize his voice.

   b.   explain as tactfully as you can that you like him, but "only as a friend."

   c.   say, "I have a lot of homework to do, but thanks for asking, and call again sometime."

   d.   consent to go out with him, then kick yourself for being so stupid.

Scoring

Are you too nice? Not nice enough? Find out your kindness quotient by circling the number following each letter you selected, then adding up your score.

	a.	b.	c.	d.
1.	a. 1	b. 3	c. 4	d. 2
2.	a. 2	b. 4	c. 3	d. 1
3.	a. 2	b. 4	c. 3	d. 1
4.	a. 3	b. 1	c. 2	d. 4
5.	a. 4	b. 3	c. 1	d. 2
6.	a. 1	b. 2	c. 3	d. 4
7.	a. 4	b. 1	c. 3	d. 2
8.	a. 2	b. 3	c. 1	d. 4
9.	a. 4	b. 3	c. 2	d. 1
10.	a. 3	b. 4	c. 1	d. 2
11.	a. 4	b. 2	c. 3	d. 1
12.	a. 2	b. 1	c. 4	d. 3
13.	a. 4	b. 2	c. 3	d. 1
14.	a. 2	b. 1	c. 3	d. 4
15.	a. 4	b. 1	c. 2	d. 3

15 to 25. Congratulations! You know what you want and you're strong enough to go after it, yet you always remember to take other people's feelings into consideration. When problems arise, you deal with them directly. Because you are courteous and confident, your peers respect you.

26 to 37. There are lions and there are lambs, and you fall somewhere in between. You usually manage to get yourself out of unpleasant predicaments, but instead of confronting an issue head on, you often escape through the back door, hemming and hawing and saying, "Uh, I don't think so" or "I can't, really." The trouble with being wishy-washy? You find yourself in the same bind again and again. Your excuse may work once, but you have to keep thinking up new ones. Be sensitive, but start speaking your mind to eliminate the guesswork.

38 to 49 Giving, thoughtful, helpful: That's you. But being a pushover isn't much better than being pushy, so don't let your sweet generosity run wild. If you lend out your only umbrella when you're caught in a rainstorm, that's being nice to another but not nice to yourself. Many love you for your soft heart, yet others try to take advantage of you. Some sucker you into doing them favors, then, instead of showing appreciation, they may treat you like a doormat. When you're too concerned with pleasing others, you forget to please yourself. So give, give, give—but don't give yourself away. After all, *you* count most of all. Develop your self-esteem by asking yourself what you want and learning to express it diplomatically.

50 to 64 Watch out! You're fearless and firm and you usually get your way, but your brusqueness may be scaring off friends. It's possible to be forceful without being rude and to make your wishes clear without hurting or alienating others. Brush up on your manners, and imagine how the other person will feel before you say or do something you may regret later. Being assertive is one thing. Being aggressive is another.

HOW WELL DO YOU KNOW YOUR BEST FRIEND?

Let's say you know your best friend adores Fitzgerald, freckles, and peppermint ice cream . . . but do you know her future plans? Or her favorite kind of party?

Take this quiz with your best friend at your side. Read each question together; then, on separate pieces of paper, write the number of the question and the letter of the answer that best describes your friend. She should choose the answer that best describes herself. When you've completed all fifteen questions, find out your score and see how much you really know (or don't know!) about her. Then take the quiz again and find out how much she really knows about you!

1. If she could specify only one quality in a computer-matched blind date, she would ask that her date be
   a. intellectual.
   b. handsome.
   c. sensitive.
   d. athletic.

2. If a guy wanted to win her over, he'd do best by giving her
   a. a framed photograph of the two of them.
   b. fresh bread that he baked himself.
   c. a roll of quarters for Pac man.
   d. a bouquet of wildflowers.

3. She'll admit she's sometimes envious of you because
   a. you get along with your parents.
   b. you're so popular with guys.

    c. you're so good at sports.

    d. you get such good grades.

4. Provided she meets the right guy, she thinks a good age to get married is
    a. 21 or younger.
    b. 22 to 26.
    c. 27 or older.
    d. never.

5. If she won a lottery, she'd probably
    a. buy a completely new wardrobe.
    b. travel around the world.
    c. contribute most of the money to a worthy cause.
    d. save most of the money for her education and future.

6. The best way to snap her out of a bad mood would be to
    a. take a walk and talk.
    b. accompany her to a movie.
    c. blast her favorite album and dance crazily together.
    d. go out and splurge on everything from ice cream to makeup.

7. As for legislating equal rights for women, she
    a. supports the concept completely.
    b. thinks it's a bad idea.
    c. thinks it has pros and cons.
    d. knows little about it.

8. Her second favorite subject at school is
    a. math.
    b. foreign language.
    c. social studies.
    d. English.

9. Which of the following situations would upset her most?
    a. if she received a D+ on a report.
    b. if a girl flirted with her boyfriend.
    c. if she saw a friend shoplifting.
    d. a political crisis in the news.

10. If someone offered her a Quaalude, she'd probably
    a. ask, "What's that?"
    b. say, "Great!"
    c. say, "No thanks."
    d. steer clear of that person from then on.

11. Her high hopes after high school include
    a. getting a job.
    b. taking time off to work or travel, then going to college.
    c. immediately beginning two or more years of college.

d.   four years of college and then on to graduate school.

12. If she could magically change one part of her body, it would be her
    a.   legs.
    b.   bosom.
    c.   hair.
    d.   nose.

13. She would most enjoy spending an afternoon
    a.   sunning at the beach.
    b.   hiking in the mountains.
    c.   shopping in the city.
    d.   playing or watching a ball game.

14. At a school dance, she's most likely to wear
    a.   khaki pants, a polo shirt, and Top-siders.
    b.   a frilly dress, high heels, and a flower in her hair.
    c.   faded jeans and a T-shirt and some zany accessory.
    d.   a prairie-style skirt and blouse.

15. Her favorite kind of party is
    a.   a slumber party, complete with séances, gossip, and raiding the refrigerator.
    b.   a big open house with old friends and new faces.
    c.   a small pizza party with her very best buddies, male and female.
    d.   a masquerade party.

Scoring

How well did you guess each other's responses? Compare your answers and add up the number of answers that match.

11 to 15 You know each other very well and you share the gift of true friendship. Your conversations are open and trusting, whether you're discussing parties, pastimes, or politics. You're both lucky. But remember, friendship is like an old house—the shelter is warm and the memories happy, but the roof may spring an occasional leak. Take care of your treasured bond and try not to let a new boyfriend, a summer apart, or any other circumstance ever weaken it.

6 to 10 You know a lot about each other, and you know you enjoy being together. Maybe the reason you can't predict every twist and turn of your best friend's personality is that her opinions change often, or that she's more comfortable keeping certain thoughts private. Perhaps, with time, you'll explore new topics of conversation and learn even more about each other. Meanwhile, your friendship is important to you both, and only you two know if it feels wonderful as is or if it needs a bit more talking, more listening, more caring.

0 to 5 Why so few answers in common? Is your friend that mysterious? That private? That shy? Or could it be that you've been doing all the talking? Maybe there's a reason she isn't opening up to you. Did she ever tell you a secret only to find out that you'd spread it? Or perhaps you never think aloud with her, so she hesitates to be the first to expose her innermost thoughts. Begin to share your thoughts and insights, and learn to ask about and listen to hers. You'll both win in the long run.

ARE YOU AND HE A GOOD MATCH?

Are you and your boyfriend really right for each other? Are you like two peas in a pod or like apples and oranges—and which makes for a more compatible couple?

Like the friendship quiz, you two take this in tandem. Unlike that quiz, you each answer for yourselves. You and your boyfriend should each number a separate piece of paper from 1 to 25. Read the questions together, then write down the letter of your answer. When you finish, add up the answers you have in common and check the scoring.

1. Your bedroom is
    a. stylish, immaculate—right out of a decorating magazine.
    b. neat but "lived in."
    c. somewhat eccentric—there may be a huge mobile hanging from the ceiling or a hand-painted mural on the wall.
    d. buried under layers of books, clothes, and records.

2. If you've planned to meet a friend at 3 P.M., you arrive
    a. ten minutes early.
    b. at 3 P.M. exactly.
    c. ten minutes late.
    d. who knows? There is no pattern to your punctuality.

3. Which best describes your attitude toward animals?
    a. You're a cat person: Happiness is a kitten purring in your arms.
    b. You're a dog person: Nothing beats walking with a tail-wagging canine.
    c. You adore horses, parakeets, turtles—any creature with fur, feathers, or fins.
    d. Animals? Yech! They bite and shed, they're noisy and messy, and some even make you sneeze.

4. On Friday, you're paid $50 for your part-time job. This weekend, you'll probably
    a. spend $60.
    b. buy one big item that costs around $40.
    c. save $25 and spend the rest on little things.
    d. put it all in the bank.

5. As far as astrology goes . . .
   a. when you learn someone's birthday, you feel you know a lot about that person's character. You read your horoscope every day, and if it says "Avoid travel," you stay home.
   b. you think sun signs have some effect on personalities, and you often read your daily horoscope.
   c. you'll admit some Virgos are perfectionists, but when you read your horoscope, it's just for kicks.
   d. you think zodiac signs and horoscopes are nonsense.

6. When it comes to clothes,
   a. you like being in style and you update your wardrobe regularly.
   b. you favor the classic and conservative (the preppy look, for instance).
   c. you take it to the limit with wild colors and surprising combinations.
   d. you've never gone to school naked, but you hardly notice what you wear.

7. Your feeling about school sports is that you
   a. would love to be the most valuable player on the team.
   b. would like to at least make the team.
   c. enjoy going to games and meets.
   d. couldn't care less about school athletics.

8. In school, you especially enjoy
   a. math and science
   b. English, foreign language, and history.
   c. art and music.
   d. lunch period and the final bell.

9. When a substitute teacher is at the desk, you
   a. help the sub figure out who's who and what's what.
   b. neither help nor hinder.
   c. slam your books on the floor and draw pictures on the blackboard. Your motto: Sink the Sub.
   d. skip class.

10. It's 11 P.M., your usual bedtime, but tonight you still have lots of homework. You
    a. go to bed; sleep is important, too.
    b. stay up another 45 minutes finishing assignments, however haphazardly.
    c. continue working conscientiously until you're satisfied with your efforts.
    d. set the alarm for 6 A.M.

11. When you see two students comparing answers during a quiz, you
    a. are appalled and tell your teacher to watch for cheating.
    b. wish you were sitting next to them—some tests are impossible!
    c. figure they're only cheating themselves and forget about it.

d. feel angry that cheating is so commonplace, and frustrated that their scores may upset the grading curve.

12. Your ideal vacation is
   a. skiing down snowy mountain trails.
   b. going to a city you've never seen and exploring its restaurants, museums, shops, parks, and sites.
   c. getting together with relatives at a family reunion.
   d. staying home and catching up on reading, seeing friends, and everything you don't usually have time for.

13. If you spent a week on a warm beach, you'd
   a. enjoy lolling around with no decisions to make except which flavor ice cream to order.
   b. use a lot of effort and oil to achieve the perfect tan.
   c. spend the whole time swimming and body surfing.
   d. complain about sand, heat, sunburn, and boredom.

14. You've won a free round-trip vacation to anywhere, so you're packing your bags for
   a. China.
   b. Kenya.
   c. France.
   d. Hawaii.

15. Of the following meals, your favorite is
   a. a cheeseburger, fries, and a pickle.
   b. stir-fried shrimp with peapods.
   c. tacos and hot chili.
   d. veal scallops in lemon butter.

16. You find swearing in public
   a. normal for guys and girls.
   b. okay for guys but not for girls.
   c. somewhat offensive.
   d. totally vulgar and off-putting.

17. Cigarette smoking is
   a. okay every once in a while, but you'd hate to be hooked.
   b. enjoyable—you don't feel guilty about smoking.
   c. not for you, but it doesn't bother you when others smoke.
   d. unattractive, unhealthy, and impolite.

18. Regular exercise? Yes, you
   a. jog daily, rain or shine.
   b. do sit-ups, pushups, or aerobic stretches every so often.
   c. practice a sport regularly, on a team or solo.
   d. make many round trips to the candy store.

19. Which do you go to most often?

    a. The symphony or ballet.
    b. Art museums.
    c. The theater.
    d. Baseball or football games.

20. When you are 18, you
    a. plan to vote in every election and campaign for candidates.
    b. plan to vote in national and local elections.
    c. plan to vote only in the presidential elections.
    d. doubt you'll vote.

21. If you found $20 on the floor of a store, you would
    a. pocket it and feel giddy.
    b. pocket it and feel guilty.
    c. quietly ask, "Did anybody lose some money?"
    d. turn it in to a salesperson.

22. How long will you be a student? You'll probably
    a. get your high school diploma.
    b. attend a two-year college.
    c. graduate from a four-year college.
    d. go to graduate school.

23. Your ideal home is a
    a. modern condominium in the heart of a bustling city.
    b. restored nineteenth-century farmhouse in the country.
    c. brick house in the suburbs.
    d. wood-shingle house at the seashore.

24. You think divorce is so common nowadays because
    a. marriage itself is too limiting. It's unrealistic to expect two people
        to stay married for decades and decades.
    b. people get married too soon and for the wrong reasons.
    c. married couples don't try hard enough to get along.
    d. women's and men's roles are changing too fast today—no one
        knows what he or she wants.

25. Children? Ideally you'd like to have
    a. none.
    b. one or two.
    c. three or four.
    d. five or more.

Scoring

How many times did your answers match? Add up and see what your score means.

17 to 25 A toast to two of a kind! You and your special guy are well suited.
You have similar values, tastes, opinions, and habits, and you are as compatible

in school as you are in your leisure time. Enjoy yourselves, perfect pair, but be careful not to lose your individuality. In the long run, you'd be bored going out with your double. Continue to grow separately and together, discussing insights, feelings, and projects. Being a good match is a good start; the future is up to you.

8 to 16 You two have your differences, but many of your priorities, character traits, and viewpoints are similar. You and your boyfriend probably complement each other well and have a dynamic, exciting relationship, with plenty to talk about all the time. If you can learn to debate politics, religion, and which movie to see without causing hard feelings, you're all set. Compromise and tolerance are the necessary glues to keep you both smiling for a long time.

0 to 7 You've just proved the old adage: Opposites attract. Lots of liberals and conservatives, spenders and savers, cat people and dog people, sloppies and neatniks do make happy couples. If you can each allow for some give or take, you may find you get along as well as the couples who seem like identical twins. But your bond *is* more challenging. Little quirks can drive you crazy, like his being late when you're always early. And big issues must be reckoned with: If you want a Ph.D. and he wants to drop out after eleventh grade, you probably aren't a heaven-made match. For now, have fun, learn from each other, and enjoy finding out why your characters, values, and tastes are often different.

ARE YOU THE JEALOUS TYPE?

Nobody is immune to jealousy. But while the green-eyed monster makes some feel blue and makes some see red, others rarely suffer the aches of envy. Test yourself honestly in the following situations. Then check the scoring to learn how you can understand and tame the monster.

1. The science teacher assigned lab partners, and your boyfriend got matched with a cute girl who, you happen to know, has a crush on him. You
   a. don't worry—after all, examining a paramecium together isn't in the same league as going out.
   b. quiz your boyfriend lightheartedly on everything the two of them say and do on lab days.
   c. are very uncomfortable with the arrangement but don't say anything.

2. You're upset, so you call a close out-of-town friend. You catch her in top spirits: She's made honor roll, has a new boyfriend, and landed a summer job on a cruise ship. You
   a. listen, mumble "That's great," swallow the lump in your throat, and tell her your saga.
   b. are delighted for her, say, "Congratulations" and ask for all the details, not mentioning your woes.

    c.   say that your mom suddenly needs to use the phone, and cut the conversation short.

3. Your sister never wears jewelry or makeup and is oblivious to fashion and diet. Yet she always looks stunning! You
    a.   wish she'd wake up, just occasionally, with a few pimples on her nose and forehead.
    b.   often remind yourself that while she's particularly pretty, you're especially bright, funny, or artistic.
    c.   are proud to have such a beautiful sister.

4. He still speaks wistfully of his former girlfriend, who moved away last year. You
    a.   hope that if she ever comes to town, he doesn't find out.
    b.   insist that if he expects a future with you, he must get over his past with her.
    c.   think she sounds nice and are curious to meet her.

5. Your teacher gave both you and another student As for your joint report on Lebanon, but in front of the class, the teacher lavished your classmate with compliments and didn't even acknowledge your contribution. You
    a.   don't mind; grades speak louder than praise.
    b.   write your classmate a note saying you resent her not reminding the teacher of your share of the work.
    c.   plan to find the teacher later and say something subtle, like, "I'm glad you liked our project. We both enjoyed writing it."

6. Your boyfriend loves bicycling. So much, in fact, that when he's not in school, at sports practice, or doing homework, he's cycling into the wild blue yonder. You
    a.   tell him you won't play second fiddle to his bicycle anymore: If things don't change, you want out.
    b.   don't mind: He's happy, you admire his athletic prowess, and better your rival be a bicycle than another girl—even if you hardly see him.
    c.   accept his cycling gusto but say that you want to be with him outside school at least twice a week.

7. You've just seen a movie together. You're raving about the special effects. Your date is raving about the teen actress. You
    a.   agree that she's a talented beauty and bring up other movies in which you've admired her.
    b.   point out that the male lead was sensitive and charming, then change the subject.
    c.   say that while she's not unattractive, you've never been impressed by her acting.

8. According to your mother, your brother can do no wrong. She recites the list of his accomplishments. You

a.   tune her out, feeling hurt.

b.   are glad to see her so proud.

c.   listen, nod, and hint that you're nothing to sneeze at yourself.

9. The guy you've secretly had your eye on for months just asked your best friend to the prom. You

a.   cry and decide you hate them both.

b.   feel hurt but since nobody really betrayed you, you try not to let it drag you down.

c.   figure it's no big deal. There are other guys out there and nothing could ever come between you and your friend.

10. You're from a middle-income family. You visit a friend's house for the first time. House? It's a mansion, complete with everything from food processor to word processor. Her room has a canopy water bed, and out back, there's even a swimming pool—into which you both dive. You

a.   say with a sigh, "This is the life," and enjoy yourself thoroughly.

b.   are so overwhelmed by the contrast between your two homes that your stomach is knotted and you can scarcely keep afloat.

c.   drift merrily but think with a passing pang, "I wish our home were half this size."

11. You and a guy you've just met have been flirting at a party. Suddenly the pretty new girl in town asks him to dance. He accepts with a big smile. You

a.   glare at her and ask a good-looking guy to dance.

b.   smile at them and go talk with another friend.

c.   study the record collection and consider cutting in if they dance the next number together.

12. The teacher hands back the papers. You can't help noticing that both classmates next to you got an A while you got a B. You

a.   are happy with your grade and don't think twice about theirs.

b.   wonder if their papers really are better than yours and why.

c.   wish you hadn't seen their grades—now you feel bad that yours wasn't higher.

Scoring

1.	a-1	b-2	c-3	7.	a-1	b-2	c-3
2.	a-2	b-1	c-3	8.	a-3	b-1	c-2
3.	a-3	b-2	c-1	9.	a-3	b-2	c-1
4.	a-2	b-3	c-1	10.	a-1	b-3	c-2
5.	a-1	b-3	c-2	11.	a-3	b-1	c-2
6.	a-3	b-1	c-2	12.	a-1	b-2	c-3

12 to 19 You are unselfish and unpossessive, and these qualities save you from many needless heartaches. But before you stick a gold star on your forehead, be sure you are being truly honest with yourself about your feelings, not just repressing emotions. Could your nonchalance be a mere facade? Don't be afraid to open up and deal with any anger and fears inside you.

20 to 27 Hurray! You are in touch with your full range of feelings, jealousy included. Sure you'd be happy if your neighbor won the lottery, but you'd be even happier if you won. You are mature enough to recognize your occasional envy as natural and legitimate, and wise enough to control it rather than letting it control you. When you are jealous, ask yourself why and explore it. For example, maybe you think your boyfriend is tempted to roam because *you're* restless and you're projecting your feelings onto him. Or maybe you're feeling insecure because things at home and at school aren't going well. If you think your jealousy is well founded, let it serve as a warning that you two need to reexamine your relationship.

28 to 36 Nobody will ever steal your friends without a fight: You're the jealous type. You are also a devoted girlfriend, and you like commitment in return. Fine. But if debilitating jealousy often gets the best of you, it's time to defuse it. Talk your jealousy out with someone you trust. And work on staying busy, building on your good points, and bolstering your self-esteem. The better you feel about yourself, the less vulnerable you'll be to jealousy.

HOW OBSERVANT ARE YOU?

Do you notice the big and little things going on around you? Are you looking and listening closely? Don't guess on this difficult quiz—just answer the questions when you know you are correct.

1. Name two expressions that one or both of your parents use all the time.
2. Were more than two people absent from your math class today?
3. What make of car were you last in besides your family's?
4. Whose face is on the five-dollar bill?
5. Describe the shirt your English teacher was wearing today.
6. Name three sounds particular to your home.
7. What is the state sales tax where you live?
8. Who is the author of your science textbook?
9. Describe the rug or carpet in your best friend's living room.
10. What is the license plate on your family's car?
11. What item of clothing in your closet is hanging farthest to the right?
12. What is the brand name of your refrigerator?
13. How many shampoo bottles are now in your shower stall?
14. Describe the plates you eat from in your school cafeteria.

15. Describe the most fragrant tree, bush, or flower in your garden or nearest your home.

Scoring

How many answers were you sure of?

12 to 15 Nothing escapes your eagle eye. Someday you may become a detective or an artist.

8 to 11 Bravo! Your good eye and good ear serve you well.

4 to 7 You may be looking both ways before crossing the street, but how much are you really seeing? Pretend you're E.T., a newcomer to this planet, and start taking it all in.

0 to 3 Have you seen your optometrist lately? Try to work on your observation skills, because you're missing too much.

GOOD-BYE

You have a lot to look forward to, and you have hurdles ahead. Sometimes I envy you. Sometimes I'm scared for you. Mostly I hope you work for and get what you want. Remember: Getting there is half the fun. And life gets easier once you get the hang of it.

If you have any questions or comments, drop me a line. You can reach me at

Carol Weston
P.O. Box 291
Planetarium Station
127 W. 83 Street
New York, N.Y. 10024

Be sure to include a *stamped self-addressed* envelope, and I'll try to answer. I may even print your letter in a future book or column. So sign it Heartbroken in Hoboken or Wild in Wichita or something, if you don't want me to use your real name.

Well, I'm signing off at last. Good luck! Give it your best shot!

Love,

Carol Weston

ABOUT THE AUTHOR

Carol Weston has been writing for teens ever since she was a teen. Her work has been published in *Young Miss, Seventeen, Glamour, Bride's, Cosmopolitan, McCall's, House & Garden*, and *The New York Times*, and translated into French, Spanish, and Japanese. Carol received her B.A. summa cum laude, Phi Beta Kappa, from Yale in 1978 and her M.A. from Middlebury in 1979. She enjoys tutoring French and Spanish to teens and frequently gives talks about writing. She and her husband, stage director Robert Ackerman, recently moved from the midwest to Manhattan.

GIRLTALK is Carol's first book.